The Editors

ROBERT M. BENDER is currently professor of English at the University of Missouri–Columbia. He has taught at Brooklyn College, New York City, and at the University of Michigan. He received his B.S. from the Illinois Institute of Technology and his Ph.D. from the University of Michigan. Professor Bender is the author of *Five Courtier Poets of the English Renaissance* and *The Shaping of Fiction*, a study of short works by Hawthorne, Melville, Conrad and Stephen Crane.

CHARLES L. SQUIER is professor of English at the University of Colorado–Boulder. He received the B.A. and M.A.T. from Harvard and his Ph.D. from the University of Michigan. He has taught as a visiting professor at the University of Liverpool and at the Tianjin Foreign Languages Institute, People's Republic of China. Professor Squier is the author of *Sir John Suckling* and *John Fletcher* and also has published poetry and fiction.

the Sonnet
An Anthology

A comprehensive selection
of British and American
sonnets from
the Renaissance to the
present

Robert M. Bender and
Charles L. Squier,
Editors

WSP

WASHINGTON SQUARE PRESS
PUBLISHED BY POCKET BOOKS

New York   London   Toronto   Sydney   Tokyo

A WASHINGTON SQUARE PRESS *Original* Publication

A Washington Square Press Publication of
POCKET BOOKS, a division of Simon & Schuster Inc.
1230 Avenue of the Americas, New York, NY 10020

ISBN: 0-671-63732-0

First Washington Square Press revised printing August 1987

10 9 8 7 6 5 4 3 2

WASHINGTON SQUARE PRESS and WSP colophon are
registered trademarks of Simon & Schuster Inc.

Printed in the U.S.A.

PERMISSIONS

Grateful acknowledgment is made to the following authors and publishers for permission to include material in this work:

Atheneum Publishers, Inc., for Anthony Hecht, "Double Sonnet" from *The Hard Hours*, copyright © 1967 by Anthony E. Hecht, reprinted by permission of Atheneum Publishers, Inc.

Beacon Press, for "Sunflower Sonnet Number One" and "Sunflower Sonnet Number Two" from *Things That I Do in the Dark* by June Jordan, copyright © 1977 by June Jordan, reprinted by permission of Beacon Press.

Gwendolyn Brooks, for "What shall I give my children?" and "the rites for Cousin Vit" from *The World of Gwendolyn Brooks*, Harper & Row, reprinted by permission of Gwendolyn Brooks.

Burns & Oates, Ltd., for the selections by Alice Meynell from *The Collected Poems of Alice Meynell*, reprinted by permission of Sir Francis Meynell and of the publishers, Burns & Oates, Ltd.

James E. Camp, for "Female Dancer" by James E. Camp, reprinted by permission of the author.

Jonathan Cape, Ltd., for the selections by C. Day-Lewis from *The Collected Works of C. Day-Lewis*, reprinted by permission of the publishers, Jonathan Cape, Ltd.

Century Hutchinson, Ltd., for "Sonnet: Equality of the Sexes" and "Sonnet: Supernatural Beings" from *The Young Pobble's Guide to His Toes*, Gavin Ewart (Hutchinson, an imprint of Century Hutchinson).

Chatto & Windus, Ltd., for the selections by Wilfred Owen from *Poems* by Wilfred Owen, reprinted by permission of Harold Owen and of the publishers, Chatto & Windus, Ltd.

The Clarendon Press, for the selections by William Alabaster from *The Sonnets of William Alabaster;* for the selections by Robert Bridges from *The Shorter Poems of Robert Bridges;* both reprinted by permission of The Clarendon Press, Oxford.

Curtis Brown, Ltd., for "The Funeral" by Donald Hall from *The Dark Houses* by Donald Hall; for the selections by Roy Fuller from *Brutus's Orchard* by Roy Fuller; both reprinted by permission of Curtis Brown, Ltd.

CONTENTS

PART ONE
The English Renaissance

PART TWO
The Seventeenth and Eighteenth Centuries

PART THREE
The Nineteenth Century

PART FOUR
The Twentieth Century

PREFACE TO THE
REVISED EDITION

When *The Sonnet* first was published in 1965, it included more than 750 poems, representing the work of 154 poets; the subtitle promised "a comprehensive anthology." Reviewers, and correspondents, immediately began to comment on poets we had neglected. For this revised edition, while we have made fairly extensive cuts, we have retained most of the poets included in the original volume, and we have added the work of some forty poets, including more than eighty new poems. Even so, the comprehensiveness of this volume once more may be questioned.

Most of the poems we have dropped—nearly two hundred—are from the earlier periods, where we have reduced the number of selections allotted to each poet. Our aim has been to achieve a sense of balance and at the same time to allow room for additions. In the Renaissance we have added two sonnets by Lady Mary Wroth; in the nineteenth century we have added sonnets by George Eliot, Frances E. W. Harper, Emma Lazarus, and Henrietta Cordelia Ray. Most of the additions, then, represent the work of poets who have written and published in the last eighty years or so. Indeed, a number of our new poets did not begin publishing until after this volume was in print. As with the original edition, we believe this anthology offers a broad historical sampling of the sonnet in English.

Our selections have been made on the basis of representativeness, historical significance, traditional popularity, and, inevitably, personal preference. Some sonnets printed here never before have been anthologized. We have included a few poems which are not, strictly speaking, sonnets—at least not the fourteen-line variety—but which nevertheless play a part in the history of the form. While we have made an attempt to include all the best sonnets in English, we have not hesitated to select outrageously bad poems when we thought they illustrate a phase of the history of the form that otherwise might have been missed. Wherever possible we have attempted to give each poet enough representation so that the full range of his or her sonnet writing may be perceived. The revival of sonnet writing, including the writing of extended sequences, in the last twenty years or so has been so great that it has been impossible to print all the poems we would like. Indeed, it is now quite possible to publish an extensive collection of sonnets for the twentieth century alone. Other editors before us, and after the publication of the original volume, have put together impressive collections of sonnets. Nevertheless, given the limitations of space, we believe this volume still offers the most comprehensive collection available.

With the exception of the Renaissance, we have arranged the poems in roughly chronological order, presenting each author according to his or her date of birth. The earliest period of sonnet writing in English presents a special case. In some instances dates of birth are impossible to determine. More significantly, the development of the sonnet as a form more often can be traced in the publication of individual sonnet sequences. To present Spenser's *Amoretti*, for example, before Sidney's *Astrophel and Stella*, even though Spenser was born a few years before Sidney, would be misleading. Sidney set the vogue for sonnet sequences; Spenser took up the form only after it had had several years of popularity.

Spelling and punctuation for earlier selections has been modernized to conform with current practice. Intentional archaisms have been retained, and glosses are provided where their meaning is unclear. Footnotes, generally, have been provided where they seemed helpful, but we have not felt it necessary to replace the services of a good dictionary. Each sonnet has been reprinted with its original title. For those with no title and for most of those originally called "Sonnet," we have supplied a title by raising the first line or part of it. Sonnets taken from sequences are numbered to show their place within the sequence where it seems appropriate.

R.M.B.
C.L.S.

INTRODUCTION

The sonnet is the most popular, enduring, and widely used poetic form in English poetry. Since its introduction in the 1530s, the sonnet has enjoyed almost unabated popularity. Nearly every major British and American poet has made use of the form. To be sure, it has had its critics as well as its defenders, in the past and in the present. In part, the vitality of the form stems from its ability to provoke controversy; but this vitality also stems from the complex and inextricable relationship which the sonnet imposes upon form and content. The sonnet is a conventional form; a full understanding and enjoyment of it begins with a recognition of its conventions.

THE STRUCTURE OF THE SONNET

To begin with, the sonnet is a fourteen-line poem, usually written in iambic pentameter, with a variety of rhyme schemes. The two main types of sonnet rhyme schemes are embodied in the Italian sonnet—sometimes called the Petrarchan sonnet—and the English or Shakespearean sonnet.

The Italian sonnet has a two-part division of eight and six lines, an octave and a sestet. The rhyme pattern for the octave is generally quite rigid, the most common rhyme being *abbaabba*. The sestet, on the other hand, provides a bit more freedom. It sometimes turns out to be a quatrain and a couplet—*cdcd ee;* it can be an alternation of two rhymes—*cdcdcd;* or it can have three rhymes—*cdecde*. The first of these sestet patterns was the favorite of Sir Philip Sidney (see p. 13); the second was often used by Keats (see p. 190); and the third is frequently found in Milton's sonnets (see p. 121).

The English sonnet consists of three quatrains and a couplet; though, of course, it too can be divided into two sections corresponding to the octave-sestet of the Italian form. The most common rhyme scheme—the one which Shakespeare habitually used—is *abab cdcd efef gg,* but some sonnets employ fewer rhymes—*abab abab abab cc*. Surrey, among earlier sonneteers, frequently used this latter pattern, though sometimes he would continue the *a* rhyme in the final couplet (see p. 6).

The sonnet, however, is not simply a fourteen-line poem having a prescribed rhyme scheme. Certainly most sonnets *are* fourteen-line poems, and most sonneteers do confine themselves to prescribed rhyme patterns. But another way of looking at the sonnet is as a kind of structural framework *within which* the poet writes. Length imposes obvious restrictions on content; it is not always possible to write expansively within so short a space. But length can just as easily force a poet to expand a trivial idea to fill the required space.

The formal pattern of rhymes within a sonnet further dictates the development of its meaning. The Italian sonnet most readily becomes a two-part poem. This is clear in Wordsworth's sonnet "Composed in the Valley near Dover, On the Day of Landing."

> Here, on our native soil, we breathe once more.
> The cock that crows, the smoke that curls, that sound
> Of bells;—those boys who in yon meadow-ground
> In white-sleeved shirts are playing; and the roar
> Of the waves breaking on the chalky shore;—
> All, all are English. Oft have I looked round
> With joy in Kent's green vales; but never found
> Myself so satisfied in heart before.
> Europe is yet in bonds; but let that pass,
> Thought for another moment. Thou are free,
> My Country! and 'tis joy enough and pride
> For one hour's perfect bliss, to tread the grass
> Of England once again, and hear and see,
> With such a dear Companion at my side.

In addition to being set off by the rhyme, the parts of the poem are divided in other ways typical of the sonnet development. Rhetorically, the poet's feelings about England, presented in the octave, are set against his reflections on these feelings in the sestet. The shift from one section to the next is marked by the rhetorical contrast of the "Here" of the first line with "Europe" in line nine. The emotions of the octave are communicated through a variety of images; the sestet, almost devoid of images, invites a response to these emotions which is directed by the invitation to "hear and see" in the thirteenth line. The sestet does not really expand upon the emotions presented in the octave, but provides something of a turn in the development of the poem, a fitting and suggestive conclusion—a set of attitudes toward the images of the octave—for the entire poem. The Italian form of the sonnet is often spoken of as an "organic" whole, the octave and the sestet fitting together like the two parts of an acorn. Certainly this is the case with Wordsworth's sonnet.

The English form, with its three distinct quatrains and concluding couplet, gives the poet somewhat more freedom. In the first of his *Amoretti* (see p. 51), using his own unique form of the English sonnet, Spenser weaves his quatrains together with interlocking rhyme, *abab bcbc cdcd,* but still keeps the content of the quatrains distinct. Each quatrain develops a different aspect of the same general analogy. Spenser entreats his mistress to deal kindly with him and his poems, and in a conceit expresses envy of the book that will reach her before he does. In the first quatrain, he calls attention to the leaves of the book; in the second, he speaks of the lines of his verse; and in the third, he focuses on his rhymes. In the couplet he draws the three quatrains together and makes his point:

> Leaves, lines, and rhymes, seek her to please alone
> Whom if ye please, I care for other none.

In constructing his poem this way, Spenser gives up both the quatrain and the octave-sestet design for a pattern of twelve lines and a couplet, a development often characteristic of the English sonnet.

Shakespeare uses a similar pattern in a great many of his sonnets. Sonnet 73, "That time of year thou mayst in me behold" (see p. 83), for example, consists of three quatrains, each containing a separate set of images, which are drawn together and commented upon in the couplet. Other patterns are possible within the confines of the English sonnet. The poet may, clearly enough, retain the standard two-part division of the Italian sonnet, treating the first two quatrains, regardless of their rhymes, as a unit and combining the third quatrain and the couplet to form a sestet. Again, Shakespeare provides numerous examples. In Sonnet 71, "No longer mourn for me when I am dead" (see

p. 83), Shakespeare marks off three quatrains and a couplet with his rhymes, but the poem is really developed in two parts. In the first two quatrains the poet counsels the person he is addressing not to mourn his death longer than the tolling of the death bell and even to forget the poet while he reads these lines. There is a full stop after the second quatrain, and then Shakespeare comments upon these instructions with the further warning that lengthy mourning can only lead to mockery. It is clear that the technical structural pattern—the rhyme scheme—does not altogether agree with the development of the meaning of the sonnet. But the structure of the sonnet is flexible enough both to support the thematic statement and to run counter to it. This tension between structure and content, instead of weakening the poem, gives it fresh vitality. And here we can see precisely how the form of the sonnet can lead to the writing of fine poetry.

The sonnet, then, can be seen both as a structural pattern *within* which the poet writes and as a framework *against* which the poet works. In either the Italian or the English form the poet can, if he or she chooses, run his or her lines over the barriers of the rhyme. Milton employs this technique in some of his best sonnets. In "On the Late Massacre in Piedmont" (see p. 124), the rhyme scheme divides the poem in an octave and a sestet. Rhetorically, however, the poem is otherwise divided into three sentences that overrun these divisions. The first sentence stops short two syllables from the end of the eighth line where presumably the "octave" should end. The next sentence runs through to the first two syllables of line ten. The remainder of the poem is just one sentence. In setting the rhetorical pattern of his thought against the pattern of his rhymes, Milton obliterates the usual divisions of the sonnet and creates a unified verse paragraph that moves from beginning to end with a broad, sweeping effect. In doing so, Milton not only breaks with the supposed confinements of the form, but also produces a poem of particular power, power in large measure attributable to the innovations made in the traditional sonnet pattern. This same sort of development can be seen in a twentieth century sonnet such as E. S. Miller's "To My Lady" (see p. 316).

Some poets are even more experimental with form than Milton. In his early blank verse translations from the French sonnets of Du Bellay (see p. 49), Edmund Spenser ignores rhymes entirely. Robert Frost, to cite a modern poet, shows great fondness for structural variations within the sonnet form. "Once by the Pacific" (see p. 277), for example, consists of seven rhymed couplets; "Acquainted with the Night" (see p. 278) is made up of four stanzas of terza rima, three-line units in which the second line of each rhymes with the first and third line of the next and so on, and a couplet; "The Oven Bird" (see p. 277) contains a series of random rhymes. Nor is Frost alone in his experimentation. Adrienne Rich's "The Insusceptibles" (see p. 367) and Marilyn Hacker's "Occasional Verses" (see p. 377), to cite just two examples, employ rhymed couplets. Peyton Houston, in "Canzone," which concludes his *Sonnet Variations*, of which only Part II is included in this anthology, employs an even more complicated rhyme scheme (see p. 328), but nevertheless adheres to the sonnet form. The point is that these poems are recognizable sonnets no matter what their rhyme schemes. Even the amusing "Aeronaut to his Lady" by Frank Sidgwick (1879–1939) is obviously intended as a sonnet—

> 'I
>   Through
>   Blue
>   Sky
>   Fly
>   To
>   You.
>   Why?
>
>   Sweet
>   Love,
>   Feet
>   Move
>   So
>   Slow!'

For another poem that makes fun of the form there is John Updike's "Love Sonnet" (see p. 371).

In *Notebook* Robert Lowell worried that he sometimes "failed to avoid the themes and giganticism of the sonnet" in his fourteen-line poems in iambic pentameter; still, they appropriately belong to the sonnet tradition. George Meredith wrote sixteen-line sonnetlike poems in his sequence *Modern Love* (see p. 234).

Alan Dugan declares his fifteen-line "To a Red-Headed Do-Good Waitress" (see p. 360) as a "wrong sonnet," but it may be considered as much a part of the experimental or varietal line as Hayden Carruth's fifteen-line poems in *The Sleeping Beauty*. Anthony Hecht's "Double Sonnet" (see p. 359) has twenty-eight lines, the traditional octave and sestet being doubled. In such sequences as Judith Moffett's "Now or Never" (see p. 373) or Richard Kenney's "The Hours of the Day" (see p. 382) it might be argued that these are only long poems employing fourteen-line stanzas, but the form of the sonnet informs the structure of each poem.

The traditional definition of the sonnet is not quite adequate to account for all the poems we can justifiably call sonnets. Exceptions can be found for almost every part of the standard definition. In general, a sonnet should retain a pattern of rhyme or a division of thought consistent with the history of the form. Not every fourteen-line poem is a sonnet, but we must pay some regard to a poet's intention and be willing to grant the flexibility of the tradition.

The really remarkable thing about the sonnet is its endurance as a form; it is, after all, virtually the only important verse form in English poetry. To be sure, there are other forms. Sestinas have had a variety of practitioners, but we would not expect much from an entire collection of them. Stanzaic forms like rhyme royal or the Spenserian stanza are generally only a part of long narrative poems. Unless we are willing to call something like the heroic couplet a distinct form, it must be admitted that the sonnet is just about the only clearly distinguishable form, with an exact and definite set of conventions, for lyrical poetry.

The endurance and the utility of the sonnet as a form stems to a great extent from the fact that the sonnet is so flexible; the pattern can be violated in many ways and yet the sonnet remains a sonnet. The sonnet is a distinctly appropriate and effective means of saying certain kinds of things; the difficulty of defining *what kinds of things* only illustrates the range of the form. Love—whether it is directed toward a woman, a dear friend, God, or one's country—is surely one of the important subjects for the sonnet, but it is not the only one. The sonnet provides the poet with a form and traditions which he or she can use nearly at will to say what he or she wants.

It would not do, however, to imply that form is necessarily the sonneteer's primary consideration. Some sonnets, to be sure, are little more than formal exercises, but there are a great number of very fine sonnets in which form appears very much a secondary consideration. Yeats's "Leda and the Swan" (see p. 270) is such a poem; one is almost surprised to discover it is a sonnet. But that surprise and the awareness of form are part of the strength of the poem. The history of the sonnet in English is at once the record of the use of a conventional artifice and departures from it. Poets have consistently altered the formal aspects of the sonnet and expanded the range of its content.

THE HISTORY OF THE SONNET IN ENGLISH

Sonnets have been written in a great many languages. The history of sonnet writing in England and America is only a small part of the story of the form. The form enjoyed great popularity during the Renaissance in most European countries—Italy, France, Spain and England—but it is no less important and ubiquitous today.

The sonnet originated in Italy. Dante (1265–1321) and Petrarch (1304–1374) are the most important of the early Italian sonneteers. Sir Thomas Wyatt encountered the form during his travels in Italy and Spain and brought it back to England in the 1530s. The impact of Petrarch on English sonnet writing cannot be overestimated. Of Wyatt's thirty-two sonnets, seventeen are adaptations from Petrarch; Henry Howard, Earl of Surrey, Wyatt's immediate successor, also adapted a number of sonnets from Petrarch. It is well to begin the history of the English sonnet by observing the impact of this great Italian poet on the earliest English sonneteers.

Petrarch wrote full sequences of sonnets to his mistress Laura. His usual technique can be observed in this example:

> Amor, che nel penser mio vive e regna
> E 'l suo seggio maggior nel mio cor tene,
> Talor armato ne la fronte vène;
> Ivi si loca et ivi pon sua insegna.
> Quella ch'amare e sofferir ne 'nsegna,
> E vòl che 'l gran desio, l'accesa spene,
> Ragion, vergogna e reverenza affrene,
> Di nostro ardir fra sè stessa si sdegna.

Onde Amor spaventoso fugge al core
   Lasciando ogni sua impresá; e piange, e trema;
   Ivi s'asconde e non appar più fòre.
Che poss'io far, temendo il mio signore,
   Se non star seco infin a l'ora estrema?
   Chè bel fin la chi ben amando more.*

Wyatt's version of this sonnet, "The long love that in my thought doth harbor" (see p. 3), follows the Petrarchan rhyme scheme quite well. While retaining a clear octave and sestet, Wyatt does alter the last rhyme to form a couplet. Surrey, on the other hand, departs from this pattern in his translation, "Love that liveth and reigneth in my thought" (see p. 7), to adopt the English form—*abab cdcd efef gg*. The final couplet of Surrey's poem, moreover, points to the turn, the witty summary, the final unifying statement that characterizes the English sonnet. The Italian sonnet, however, is more than simply a form, and along with it Wyatt imported a whole battery of poetic conventions for writing about love.

The mistresses addressed in the Italian sonnets are beautiful, starry-eyed, rosy-cheeked, unattainable, and cold. The poet ordinarily praises his mistress's beauty, laments her coldness, and makes clear his own suffering. Wyatt, then, made use of both the Petrarchan form and its accompanying conventions while the next great English sonneteer, Surrey, more readily abandoned the Petrarchan mold. With Surrey, the sonnet becomes truly English in form, and even in the handling of subject matter.

Although the English lyric flourished, poets neglected the sonnet for a number of years after Wyatt and Surrey. Perhaps its

---

*Love, which lives and reigns in my thought, and makes his estate in my heart, thus armed opposes me face to face; there he stands, and there he plants his banner.

She who taught me to love and to suffer, and wishes that our great desire, the ardent hope, be reined by reason, shame, and reverence, feels disdain within herself for our burning passion.

Whence fearful Love flees into the heart, deserting all such undertakings, and cries, and trembles; there he hides and no longer shows himself.

What can I do, since my master is so fearful, but stay with him until the last hour? For he ends well who dies loving well.

neglect may be attributed to its foreign origin. Importations were not popular in the ensuing years; the great burst of English lyricism was for a while essentially native in its origins. But whatever the reason, the sonnet was seldom written; and indeed, most poets had no clear idea of the exact nature of the form. They used the word "sonnet" to indicate a wide variety of short lyrics, the "little song" of the word's origin. The long series of Elizabethan miscellanies published after Tottel's *Songs and Sonnets* (1557), despite the promise of their titles, often contained very few poems that we would call sonnets. Although our normal definition of the sonnet requires fourteen lines of iambic pentameter verse, the Elizabethans were not so certain of line length. Many of Sidney's sonnets, written in the 1580s, are in hexameters (see p. 13), and Shakespeare's "Those lips that Love's own hand did make" (see p. 89) is written in octosyllabic meter.

Within this period George Gascoigne (c. 1539–1577) stands out as one of the few poets concerned with the technical nature of the sonnet. "I can best allow to call those sonnets," he declares, "which are of fourteen lines, every line containing ten syllables." Gascoigne generally avoids the Petrarchan conventions of love, and his sequence of seven sonnets (see p. 9) is really a linked narrative of his experiences at court.

The real flowering of the form came later and probably owes more to the new interest in foreign writing than to the earlier efforts of Wyatt and Surrey. Indeed, it is often asserted that the development of the sonnet in England might have been much the same had Wyatt and Surrey never used the form. The sonnet as a love poem reached its heights and sometimes its depths in the 1590s in the great vogue of sonnet sequences that followed Sir Philip Sidney's extremely popular sequence *Astrophel and Stella* (1591). While Thomas Watson (c. 1557–1592) introduced the idea of the sequence in his *Hecatompathia, or a Passionate Century of Love* (1582), which contains no true sonnets, it remained for Sidney to fire the imagination of his contemporaries with the possibilities of the sonnet in sequence.

The sonnet sequence attracted the greatest poets of the century—including Shakespeare and Spenser—as well as some of the worst. Most sonnet sequences were dedicated to ladies, either fictional or real, possessed of hyperbolic charms and hard hearts. The sequences were not ordinarily intended as love stories or narratives but as accounts of emotional states. Nor were all the sonnet sequences composed entirely of "sonnets." Sidney included eleven songs among the sonnets of *Astrophel and Stella,* and other poets followed suit, varying the sonnet with poems in other forms. Thomas Lodge, for example, freely included in *Phyllis* (1593) many poems that were not fourteen lines long (see p. 28).

The vogue for sonnet writing became so widespread and the form was used by so many poets, both good and bad, that it was bound to dissipate quickly. Though sonnet sequences were written well beyond the turn of the century, by 1595 poets were already turning against the sequence and the sonnet. The *Gulling Sonnets* (1595) of Sir John Davies (1569–1626) effectively parodied the excesses found in the apparently unending gush of praise to regiments of astonishingly similar ladies. Shakespeare pokes fun at the absurdities of the Petrarchan conventions in his plays and in such a sonnet as "My mistress' eyes are nothing like the sun" (see p. 88), which uses the conventions while laughing at them.

Though love remained the chief subject for the sonnet well into the seventeenth century, sonneteers were beginning to write more and more of other things. To be sure, the Elizabethans wrote sonnets about politics, religion, falconry, hunting, and sonnet writing itself. Ben Jonson (see p. 106) and other poets realized the sonnet could be used as a form for epigrams, but Gascoigne had realized that several years before them. The really significant change, however, occurred toward the end of the sixteenth century when religion became almost as important a subject for the sonneteer as secular love.

The extension is logical and natural, and several religious sequences were written before the end of the century. Nevertheless, John Donne in *La Corona* (composed c.1608) was really the first to fully develop the potential of the form for religious expression. Like Milton afterward, though to a lesser extent, Donne experimented with the structure of the sonnet; many of his sonnets depart from the conventional dictates of the octave-sestet division. Donne's contribution, however, is in showing that the sonnet, so often merely the showcase of the poet's wit and technical facility, the vehicle for insincere expressions of love, could be used to express religious sentiments of the greatest intensity.

Though Milton wrote relatively few sonnets, he took keen interest in the form and used it throughout his writing career. He departed from the usual conventions and experimented freely with both the form and the content of the sonnet. His influence on the later development of the sonnet tradition was tremendous. Milton was really the first English poet who consistently adhered to the Italian rhyme scheme as a means of playing the development of his thought against the pattern of his rhymes. He also broadened the range of subject matter for the sonnet: in his hands, the sonnet became the vehicle for political protests, for satirical exclamations, and for meditations on the poet's own condition. Admittedly Milton must be blamed for such vocative openings as "Vane, young in years . . ." (see p. 124) and "Cyriack, this three years' day . . ." (see p. 125) which led to unfortunate excesses of the apostrophe in the sonnet tradition, typified by William Bowles's "O Tweed! a stranger . . ." (see p. 152) and Wordsworth's exceptionally unhappy "Jones! as from Calais . . ." (not included in this collection); but more important, with Milton the sonnet takes on a wider range of expression.

English poets did not at first follow Milton's example, and very few sonnets were written in the years between 1660 and 1740. Pope and his contemporaries were far more interested in imitating Horace than Petrarch. Despite Ben Jonson's use of the sonnet in writing epigrams, the eighteenth century ignored the form as nonclassical. The neoclassicism of the eighteenth century was accompanied, moreover, by the self-conscious view that the times were particularly "modern." The Augustan Age rejected the "barbarism" of its Elizabethan forebears, and the sonnets of Sidney and Spenser as well as Shakespeare were not read, or if read, were not understood.

The sonnets of Charles Cotton and Philip Ayres represent the end of a tradition, but neither is Elizabethan in spirit nor do they show the influence of Milton. The revival of the sonnet is frequently attributed to Thomas Gray, yet his sonnet "On the Death of Richard West" (see p. 137), although written early in the decade of the 1740s, was not published until 1775. A more likely candidate for the title of reviver of the sonnet is the cantankerous critic Thomas Edwards, whose sonnets first appeared in the second volume of Dodsley's *A Collection of Poems, by Several Hands* in 1748. Edwards's sonnets are for most readers not much more than lively historical curiosities. A less exciting, but more competent and surely more influential poet is Thomas Warton, the Younger, who helped to give direction to the subsequent thematic development of the sonnet by using it as a means of making reflections on places of scenic beauty and historic interest.

The revival of the sonnet in popularity is thoroughly established in the voluminous outpourings of sentimental melancholy by writers like Charlotte Smith and Anna Seward. It is hard, however, to argue that the productivity of the late eighteenth century resulted in many sonnets of real excellence. Nonetheless, the sonnet is restored to its position as a major poetic form in this period. An important influence on the sonnet is seen in the poems of William Lisle Bowles. Both Wordsworth and Coleridge admired him, and Coleridge cited his influence on his own sonnet writing in the *Biographia Literaria*. Fortunately, Coleridge was able to recognize and satirize the weaknesses of his own sonnets in his Nehemiah Higginbottom parodies (see p. 167); in general, these weaknesses are shared by the age.

Wordsworth obviously found the sonnet highly congenial; he wrote over 520 of them. In *The River Duddon* (1820) and the *Ecclesiastical Sonnets* (1822) he used the form for a long series, but readers turn most frequently to the highly charged sonnets of his early years—perhaps in particular to those sonnets in *Poems in Two Volumes* (1807) written in the Miltonic vein and dealing with the themes of liberty and England. For Wordsworth the sonnet is "a scanty plot of ground" in which the poet can express lofty sentiments (see p. 157). The influence of Milton noted in Wordsworth is also evident in the impassioned political verses of the "Corn Law Rhymer," Ebenezer Elliott, while the reestablished interest in Elizabethan poetry is obvious in Lamb, Darley, and, of course, Keats, to cite only a few names. In general, poets of the Romantic period preferred the Italian to the English form. Coleridge, Southey, Lamb, Hunt, and many others all wrote numerous Italian sonnets and were most often content with the established rhetorical pattern of the octave-sestet structure. The very volume of sonnet production, following Wordsworth's lead, in the Romantic period assured the continued popularity of the form.

The main contribution of the Victorians is in the firm reestablishment of the sonnet sequence. Elizabeth Barrett Browning's *Sonnets from the Portuguese* (1850), although sometimes filled with overstatement, retains a popularity; both Dante Gabriel Rossetti in *The House of Life* (1870) and George Meredith in his sequence of sixteen-line sonnets, *Modern Love* (1862), bring to the revived sonnet sequence not merely heightened emotions and a sensitive depiction of love but acute psychological awareness and analysis. Whether one calls Gerard Manley Hopkins a late Victorian or an early Modern, his religious sonnets are among the finest in the language; and his experiments with the shortened "curtal sonnet" and the "with-a-tail" or "caudated" sonnet (see p. 252) point to the continuation of experimentation, of playing form against content in the sonnet tradition.

The experiments in form found in Hopkins are continued in the years since 1900 in the sonnets of a great many poets; innovation in structure, in rhyme, in line length, can be found in the work of Robert Frost, Robinson Jeffers, E. E. Cummings, Peyton Houston, Gavin Ewart, Dylan Thomas, Hayden Carruth, Anthony Hecht, Alan Dugan, Adrienne Rich, John Updike, and Marilyn Hacker. The twenties and thirties witnessed an incredible outpouring of sonnet sequences—in William Ellery Leonard's *Two Lives* (see p. 282), Anna Hempstead Branch's *Sonnets from a Lock Box* (see p. 281), Elinor Wylie's *One Person* (see p. 285), and in several sequences by Edna St. Vincent Millay, including *Fatal Interview* (see p. 300) and her *Sonnets from an Ungrafted Tree*.

Indeed, it now seems clear that our own century may well rival the Renaissance as one of the great ages of the sonnet. The roster of poets in the twentieth century who have written sonnets is enormous. To be sure, the sonnet has been ignored or scorned by many modern and contemporary poets; one thinks immediately of T. S. Eliot and William Carlos Williams, of Robert Creeley, Denise Levertov and Allen Ginsberg. Theodore Roethke called the sonnet "a great form to pick your nose in." But in a curious way the sonnet has endured, and as poets have returned to formal poetry it has become more prevalent than ever.

Edna St. Vincent Millay provides an instance of a poet who has now survived shifts in fashion. Enormously popular and successful in the twenties and thirties, she often chose the sonnet as a means of expression and excelled in her use of the form. By 1941, when she published her *Collected Sonnets*, she began to lose favor, her work was seen as too conventional in her use of form, outshadowed by the brilliance of more "modernist" poets. In recent years, there has been renewed interest in her work, and now it is clear that she not only participated in a vital tradition but is one of the major sonneteers of the century.

The revived interest in Millay, in part, derives from the feminist movement of the sixties. This movement also has led to the rediscovery of a number of writers from the past and has enabled us to appreciate the work of present writers. Lady Mary Wroth's sequence *Pamphilia to Amphilanthus*, first published in 1621 (see p. 114), while written after the great Elizabethan vogue for sonnet sequences, continues in that tradition and offers us sonnets, written from the vantage point of a woman, that can stand with all but the very best of the earlier sonnets. George Eliot's sequence of eleven sonnets, *Brother and Sister* (see p. 220), enhances our sense of sonnet writing in the nineteenth century. Emma Lazarus's use of the form for her famous lines engraved on the pedestal of the Statue of Liberty (see p. 256) again suggests the vitality of the form and the basis of a continuing tradition. It is now clear that such major writers as Amy Lowell and Muriel Rukeyser as well as more recent poets such as Adrienne Rich and Marilyn Hacker not only have employed the form with enormous success but contribute to our understanding of the tradition of women writing in English.

The sixties also saw a revival of interest in black poetry. Here, again, we can see the sonnet being used for yet another tradition. Poems like Frances E. W. Harper's "She's Free!" (see p. 229) and Henrietta Cordelia Ray's "Robert G. Shaw" (see p. 257) are sonnets of protest and celebration that derive from the tradition Milton set in motion and lead to later sonnets such as those by Paul Laurence Dunbar (see p. 274), Claude McKay (see p. 295), Countee Cullen (see p. 314), Robert Hayden (see p. 335), Margaret Walker (see p. 345), and Gwendolyn Brooks (see p. 350). Indeed, such sonnets as Cullen's "Yet Do I Marvel" (see p. 314), Brooks's "What Shall I Give My Children?" (p. 350), and Walker's "For Malcolm X" (see p. 346) are among the major sonnets of this century.

Merrill Moore may well stand in splendid isolation for having written over a thousand sonnets, but it is nonetheless true that the sonnet remains a vital and flourishing form of poetic expression today. The last two decades have witnessed a great renewal in sonnet writing, not simply of individual poems on an amazing variety of topics, but in the sonnet sequence, which has not only remained popular but has undergone a remarkable resurgence and expansion of subject matter. David Huddle's Viet Nam sequence *Tour of Duty* (see p. 378), for example, not only continues in the tradition of Auden's *In Time of War* (see p. 322), but suggests war as an inevitable theme, or particular speciality, of the twentieth century. Sherod Santos's sequence *The Sheltering Ground* (see p. 384), dealing with the birth of a child, reminds us of Rukeyser's *Nine Poems for the Unborn Child* (see p. 334). The sequences of Richard Moore and Judith Moffett, Richard Kenney and Julia Alvarez, to cite only four contemporary poets, delineate a wide range of subject matter that was only suggested by some of the earlier sequences written in this century by such poets as Edna St. Vincent Millay and Conrad Aiken, Allen Tate and Dylan Thomas.

This introduction has no more than touched upon the history of the sonnet. In one sense an adequate history of the form would be a history of poetry in English; the sonnet suffers a brief eclipse, after all, only in the period of the dominance of the couplet. The changes in subject matter of the sonnet are the changes in the concerns of the stream of English and American poetry. The form has proved large enough to accommodate most of our traditions.

It is sometimes argued that the sonnet is an historical form; that its great period begins with Wyatt and ends with Milton, if not earlier. To be sure, the Renaissance is a great age of sonnet writing and it is in this period that the traditions of the sonnet are established. But great sonnets have been written after Milton; and they continue to be written, for the sonnet is a living form. Its strength and endurance stem from the richness and solidity of its tradition. Undoubtedly, the sonnet will also be, as it always has been, the test of a poet's agility, wit, and technical skill. But in the right hands it will be something more. It is remarkably easy to write a bad sonnet; good sonnets are something else. The curious point is that the sonnet form can call forth some exceedingly fine poems from ordinarily middling poets. For clearly major poets it can provide the frame for truly great poetry.

Yeats wrote few sonnets, and yet "Leda and the Swan" is surely one of his finest poems. A reading of Robert Frost as a sonneteer will lead to the conclusion that he is, in fact, a major one. One might continue the argument with Millay and Auden and a host of other poets in this century. The sonnet provides the poetic equivalent of the high hurdle, but because it pits the poet against a long formal tradition, and because of the intrinsic shape of the form and the kind of lyric sense it makes, it can push the poet to great heights of achievement. The sonnet is not, finally, the pedagogue's pride or the pedant's last resort. It is a vital and living form, a test of poetic mettle, but primarily the shaping pattern for some of the finest poems in the English language.

The English Renaissance

SIR THOMAS WYATT
(c.1503–1542)

Wyatt was born in Kent and educated at Cambridge. A courtier-poet, he served King Henry VIII as Marshal of Calais, Ambassador to Spain, and member of the Privy Council. In the course of his tumultuous career he was imprisoned and charged with treason; yet, through his translations of Petrarch, he was the first English poet to use the sonnet form.

The Lover for Shamefastness Hideth His Desire Within His Faithful Heart

The long love that in my thought doth harbor,
And in mine heart doth keep his residence,
Into my face presseth with bold pretense
And therein campeth, spreading his banner.
She that me learneth to love and suffer
And wills that my trust and lust's negligence
Be reined by reason, shame, and reverence,
With his hardiness taketh displeasure.
Wherewithall unto the heart's forest he fleeth,
Leaving his enterprise with pain and cry,
And there him hideth, and not appeareth:
What may I do when my master feareth
But in the field with him to live and die?
For good is in the life ending faithfully.

How the Lover Perisheth in His Delight, As the Fly in the Fire

Some fowls there be that have so perfect sight
Against the sun their eyes for to defend;
And some, because the light doth them offend,
Never appear but in the dark or night.
Other rejoice to see the fire so bright
And ween[1] to play in it, as they pretend,
But find contrary of it they intend.
Alas, of that sort may I be by right.
For to withstand her look I am not able;

3

Yet can I not hide me in no dark place;
So followeth me remembrance of that face,
That with my teary eye, swollen, and unstable,
My destiny to behold her doth me lead;
And yet I know, I run into the glede.[2]

[1] ween/think   [2] glede/fire

Description of the Contrarious Passions of a Lover

I find no peace, and all my war is done;
I fear and hope; I burn, and freeze like ice;
I fly above the wind, yet can I not arise;
And nought I have, and all the world I season.
That looseth nor locketh holdeth me in prison,
And holdeth me not, yet can I 'scape no wise;
Nor letteth me live, nor die, at my devise,
And yet of death it giveth none occasion.
Without eyen,[1] I see; and without tongue, I plain[2];
I desire to perish, and yet I ask health;
I love another, and thus I hate myself;
I feed me in sorrow, and laugh in all my pain.
Likewise displeaseth me both death and life,
And my delight is causer of this strife.

[1] eyen/eyes   [2] plain/complain

The Lover Compareth His State to a Ship in Perilous Storm Tossed on the Sea

My galley, charged with forgetfulness,
Thorough[1] sharp seas in winter nights doth pass
'Tween rock and rock; and eke[2] my foe, alas,
That is my lord, steereth with cruelness;
And every oar, a thought in readiness,
As though that death were light in such a case;
An endless wind doth tear the sail apace
Of forced sighs, and trusty fearfulness;
A rain of tears, a cloud of dark disdain,
Hath done the wearied cords great hinderance;
Wreathed with error and eke with ignorance,

The stars be hid that led me to this pain.
Drowned is reason that should me comfort,
And I remain, despairing of the port.

¹thorough/through   ²eke/also

A Renouncing of Love

Farewell, love, and all thy laws for ever,
Thy baited hooks shall tangle me no more;
Senec and Plato call me from thy lore
To perfect wealth, my wit for to endeavor;
In blind error when I did persever,
Thy sharp repulse that pricketh aye so sore
Hath taught me to set in trifles no store,
And scape forth, since liberty is lever.¹
Therefore, farewell! Go trouble younger hearts,
And in me claim no more authority;
With idle youth go use thy property,
And thereon spend thy many brittle darts.
For hitherto though I have lost all my time,
Me lusteth² no longer rotten boughs to climb.

¹lever/dearer   ²lusteth/I want, care

"Divers doth use . . ."

Divers doth use, as I have heard and know,
  (When that to change their ladies do begin),
  To mourn and wail, and never for to lin,¹
  Hoping thereby to pease² their painful woe.
And some there be, that when it chanceth so
  That women change, and hate where love hath been,
  They call them false, and think with words to win
  The hearts of them which overwhere doth grow.
But as for me, though that by chance indeed
  Change hath outworn the favor that I had,
  I will not wail, lament, nor yet be sad,
Nor call her false that falsely did me feed;
  But let it pass, and think it is of kind³
  That often change doth please a woman's mind.

¹lin/cease   ²pease/appease   ³of kind/natural

"Whoso list to hunt . . ."

Whoso list to hunt, I know where is an hind,
  But as for me—alas, I may no more.
  The vain travail hath wearied me so sore,
  I am of them that farthest cometh behind.
Yet may I, by no means, my wearied mind
  Draw from the deer; but as she fleeth afore
  Fainting I follow. I leave off therefore,
  Since in a net I seek to hold the wind.
Who list her hunt, I put him out of doubt,
  As well as I, may spend his time in vain.
  And graven with diamonds in letters plain
There is written, her fair neck round about:
  Noli me tangere,[1] for Cæsar's I am,
  And wild for to hold, though I seem tame.

[1] *Noli me tangere*/Do not touch me. The poem is often taken to refer to Anne Boleyn and to Henry VIII.

HENRY HOWARD, EARL OF SURREY
(c.1517–1547)

Of royal birth, Surrey was active in the court of Henry VIII. He was twice commander of English forces. Accused of treason, he was beheaded in 1547 just a week before Henry died. As a poet, Surrey's fame stems from his translation of the *Aeneid*, in which he introduced blank verse to English poetry. He was a friend of Wyatt; with him he introduced the sonnet form to England.

Description of the Spring, Wherein Each Thing Renews Save Only the Lover

The soote[1] season that bud and bloom forth brings
With green hath clad the hill and eke[2] the vale,
The nightingale with feathers new she sings,
The turtle to her make[3] hath told her tale.

Summer is come, for every spray now springs,
The hart hath hung his old head on the pale,
The buck in brake[4] his winter coat he flings,
The fishes float with new repaired scale,
The adder all her slough away she slings,
The swift swallow pursueth the flyes smale,[5]
The busy bee her honey now she mings,—[6]
Winter is worn, that was the flowers' bale:
And thus I see, among these pleasant things
Each care decays—and yet my sorrow springs.

[1] soote/sweet [2] eke/also [3] make/mate
[4] brake/thicket [5] smale/small [6] mings/mingles

Complaint of a Lover Rebuked

Love that liveth and reigneth in my thought,
That built his seat within my captive breast,
Clad in the arms wherein with me he fought,
Oft in my face he doth his banner rest.
She that me taught to love and suffer pain,
My doubtful hope and eke my hot desire
With shamefast cloak to shadow and refrain,
Her smiling grace converteth straight to ire;
And coward love then to the heart apace
Taketh his flight, whereas he lurks and plains
His purpose lost, and dare not show his face.
For my lord's guilt thus faultless bide I pains;
Yet from my lord shall not my foot remove,—
Sweet is his death that takes his end by love.

A Complaint by Night of the Lover Not Beloved

Alas, so all things now do hold their peace,
Heaven and earth disturbed in nothing;
The beasts, the air, the birds their song do cease.
The night's[1] chair the stars about doth bring;
Calm is the sea, the waves work less and less.

So am not I, whom love, alas, doth wring,
Bringing before my face the great increase
Of my desires, whereat I weep and sing
In joy and woe, as in a doubtful ease.
For my sweet thoughts sometime do pleasure bring,
But by and by the cause of my disease
Gives me a pang that inwardly doth sting,
When that I think what grief it is again
To live and lack the thing should rid my pain.

[1] night's/pronounced with two syllables

How Each Thing Save the Lover in Spring Reviveth to Pleasure

When Windsor walls sustained my wearied arm,
My hand my chin, to ease my restless head,
The pleasant plot revested[1] green with warm,
The blossomed boughs with lusty Ver[2] yspred,[3]
The flowered meades,[4] the wedded birds so late
Mine eyes discover; and to my mind resort
The jolly woes, the hateless short debate,
The rakhell[5] life that longs to love's disport.[6]
Wherewith (alas) the heavy charge of care,
Heaped in my breast, breaks forth against my will,
In smoky sighs that overcast the air.
My vapored eyes such dreary tears distill,
The tender spring which quicken where they fall,
And I half bent to throw me down withall.

[1] revested/reclothed   [2] Ver/spring   [3] yspred/spread
[4] meades/meadows   [5] rakhell/careless   [6] disport/diversion

GEORGE GASCOIGNE
(c.1539–1577)

Gaining prominence as a poet and a dramatist in the 1570s, Gascoigne also had a career as a soldier and a courtier. Long recognized for his versatility, Gascoigne is more and more appreciated for the quality of his work. Though he wrote in a time when sonnets were not very much in vogue, he was the first British poet to attempt a linked sonnet sequence. Gascoigne's poems first appeared in *A Hundred Sundry Flowers* (1573). He published *The Posies of George Gascoigne* in 1575.

Seven Sonnets in Sequence on a theme suggested to Gascoigne by Sir Alexander Nevil[1]

1. "In haste, post haste . . ."

In haste, post haste, when first my wandering mind
Beheld the glistring[2] Court with gazing eye,
Such deep delights I seemed therein to find,
As might beguile a graver guest than I.
The stately pomp of Princes and their peers
Did seem to swim in floods of beaten gold;
The wanton world of young delightful years
Was not unlike a heaven for to behold,
Wherein did swarm (for every saint) a Dame
So fair of hue, so fresh of their attire,
As might excell Dame *Cynthia* for Fame,
Or conquer *Cupid* with his own desire.
These and such like baits that blazed still
Before mine eye, to feed my greedy will.

[1] Sir Alexander Nevil (1544–1614), a scholar and author of a number of Latin works
[2] glistring/glittering

2. *"Before mine eye . . ."*

Before mine eye, to feed my greedy will,
Gan[1] muster eke mine old acquainted mates,
Who helped the dish (of vain delight) to fill
My empty mouth with dainty delicates;
And foolish boldness took the whip in hand
To lash my life into this trustless trace,
Till all in haste I leapt a loof[2] from land
And hoist up sail to catch a Courtly grace.
Each lingering day did seem a world of woe,
Till in that hapless haven my head was brought;
Waves of wanhope[3] so tossed me to and fro
In deep despair to drown my dreadful thought;
Each hour a day, each day a year, did seem,
And every year a world my will did deem.

[1] Gan/began
[2] loof/a nautical term meaning to sail a ship close to the wind; here,
a distance
[3] wanhope/despair

3. *"And every year a world . . ."*

And every year a world my will did deem,
Till lo! at last, to Court now am I come,
A seemly swain that might the place beseem,
A gladsome guest embraced by all and some.
Not there content with common dignity,
My wandering eye in haste (yea post post haste)
Beheld the blazing badge of bravery,
For want whereof I thought my self disgraced.
Then peevish pride puffed up my swelling heart,
To further forth so hot an enterprise;
And comely cost began to play his part
In praising patterns of mine own devise.
Thus all was good and might be got in haste,
To prink[1] me up, and make me higher placed.

[1] prink/adorn

4. "To prink me up . . ."

To prink me up, and make me higher placed,
All came too late that tarried any time;
Piles of provision pleased not my taste,
They made my heals too heavy for to climb.
Methought it best that boughs of boistrous oak
Should first be shread to make my feathers gay,
Till at the last a deadly dinting[1] stroke
Brought down the bulk with edgetools of decay.
Of every farm I then let fly a leaf
To feed the purse that paid for peevishness,
Till rent and all were fallen in such disease,
As scarce could serve to maintain cleanliness;
They bought the body, fine, farm, leaf, and land;
All were too little for the merchant's hand.

[1] dinting/crushing

5. "All were too little . . ."

All were too little for the merchant's hand,
And yet my bravery bigger than his book;
But when this hot account was coldly scanned,
I thought high time about me for to look.
With heavenly cheer I cast my head aback
To see the fountain of my furious race,
Compared my loss, my living, and my lack
In equal balance with my jolly grace,
And saw expenses grating on the ground
Like lumps of lead to press my purse full oft,
When light reward and recompense were found,
Fleeting like feathers in the wind aloft.
These thus compared, I left the Court at large,
For why[1] the gains doth seldom quit the charge.

[1] For why/because

6. "For why the gains . . ."

For why the gains doth seldom quit the charge;
And so say I by proof too dearly bought,
My haste made waste; my brave and brainsick barge
Did float too fast to catch a thing of naught.
With leisure, measure, mean, and many moe[1]
I mought[2] have kept a chair of quiet state.
But hasty heads cannot be settled so,
Till crooked Fortune give a crabbed mate.
As busy brains must beat on tickle[3] toys.
As rash invention breeds a raw devise,
So sudden falls do hinder hasty joys;
And as swift baits do fleetest fish entice,
So haste makes waste, and therefore now I say,
No haste but good, where wisdom makes the way.

[1] moe/more   [2] mought/might   [3] tickle/uncertain, capricious

7. "No haste but good . . ."

No haste but good, where wisdom makes the way.
For proof whereof behold the simple snail
(Who sees the soldier's carcass cast away,
With hot assault the Castle to assail)
By line and leisure climbs the wall,
And wins the turret's top more cunningly
Than doughty Dick, who lost his life and all
With hoisting up his head so hastily.
The swiftest bitch brings forth the blindest whelps;
The hottest Fevers coldest cramps ensue;
The nakedest need hath ever latest helps.
With *Nevil* then I find this proverb true,
That *haste makes waste,* and therefore still I say,
No haste but good, where wisdom makes the way.

Sir Philip Sidney
(1554–1586)

Born at Penshurst, educated at Oxford, Sidney was the most notable gentleman his age produced. A real-life counterpart of Hamlet, Sidney was truly "the glass of fashion and the mold of form." At once a poet and a patron of poets, he also distinguished himself as scholar, soldier, courtier, and statesman. The great popularity of the sonnet in England stems directly from the publication of his *Astrophel and Stella* (1591).

FROM ASTROPHEL AND STELLA

1. *"Loving in truth . . ."*

Loving in truth, and fain in verse my love to show,
  That she, dear she, might take some pleasure of my pain,
  Pleasure might cause her read, reading might make her know,
  Knowledge might pity win, and pity grace obtain,—
I sought fit words to paint the blackest face of woe;
  Studying inventions fine, her wits to entertain,
  Oft turning others' leaves to see if thence would flow
  Some fresh and fruitful showers upon my sun-burned brain.
But words came halting forth, wanting invention's stay;
  Invention, nature's child, fled step-dame Study's blows,
  And others' feet still seemed but strangers in my way.
Thus, great with child to speak, and helpless in my throes,
  Biting my truant pen, beating myself for spite,
  Fool, said my muse to me, look in thy heart and write.

3. *"Let dainty wits cry on the sisters nine"*

Let dainty wits cry on the sisters nine,
  That, bravely masked, their fancies may be told;
  Or Pindar's apes[1] flaunt they in phrases fine,
  Enam'ling with pied flowers their thoughts of gold;
Or else let them in statelier glory shine,
  Ennobling new-found tropes with problems old;
  Or with strange similes enrich each line,
  Of herbs or beasts which Ind or Afric hold.

For me, in sooth, no Muse but one I know;
  Phrases and problems from my reach do grow,
  And strange things cost too dear for my poor sprites.
How then? even thus,—in Stella's face I read
  What love and beauty be, then all my deed
  But copying is, what in her Nature writes.

[1] Pindar's apes/imitators of Pindar

5. "It is most true . . ."

It is most true that eyes are formed to serve
  The inward light, and that the heavenly part
  Ought to be king, from whose rules who do swerve,
  Rebels to nature, strive for their own smart.
It is most true what we call Cupid's dart
  An image is which for ourselves we carve,
  And, fools, adore in temple of our heart
  Till that good god make church and churchman starve.
True, that true beauty virtue is indeed,
  Whereof this beauty can be but a shade,
  Which elements with mortal mixture breed.
True, that on earth we are but pilgrims made,
  And should in soul up to our country move;
  True, and yet true that I must Stella love.

6. "Some lovers speak . . ."

Some lovers speak, when they their muses entertain,
  Of hopes begot by fear, of wot[1] not what desires,
  Of force of heav'nly beams infusing hellish pain,
  Of living deaths, dear wounds, fair storms, and freezing fires;
Someone his song in Jove and Jove's strange tales attires,
  Bordered with bulls and swans, powdered with golden rain;
  Another humbler wit to shepherd's pipe retires,
  Yet hiding royal blood full oft in rural vein;
To some a sweetest plaint a sweetest style affords,
  While tears pour out his ink, and sighs breathe out his words,
  His paper pale despair, and pain his pen doth move.
I can speak what I feel, and feel as much as they,
  But think that all the map of my state I display
  When trembling voice brings forth that I do Stella love.

[1] wot/know

7. *"When nature made her chief work . . ."*

When nature made her chief work, Stella's eyes,
    In color black why wrapped she beams so bright?
    Would she in beamy black, like painter wise,
    Frame daintiest luster mixed of shades and light?
Or did she else that sober hue devise
    In object best to knit and strength our sight,
    Lest, if no veil these brave gleams did disguise,
    They, sunlike, should more dazzle than delight?
Or would she her miraculous power show,
    That, whereas black seems beauty's contrary,
    She even in black doth make all beauties flow?
Both so, and thus,—she, minding Love should be
    Placed ever there, gave him this mourning weed
    To honor all their deaths who for her bleed.

15. *"You that do search for every purling spring"*

You that do search for every purling spring
    Which from the ribs of old Parnassus flows,
    And every flower, not sweet perhaps, which grows
    Near thereabouts into your poesy wring;
You that do dictionary's method bring
    Into your rhymes, running in rattling rows;
    You that poor Petrarch's long-deceased woes
    With new-born sighs and denizened[1] wit do sing;
You take wrong ways, those far-fet helps be such
    As do bewray a want of inward touch,
    And sure at length stolen goods do come to light.
But if, both for your love and skill, your name
    You seek to nurse at fullest breasts of Fame,
    Stella behold, and then begin to endite.

[1] denizened/naturalized

22. *"In highest way of heaven . . ."*

In highest way of heaven the Sun did ride,
    Progressing then from fair twins'[1] golden place;
    Having no scarf of clouds before his face,
    But shining forth of heat in his chief pride;
When some fair ladies, by hard promise tied,
    On horseback met him in his furious race,
    Yet each prepared, with fan's well-shading grace,
    From that foe's wounds their tender skins to hide.
Stella alone with face unarmed marched,
    Either to do like him, which open shone,
    Or careless of the wealth because her own;
Yet were the hid and meaner beauties parched,
    Her daintiest bare went free; the cause was this,
    The Sun which others burned, did her but kiss.

[1] twins'/the sign of Gemini

26. *"Though dusty wits dare scorn astrology"*

Though dusty wits dare scorn astrology,
    And fools can think those lamps of purest light,
    Whose numbers, ways, greatness, eternity,
    Promising wonders, wonder to invite,
To have for no cause birthright in the sky,
    But for to spangle the black weeds of night;
    Or for some brawl,[1] which in that chamber high,
    They should still dance to please a gazer's sight.
For me, I do nature unidle know,
    And know great causes, great effects procure;
    And know those bodies high reign on the low.
And if these rules did fail, proof makes me sure,
    Who oft fore-judge my after-following race,
    But only those two stars in Stella's face.

[1] brawl/a dance

31. "With how sad steps . . ."

With how sad steps, O moon, thou climb'st the skies!
 How silently, and with how wan a face!
 What! may it be that even in heavenly place
 That busy archer his sharp arrows tries?
Sure, if that long-with-love-acquainted eyes
 Can judge of love, thou feel'st a lover's case;
 I read it in thy looks,—thy languished grace
 To me, that feel the like, thy state descries.
Then, even of fellowship, O moon, tell me,
 Is constant love deemed there but want of wit?
 Are beauties there as proud as here they be?
Do they above love to be loved, and yet
 Those lovers scorn whom that love doth possess?
 Do they call virtue there ungratefulness?

37. "My mouth doth water . . ."

My mouth doth water, and my breast doth swell,
 My tongue doth itch, my thoughts in labor be;
 Listen then, lordings, with good ear to me,
 For of my life I must a riddle tell.
Toward Aurora's court a nymph doth dwell,
 Rich in all beauties which man's eye can see;
 Beauties so far from reach of words that we
 Abase her praise saying she doth excel;
Rich in the treasure of deserved renown,
 Rich in the riches of a royal heart,
 Rich in those gifts which give th' eternal crown;
Who, though most rich in these and every part
 Which make the patents of true worldly bliss,
 Hath no misfortune but that Rich[1] she is.

[1] Rich/Sidney's Stella, Penelope Devereux, married Lord Rich.

39. *"Come sleep! O sleep, the certain knot of peace"*

Come sleep! O sleep, the certain knot of peace,
  The baiting place of wit, the balm of woe,
  The poor man's wealth, the prisoner's release,
  Th' indifferent judge between the high and low;
With shield of proof shield me from out the prease[1]
  Of those fierce darts despair at me doth throw;
  O make in me those civil wars to cease;
  I will good tribute pay, if thou do so.
Take thou of me smooth pillows, sweetest bed,
  A chamber deaf to noise and blind to light,
  A rosy garland and a weary head;
And if these things, as being thine by right,
  Move not thy heavy grace, thou shalt in me,
  Livelier than elsewhere, Stella's image see.

[1] prease/press

41. *"Having this day my horse . . ."*

Having this day my horse, my hand, my lance
  Guided so well that I obtained the prize,
  Both by the judgment of the English eyes
  And of some sent from that sweet enemy, France;
Horsemen my skill in horsemanship advance,
  Town-folks my strength; a daintier judge applies
  His praise to sleight, which from good use doth rise;
  Some lucky wits impute it but to chance;
Others, because of both sides I do take
  My blood from them, who did excel in this,
  Think nature me a man of arms did make.
How far they shot awry! The true cause is,
  Stella looked on, and from her heavenly face
  Sent forth the beams which made so fair my race.

65. "Love, by sure proof I may call thee unkind"

Love, by sure proof I may call thee unkind,
   That giv'st no better ear to my just cries;
   Thou whom to me such my good turns should bind,
   As I may well recount, but none can prize;
For when, naked boy, thou couldst no harbor find
   In this old world, grown now so too too wise,
   I lodged thee in my heart, and being blind
   By nature born, I gave to thee mine eyes.
Mine eyes, my light, my heart, my life, alas,
   If so great services may scorned be;
   Yet let this thought thy tigerish courage pass:
That I perhaps am somewhat kin to thee;
   Since in thine arms, if learned fame truth hath spread,
   Thou bear'st the arrow, I the arrow head.

73. "Love still a boy, and oft a wanton is"

Love still a boy, and oft a wanton is,
   Schooled only by his mother's tender eye;
   What wonder then if he his lesson miss,
   When for so soft a rod dear play he try?
And yet my Star,[1] because a sugared kiss
   In sport I sucked, while she asleep did lie,
   Doth lower, nay, chide; nay, threat for only this:
   Sweet, it was saucy Love, not humble I.
But no scuse[2] serves, she makes her wrath appear
   In Beauty's throne, see now who dares come near
   Those scarlet judges, threatening bloody pain?
O heavenly fool, thy most kiss-worthy face,
   Anger invests with such a lovely grace,
   That Anger's self I needs must kiss again.

[1] Star/i.e., Stella   [2] scuse/excuse

74. "I never drank of Aganippe well"

I never drank of Aganippe well,[1]
   Nor ever did in shade of Tempe[2] sit,
   And Muses scorn with vulgar brains to dwell;
   Poor layman I, for sacred rites unfit.

Some do I hear of poets' fury tell,
   But, God wot, wot not what they mean by it;
   And this I swear by blackest brook of hell,
   I am no pick-purse of another's wit.
How falls it then, that with so smooth an ease
   My thoughts I speak, and what I speak doth flow
   In verse, and that my verse best wits doth please?
Guess we the cause? What, is it thus? Fie, no.
   Or so? Much less. How then? Sure thus it is:
   My lips are sweet, inspired with Stella's kiss.

[1] Aganippe well/at the foot of Mt. Helicon in Greece and sacred to the Muses
[2] Tempe/valley near Mt. Olympus and sacred to Apollo

81. "O kiss, which dost those ruddy gems impart"

O kiss, which dost those ruddy gems impart,
   Or gems, or fruits or new-found Paradise,
   Breathing all bliss and sweetening to the heart,
   Teaching dumb lips a nobler exercise.
O kiss, which souls, even souls together ties
   By links of Love, and only Nature's art,
   How fain would I paint thee to all men's eyes,
   Or of thy gifts at least shade out some part.
But she forbids, with blushing words, she says,
   She builds her fame on higher seated praise;
   But my heart burns, I cannot silent be.
Then since (dear life) you fain would have me peace,
   And I, mad with delight, want wit to cease,
   Stop you my mouth with still still kissing me.

99. "When far spent night persuades each mortal eye"

When far spent night persuades each mortal eye,
   To whom nor art nor nature granteth light,
   To lay his then mark wanting shafts of sight,
   Closed with their quivers in sleep's armory;

With windows ope[1] then most my mind doth lie,
   Viewing the shape of darkness and delight,
   Takes in that sad hue, which with th' inward night
Of his mazed powers keeps perfect harmony.
But when birds charm, and that sweet air, which is
   Morn's messenger, with rose enameled skies
   Calls each wight[2] to salute the flower of bliss;
In tomb of lids then buried are mine eyes,
   Forced by their Lord, who is ashamed to find
   Such light in sense, with such a darkened mind.

[1]ope/open   [2]wight/creature

100. "O tears, no tears, but rain from beauty's skies"

O tears, no tears, but rain from beauty's skies,
   Making those Lilies and those Roses grow,
   Which ay[1] most fair, now more than most fair show,
   While graceful pity beauty beautifies.
O honeyed sighs, which from that breast do rise,
   Whose pants do make unspilling cream to flow,
   Winged with whose breath, so pleasing Zephyrs blow,
   As can refresh the hell where my soul fries.
O plaints[2] conserved in such a sugared phrase,
   That eloquence itself envies your praise,
   While sobbed out words a perfect Music give.
Such tears, sighs, plaints, no sorrow is, but joy;
   Or if such heavenly signs must prove annoy,
   All mirth farewell, let me in sorrow live.

[1]ay/before   [2]plaints/complaints

104. "Envious wits, what hath been mine offence"

Envious wits, what hath been mine offence,
   That with such poisonous care my looks you mark,
   That to each word, nay sigh of mine, you hark,
   As grudging me my sorrow's eloquence?

Ah, is it not enough that I am thence,
   Thence, so far thence, that scarcely any spark
   Of comfort dare come to this dungeon dark,
   Where rigor's exile locks up all my sense?
But if I by a happy window pass,
   If I but stars upon mine armor bear—
   Sick, thirsty, glad, though but of empty glass—
Your moral notes straight my hid meaning tear
   From out my ribs, and, puffing, proves that I
   Do Stella love; fools, who doth it deny?

"Thou blind man's mark . . ."

Thou blind man's mark, thou fool's self-chosen snare,
Fond fancy's scum, and dregs of scattered thought;
Band of all evils, cradle of causeless care;
Thou web of will, whose end is never wrought;
Desire, desire! I have too dearly bought,
With price of mangled mind, thy worthless ware;
Too long, too long, asleep thou hast me brought,
Who should my mind to higher things prepare.
But yet in vain thou hast my ruin sought;
In vain thou madest me to vain things aspire;
In vain thou kindlest all thy smoky fire;
For virtue hath this better lesson taught,—
Within myself to seek my only hire,
Desiring nought but how to kill desire.

"Leave me, O love . . ."

Leave me, O love which reachest but to dust;
And thou, my mind, aspire to higher things;
Grow rich in that which never taketh rust,
Whatever fades but fading pleasure brings.
Draw in thy beams, and humble all thy might
To that sweet yoke where lasting freedoms be;
Which breaks the clouds and opens forth the light,
That doth both shine and give us sight to see.
O take fast hold; let that light be thy guide
In this small course which birth draws out to death,
And think how evil becometh him to slide,

Who seeketh heaven, and comes of heavenly breath.
  Then farewell, world; thy uttermost I see;
  Eternal Love, maintain thy life in me.

FULKE GREVILLE, LORD BROOKE
(1554–1628)

Born in the same year as Sir Philip Sidney, Greville's career parallels that of his more famous friend. Sidney and Greville began writing poetry together sometime before 1580. After Sidney's death, Greville became an influential man at court, serving under both Elizabeth and James. In later life he wrote a biography of Sidney. His affection for Sidney is reflected in his famous epitaph, "Servant to Queen Elizabeth, Councillor to King James, and friend to Sir Philip Sidney."

FROM CÆLICA

12. *"Cupid, thou naughty boy . . ."*

Cupid, thou naughty boy, when thou wert loathed,
Naked and blind, for vagabonding noted,
Thy nakedness I in my reason clothed,
Mine eyes I gave thee, so was I devoted.

Fie, wanton, fie! who would show children kindness?
No sooner he into mine eyes was gotten
But straight he clouds them with a seeing blindness,
Makes reason wish that reason were forgotten.

From thence to Myra's eyes the wanton strayeth,
Where while I charge him with ungrateful measure,
So with fair wonders he mine eyes betrayeth,
That my wounds and his wrongs become my pleasure;
  Till for more spite to Myra's heart he flyeth,
  Where living to the world, to me he dieth.

16. "Fie, foolish earth . . ."

Fie, foolish earth, think you the heaven wants glory
Because your shadows do yourself benight?
All's dark unto the blind, let them be sorry;
The heavens in themselves are ever bright.

Fie, fond desire, think you that love wants glory
Because your shadows do yourself benight?
The hopes and fears of lust may make men sorry,
But love still in herself finds her delight.

Then earth, stand fast, the sky that you benight
Will turn again and so restore your glory;
Desire, be steady, hope is your delight,
An orb wherein no creature can be sorry,
  Love being placed above these middle regions
  Where every passion wars itself with legions.

38. "Cælica, I overnight was finely used"

Cælica, I overnight was finely used,
Lodged in the midst of paradise, your heart;
Kind thoughts had charge I might not be refused,
Of every fruit and flower I had part.

But curious knowledge, blown with busy flame,
The sweetest fruits had in down shadows hidden,
And for it found mine eyes had seen the same,
I from my paradise was straight forbidden.

Where that cur, rumor, runs in every place,
Barking with care, begotten out of fear;
And glassy honor, tender of disgrace,
Stand seraphim to see I come not there;
  While that fine soil which all these joys did yield,
  By broken fence is proved a common field.

84. *"Farewell, sweet boy . . ."*

Farewell, sweet boy; complain not of my truth;
Thy mother loved thee not with more devotion;
For to thy boy's play I gave all my youth;
Young master, I did hope for your promotion.

While some sought honors, princes' thoughts observing,
Many wooed Fame, the child of pain and anguish;
Others judged inward good a chief deserving;
I in thy wanton visions joyed to languish.

I bowed not to thy image for succession,
Nor bound thy bow to shoot reformed kindness;
Thy plays of hope and fear were my confession,
The spectacles to my life was thy blindness.
   But, Cupid, now farewell; I will go play me
   With thoughts that please me less, and less betray me.

100. *"In night, when colors all to black are cast"*

In night, when colors all to black are cast,
Distinction lost, or gone down with the light,
The eye, a watch to inward senses placed,
Not seeing, yet still having power of sight,

Gives vain alarums to the inward sense,
Where fear, stirred up with witty tyranny,
Confounds all powers, and through self-offence
Doth forge and raise impossibility,

Such as in thick depriving darknesses
Proper reflections of the error be,
And images of self-confusedness,
Which hurt imaginations only see:—
   And from this nothing seen, tells news of devils,
   Which but expressions be of inward evils.

Sir Walter Ralegh
(c.1552–1618)

Celebrated as a soldier, sailor, courtier, and poet, Ralegh [Raleigh] was active in the early colonization of Virginia and in the British wars against Spain. Although he had been the favorite of Queen Elizabeth, he was imprisoned in the Tower of London and finally executed by King James. During his long imprisonment he wrote his *History of the World*. Though Ralegh did not participate in the vogue of the sonnet sequences, he wrote a number of single sonnets of high quality.

"Like truthless dreams . . ."

Like truthless dreams, so are my joys expired,
And past return are all my dandled days;
My love misled, and fancy quite retired—
Of all which passed the sorrow only stays.

My lost delights, now clean from sight of land,
Have left me all alone in unknown ways;
My mind to woe, my life in fortune's hand—
Of all which passed the sorrow only stays.

As in a country strange, without companion,
I only wail the wrong of death's delays,
Whose sweet spring spent, whose summer well nigh done—
Of all which passed the sorrow only stays.

Whom care forewarns, ere age and winter cold,
To haste me hence to find my fortune's fold.

FROM "COMMENDATORY VERSES" TO EDMUND
SPENSER'S FAIRY QUEEN

A Vision upon This Conceit of the Fairy Queen

Methought I saw the grave where Laura lay,
Within that temple where the vestal flame
Was wont to burn; and passing by that way
To see that buried dust of living fame,
Whose tomb fair Love and fairer Virtue kept,
All suddenly I saw the Fairy Queen;
At whose approach the soul of Petrarch wept,
And from thenceforth those graces were not seen,
For they this Queen attended; in whose stead
Oblivion laid him down on Laura's hearse.
Hereat the hardest stones were seen to bleed,
And groans of buried ghosts the heavens did pierce;
  Where Homer's sprite did tremble all for grief,
  And cursed th' access of that celestial thief.

Sir Walter Ralegh to His Son

Three things there be that prosper up apace
And flourish, whilst they grow asunder far;
But on a day, they meet all in one place,
And when they meet, they one another mar.
And they be these: the wood, the weed, the wag.
The wood is that which makes the gallow tree;
The weed is that which strings the hangman's bag;
The wag, my pretty knave, betokeneth thee.
Mark well, dear boy, whilst these assemble not,
Green springs the tree, hemp grows, the wag is wild;
But when they meet, it makes the timber rot,
It frets the halter, and it chokes the child.
  Then bless thee, and beware, and let us pray
  We part not with thee at this meeting day.

Thomas Lodge
(c.1558–1625)

The son of a Lord Mayor of London, Lodge devoted himself to a number of careers. After receiving a degree at Oxford, he studied law but soon gave it up for writing. After a full career as a writer of tracts, romances, and poetry, he turned to medicine. Like other Elizabethan sonnet sequences, *Phyllis* (1593) contains a variety of poems, not all fourteen lines long.

FROM PHYLLIS

1. *"O pleasing thoughts . . ."*

O pleasing thoughts, apprentices of love,
Forerunners of desire, sweet mithridates[1]
The poison of my sorrows to remove,
With whom my hopes and fear full oft debates,—
　Enrich yourselves and me by your self riches
Which are the thoughts you spend on heaven-bred beauty,
Rouse you my muse beyond our poets' pitches,
And working wonders, yet say all is duty;
　Use you no eaglets' eyes nor phoenix' feathers
To tower the heaven from whence heaven's wonder sallies,
For why, your sun sings sweetly to her weathers,
Making a spring of winter in the valleys.
　　Show to the world, though poor and scant my skill is,
　　How sweet thoughts be that are but thought on Phyllis.

[1] mithridates/antidotes

8. *"No stars her eyes . . ."*

No stars her eyes, to clear the wandering night,
But shining suns of true divinity,
That make the soul conceive her perfect light;
No wanton beauties of humanity
　Her pretty brows, but beams that clear the sight
Of him that seeks the true philosophy;

No coral is her lip, no rose her fair,
But even that crimson that adorns the sun;
   No nymph is she, but mistress of the air,
By whom my glories are but new begun.
     But when I touch and taste as others do,
     I then shall write and you shall wonder too.

13. *"Love guides the roses of thy lips"*

Love guides the roses of thy lips
And flies about them like a bee;
If I approach he forward skips,
And if I kiss he stingeth me.
   Love in thine eyes doth build his bower
And sleeps within their pretty shine;
And if I look, the boy will lour
And from their orbs shoot shafts divine.
   Love works thy heart within his fire,
And in my tears doth firm the same;
And if I tempt it will retire,
And of my plaints doth make a game.
   Love, let me cull her choicest flowers,
And pity me, and calm her eye,
Make soft her heart, dissolve her lours,
Then will I praise thy deity.
     But if thou do not, Love, I'll truly serve her
     In spite of thee, and by firm faith deserve her.

35. *"I hope and fear . . ."*[1]

I hope and fear, I pray and hold my peace,
Now freeze my thoughts and straight they fry again,
I now admire and straight my wonders cease,
I loose my bonds and yet myself restrain;
   This likes me most that leaves me discontent,
My courage serves and yet my heart doth fail,
My will doth climb whereas my hopes are spent,
I laugh at love, yet when he comes I quail;

The more I strive, the duller bide I still,
I would be thralled, and yet I freedom love,
I would redress, yet hourly feed mine ill,
I would repine, and dare not once reprove;
 And for my love I am bereft of power,
 And strengthless strive my weakness to devour.

[1] "I hope and fear . . ."/cf. Wyatt's "Description of the Contrarious Passions of a Lover," p. 4.

GILES FLETCHER, THE ELDER
(c.1549–1611)

The father of two poets, Giles, the Younger and Phineas, Fletcher was educated at Cambridge and employed on diplomatic missions in Scotland and Russia. His *Licia* is one of the earliest sonnet sequences, written when the fashion was still new. Worth noting is his declaration in the dedication that "a man may write of love, and not be in love, as well as of husbandrie and not goe to plough."

FROM LICIA

1. *"Sad, all alone, not long I musing sat"*

Sad, all alone, not long I musing sat,
But that my thoughts compelled me to aspire;
A laurel garland in my hand I gat,
So the Muses I approached the nigher.
My suit was this, a poet to become,
To drink with them, and from the heavens be fed.
Phœbus denied, and swore there was no room,
Such to be poets as fond fancy led.
With that I mourned and sat me down to weep;
Venus she smiled, and smiling to me said,
Come drink with me, and sit thee still, and sleep.
This voice I heard; and Venus I obeyed.
That poison sweet hath done me all this wrong,
For now of love must needs be all my song.

20. "First did I fear . . ."

First did I fear, when first my love began,
Possessed in fits by watchful jealousy;
I sought to keep what I by favor wan,
And brooked no partner in my love to be.
But tyrant sickness fed upon my love,
And spread his ensigns, dyed with color white;
Then was suspicion glad for to remove,
And, loving much, did fear to lose her quite.
Erect, fair sweet, the colors thou didst wear;
Dislodge thy griefs, the short'ners of content;
For now of life, not love, is all my fear,
Lest life and love be both together spent.
   Live but, fair love, and banish thy disease,
    And love, kind heart, both when and whom thou please.

43. "Are those two stars . . ."

Are those two stars, her eyes, my life's light gone,
By which my soul was freed from all dark?
And am I left distressed to live alone,
Where none my tears and mournful tale shall mark?
Ah sun, why shine thy looks, thy looks like gold,
When horsemen brave thou risest in the east?
Ah Cynthia pale, to whom my griefs I told,
Why do you both rejoice both man and beast?
And I alone, alone that dark possess
By Licia's absence brighter than the sun,
Whose smiling light did ease my sad distress,
And broke the clouds, when tears like rain begun.
   Heavens, grant that light and so me waking keep,
    Or shut my eyes and rock me fast asleep!

Barnabe Barnes
(?1569–1609)

Barnes was the fourth son of the bishop of Durham. He was educated at Brasenose College, Oxford, and served in France with the Earl of Essex. He managed to escape sentencing for attempting to murder the recorder of Berwick with poisoned claret, but not the ridicule of other poets, in particular of Thomas Nashe. His antipopish tragedy, *The Devil's Charter* (1607) was probably acted before King James. His sonnet sequences, *Parthenophil and Parthenophe* (1593) and *A Divine Century of Spiritual Sonnets* (1595), were written at the height of the sonnet vogue.

————————

FROM PARTHENOPHIL AND PARTHENOPHE

1. "Mistress, behold, in this true-speaking glass"

Mistress, behold in this true-speaking glass
   Thy beauty's graces, of all women rarest,
   Where thou mayst find how largely they surpass
   And stain in glorious loveliness the fairest.
But read, sweet mistress, and behold it nearer,
   Pond'ring my sorrow's outrage with some pity;
   Then shalt thou find no worldly creature dearer
   Than thou to me, thyself in each love ditty.
But in this mirror equally compare
   Thy matchless beauty with mine endless grief;
   There like thyself none can be found so fair,
Of chiefest pains there, are my pains the chief.
   Betwixt these both, this one doubt shalt thou find:
   Whether are here extremest in their kind?

18. "Write! write! help! help . . ."

Write! write! help! help, sweet Muse! and never cease!
   In endless labors, pens and paper tire!
   Until I purchase my long wished desire.

Brains, with my reason, never rest in peace!
    Waste breathless words! and beautiful sighs increase!
    Till of my woes, remorseful, you espy her;
Till she with me, be burnt in equal fire.
    I never will, from labor, wits release!
    My senses never shall in quiet rest;
    Till thou be pitiful, and love alike!
And if thou never pity my distresses;
    Thy cruelty, with endless force shall strike
    Upon my wits, to ceaseless writs addrest!
    My cares, in hope of some revenge, this lesses.

FROM A DIVINE CENTURY OF SPIRITUAL SONNETS

1. *"No more lewd lays . . ."*

No more lewd lays of lighter loves I sing,
    Nor teach my lustful muse abused to fly
    With sparrows' plumes, and for compassion cry
    To mortal beauties which no succor bring.
But my muse, feathered with an angel's wing,
    Divinely mounts aloft unto the sky,
    Where her love's subjects, with my hopes, do lie.
    For Cupid's darts prefigurate hell's sting;
His quenchless torch foreshows hell's quenchless fire,
    Kindling men's wits with lustful lays of sin—
    Thy wounds my cure, dear Savior! I desire,
To pierce my thoughts, thy fiery cherubin,
    By kindling my desires true zeal t'infuse,
    Thy love my theme, and Holy Ghost my muse!

Thomas Watson
(c.1557–1592)

Though his own verse offers little to admire, Watson exerted a considerable influence over his contemporaries. Possibly educated at Oxford, he was responsible for introducing a number of foreign influences into English literature. His *Hecatompathia, or a Passionate Century of Love* (1582), though it contains no fourteen-line sonnets, is usually credited with introducing the sequence to England. *The Tears of Fancy* appeared in 1593.

FROM THE TEARS OF FANCY

"Go idle lines . . ."

Go idle lines unpolished rude and base,
Unworthy words to blazon beauty's glory:
(Beauty that hath my restless heart in chase,
Beauty the subject of my rueful story.)
I warn thee shun the bower of her abiding,
Be not so bold ne[1] hardy as to view her:
Lest she enraged with thee fall a chiding,
And so her anger prove thy woe's renewer.
Yet if she deign to rue thy dreadful smart,
And reading laugh, and laughing so mislike thee:
Bid her desist, and look within my heart,
Where she may see how ruthless she did strike me.
If she pleased though she reward thee not,
What other say of me regard it not.

[1] ne/nor

22. *"I saw the object . . ."*

I saw the object of my pining thought
Within a garden of sweet nature's placing,
Wherein an arbor, artificial wrought
By workman's wondrous skill, the garden gracing,
Did boast his glory, glory far renowned,
For in his shady boughs my mistress slept;

And with a garland of his branches crowned,
Her dainty forehead from the sun ykept.
Imperious love upon her eyelids tending,
Playing his wanton sports at every beck
And into every finest limb descending
From eyes to lips, from lips to ivory neck,
And every limb supplied, and t'every part
Had free access, but durst not touch her heart.

HENRY CONSTABLE
(1562–1613)

Constable was born in Warwickshire of a good family, and while
still young embraced the Catholic faith. Educated at Oxford, he
later spent many years abroad. His sequence *Diana,* published
in 1592, originally contained only twenty-three sonnets. It was
reissued in 1594, considerably enlarged and organized into eight
"Decades."

———————————————

FROM DIANA

The First Decade, 1. "Resolved to love . . ."

Resolved to love, unworthy to obtain,
    I do no favor crave; but, humble wise,
    To thee my sighs in verse I sacrifice,
    Only some pity, and no help to gain.
Hear then! and as my heart shall aye remain
    A patient object to thy lightening eyes;
    A patient ear bring thou to thundering cries!
    Fear not the crack! when I the blow sustain.
So as thine eye bred mine ambitious thought;
    So shall thine ear make proud my voice for joy.
    Lo, dear! what wonders great by thee are wrought,
    When I but little favors do enjoy.
The voice is made the ear for to rejoice:
And your ear giveth pleasure to my voice.

The Fourth Decade, 10. "Hope, like the hyena . . ."

Hope, like the hyena,[1] coming to be old,
  Alters his shape; it is turned into despair.
  Pity my hoary hopes! Maid of clear mould!
  Think not that frowns can ever make thee fair!
What harm is it to kiss, to laugh, to play?
  Beauty's no blossom, if it be not used.
  Sweet dalliance keeps the wrinkles long away:
  Repentance follows them that have refused.
To bring you to the knowledge of your good
  I seek, I sue. O try, and then believe!
  Each image can be chaste that's carved of wood.
  You show you live, when men you do relieve.
Iron with wearing shines. Rust wasteth treasure.
On earth, but love there is no other pleasure.

[1] hyena/The hyena was traditionally reputed to be able to change its sex at will.

The Sixth Decade, 2. "To live in hell . . ."

To live in hell and heaven to behold;
  To welcome life and die a living death;
  To sweat with heat, and yet be freezing cold;
  To grasp at stars and lie the earth beneath;
To tread a maze that never shall have end;
  To burn in sighs and starve in daily tears;
  To climb a hill and never to descend;
  Giants to kill, and quake at childish fears;
To pine for food, and watch th' Hesperian tree;
  To thirst for drink, and nectar still to draw;
  To live accursed, whom men hold blest to be,
  And weep those wrongs which never creature saw:
If this be love, if love in these be founded,
My heart is love, for these in it are grounded.

To St. Peter and St. Paul

He that for fear his Master did deny,
   And at a maiden's voice amazed stood,
   The mightiest monarch of the earth withstood,
   And on his Master's cross rejoiced to die.
He whose blind zeal did rage with cruelty
   And helped to shed the first of martyrs' blood,
   By light from heaven his blindness understood,
   And with the chief apostle slain doth lie.
O three times happy two! O golden pair!
   Who with your blood did lay the church's ground
   Within the fatal town which twins did found,
And settled there the Hebrew fisher's chair
   Where first the Latin shepherd raised his throne,
   And since, the world and church were ruled by one.

To St. Mary Magdalen

Such as, retired from sight of men, like thee
   By penance seek the joys of heaven to win,
   In deserts make their paradise begin
   And even among wild beasts do angels see.
In such a place my soul doth seem to be,
   When in my body she laments her sin
   And none but brutal passions finds therein,
   Except they be sent down from heaven to me.
Yet if those graces God to me impart
   Which he inspired thy blessed breast withal,
   I may find heaven in my retired heart;
And if thou change the object of my love,
   The winged affection which men Cupid call
   May get his sight, and like an angel prove.

WILLIAM PERCY
(1575–1648)

A younger son of Henry Percy, eighth Earl of Northumberland, Percy attended Oxford where he was friendly with Barnabe Barnes. The author of a number of plays extant only in manuscript, he seems to have published nothing other than his *Sonnets to the Fairest Cœlia* (1594).

FROM CŒLIA

1. *"Judged by my goddess' doom . . ."*

Judged by my goddess' doom to endless pain,
Lo, here I ope my sorrow's passion,
That every silly eye may view most plain
A sentence given on no occasion.
    If that by chance they fall (most fortunate)
Within those cruel hands that did enact it,
Say but, Alas, he was too passionate,
My doom is passed, nor can be now unactit.[1]
    So mayst thou see I was a spotless lover,
And grieve withal that e'er thou dealt so sore;
Unto remorse who goes about to move her,
Pursues the winged winds, and tills the shore.
        Lovely is her semblance, hard is her heart,
        Wavering is her mind, sure is her dart.

[1] unactit/undone

17. *"Relent, my dear . . ."*

Relent, my dear yet unkind Cœlia,
At length relent, and give my sorrows end.
So shall I keep my long-wished holiday,
And set a trophy on a froward friend.
    Nor tributes, nor imposts, nor other duties
Demand I will, as lawful conqueror;
Duties, tributes, imposts unto thy beauties
Myself will pay as yielded servitor.

Then quick relent, thyself surrender us.
Brave sir, and why (quoth she) must I relent?
Relent (cried I), thyself doth conquer us.
When eftsoons[1] with my proper instrument
  She cut me off, ay me, and answered,
  You cannot conquer, and be conquered.

[1] eftsoons/forthwith

ANONYMOUS

The author of the sequence *Zepheria* (1594) has never been identified. Because of the abundance of legal terminology in these sonnets, it is usually assumed that he was a member of one of the Inns of Court. The excessive use of this terminology provoked Sir John Davies to satirize these sonnets in his own sonnet to Zepheria (see p. 65).

(see p. 65)

FROM ZEPHERIA

13. "Proud in thy love . . ."

Proud in thy love, how many have I cited
Impartial thee to view, whose eyes have lavished
Sweet beauteous objects oft have men delighted;
But thou above delight their sense hast ravished.
  They, amorous artists, thee pronounced love's queen,
And unto thy supremacy did swear;
(Venus, at Paphos keep, no more be seen!)
Now Cupid after thee his shafts shall bear.
  How have I spent my spirit of invention
In penning amorous stanzas to thy beauty,
But heavenly graces may not brook dimension;
Nor more may thine, for infinite they be.
  But now in harsh tune I of amours sing,
  My pipe for them grows hoarse, but shrill to plaining.

26. *"When we, in kind embracements . . ."*

When we, in kind embracements, had agreed
To keep a royal banquet on our lips,
How soon have we another feast decreed,
And how, at parting, have we mourned by fits!
    Eftsoons, in absence have we wailed much more
Till those void hours of intermission
Were spent, that we might revel as before.
How have we bribed time for expedition!
    And when remitted to our former love-plays,
How have we, overweening in delight,
Accused the father sexton of the days
That then with eagle's wings he took his flight.
        But now, old man, fly on as swift as thought,
        Sith eyes from love, and hope from heart, is wrought.

SAMUEL DANIEL
(1562–1619)

Born in Somerset, educated at Oxford, Daniel devoted his life to writing, producing a number of works in both prose and verse. His treatise *The Defence of Rhyme* (1603) ranks high among Elizabethan critical essays. Though criticized by Ben Jonson, his poetry was admired by a large number of his contemporaries. The sonnets from *Delia* (1592) are among the best produced in the period.

FROM DELIA

6. *"Fair is my love . . ."*

Fair is my love, and cruel as she's fair:
    Her brow shades frowns, although her eyes are sunny,
    Her smiles are lightning, though her pride despair,
    And her disdains are gall, her favors honey.
A modest maid, decked with a blush of honor,
    Whose feet do tread green paths of youth and love;
    The wonder of all eyes that look upon her,
    Sacred on earth, designed a saint above.

Chastity and beauty, which were deadly foes,
  Live reconciled friends within her brow;
  And had she pity to conjoin with those,
  Then who had heard the plaints I utter now?
For had she not been fair and thus unkind,
My muse had slept, and none had known my mind.

17. *"Why should I sing in verse . . ."*

Why should I sing in verse, why should I frame
  These sad neglected notes for her dear sake?
  Why should I offer up unto her name
  The sweetest sacrifice my youth can make?
Why should I strive to make her live forever,
  That never deigns to give me joy to live?
  Why should m' afflicted muse so much endeavor
  Such honor unto cruelty to give?
If her defects have purchased her this fame,
  What should her virtues do, her smiles, her love?
  If this her worst, how should her best inflame?
  What passions would her milder favors move?
Favors, I think, would sense quite overcome,
And that makes happy lovers ever dumb.

36. *"When men shall find thy flower, thy glory, pass"*

When men shall find thy flower, thy glory, pass,
  And thou with careful brow sitting alone,
  Received hast this message from thy glass,
  That tells the truth and says that all is gone;
Fresh shalt thou see in me the wounds thou mad'st,
  Though spent thy flame, in me the heat remaining;
  I that have loved thee thus before thou fad'st,
  My faith shall wax when thou art in thy waning.
The world shall find this miracle in me,
  That fire can burn when all the matter's spent;
  Then what my faith hath been, thyself shall see,
  And that thou wast unkind, thou mayst repent.
Thou mayst repent that thou hast scorned my tears,
When winter snows upon thy sable hairs.

37. *"When winter snows upon thy sable hairs"*

When winter snows upon thy sable hairs,
   And frost of age hath nipped thy beauties near,
   When dark shall seem thy day that never clears,
   And all lies withered that was held so dear,
Then take this picture which I here present thee,
   Limned[1] with a pencil not all unworthy;
   Here see the gifts that God and nature lent thee,
   Here read thyself and what I suffered for thee.
This may remain thy lasting monument,
   Which happily posterity may cherish;
   These colors with thy fading are not spent,
   These may remain when thou and I shall perish.
If they remain, then thou shalt live thereby;
They will remain, and so thou canst not die.

[1] limned/drawn, i.e., painted with words

38. *"Thou canst not die whilst any zeal abound"*

Thou canst not die whilst any zeal abound
   In feeling hearts that can conceive these lines;
   Though thou, a Laura, hast no Petrarch found,
   In base attire yet clearly beauty shines.
And I, though born within a colder clime,
   Do feel mine inward heat as great (I know it)
   He never had more faith, although more rhyme;
   I love as well, though he could better show it.
But I may add one feather to thy fame,
   To help her flight throughout the fairest isle,
   And if my pen could more enlarge thy name,
   Then shouldst thou live in an immortal style.
For though that Laura better limned be,
Suffice, thou shalt be loved as well as she.

49. *"Care-charmer sleep . . ."*

Care-charmer sleep, son of the sable night,
   Brother to death, in silent darkness born,
   Relieve my languish and restore the light;
   With dark forgetting of my care, return.

And let the day be time enough to mourn
  The shipwreck of my ill-adventured youth;
  Let waking eyes suffice to wail their scorn
  Without the torment of the night's untruth.
Cease, dreams, th' images of day-desires,
  To model forth the passions of the morrow;
  Never let rising sun approve you liars,
  To add more grief to aggravate my sorrow.
Still let me sleep, embracing clouds in vain,
And never wake to feel the day's disdain.

50. *"Let others sing of knights and paladins"*

Let others sing of knights and paladins
  In aged accents and untimely words,
  Paint shadows in imaginary lines
  Which well the reach of their high wits records;
But I must sing of thee, and those fair eyes
  Authentic shall my verse in time to come,
  When yet th' unborn shall say, Lo where she lies,
  Whose beauty made him speak that else was dumb.
These are the arks, the trophies I erect,
  That fortify thy name against old age;
  And these thy sacred virtues must protect
  Against the dark and time's consuming rage.
Though th' error of my youth in them appear,
Suffice, they show I lived and loved thee dear.

MICHAEL DRAYTON
(1563–1631)

Michael Drayton was born in Warwickshire, and tradition counts
him as the friend of Shakespeare and Ben Jonson. A professional
writer, Drayton was one of the most prolific of the Elizabethan
poets, writing in almost every conceivable form. His sequence
first appeared as *Idea's Mirror* in 1594 and after revisions as *Idea*
in 1619. His facile style is representative of the best—and often
the worst—sonnet writing in his time.

———————————

FROM IDEA

To the Reader of These Sonnets

Into these loves who but for passion looks,
At this first sight here let him lay them by,
And seek elsewhere, in turning other books
Which better may his labor satisfy.
No farfetched sigh shall ever wound my breast,
Love from mine eye a tear shall never wring,
Nor in *Ah me's* my whining sonnets dressed.
A libertine, fantastically I sing;
My verse is the true image of my mind,
Ever in motion, still desiring change.
And as thus to variety inclined,
So in all humors sportively I range;
    My muse is rightly of the English strain,
    That cannot long one fashion entertain.

1. "Like an adventurous seafarer am I"

Like an adventurous seafarer am I,
Who hath some long and dang'rous voyage been,
And called to tell of his discovery,
How far he sailed, what countries he had seen;
Proceeding from the port whence he put forth,
Shows by his compass how his course he steered,
When east, when west, when south, and when by north,
As how the pole to ev'ry place was reared,

What capes he doubled, of what continent,
The gulfs and straits that strangely he had passed,
Where most becalmed, where with foul weather spent,
And on what rocks in peril to be cast:
    Thus in my love, time calls me to relate
    My tedious travels and oft-varying fate.

9. *"As other men, so I myself do muse"*

As other men, so I myself do muse
Why in this sort I wrest invention so,
And why these giddy metaphors I use,
Leaving the path the greater part do go.
I will resolve you: I am lunatic,
And ever this in madmen you shall find—
What they last thought of, when the brain grew sick,
In most distraction they keep that in mind.
Thus talking idly in this bedlam fit,
Reason and I, you must conceive, are twain;
'Tis nine years now since first I lost my wit,
Bear with me, then, though troubled be my brain.
    With diet and correction, men distraught
    (Not too far past) may to their wits be brought.

10. *"To nothing fitter can I thee compare"*

To nothing fitter can I thee compare
Than to the son of some rich penny-father,[1]
Who having now brought on his end with care,
Leaves to his son all he had heaped together;
This new-rich novice, lavish of his chest,
To one man gives, doth on another spend,
Then here he riots; yet amongst the rest
Haps to lend some to one true honest friend.
Thy gifts thou in obscurity dost waste,
False friends thy kindness, born but to deceive thee;
Thy love, that is on the unworthy placed;
Time hath thy beauty, which with age will leave thee;
    Only that little which to me was lent,
    I give thee back, when all the rest is spent.

[1] penny-father/miser

31. "Methinks I see some crooked mimic jeer"

Methinks I see some crooked mimic jeer,
And tax my muse with this fantastic grace;
Turning my papers, asks, What have we here?
Making withal some filthy antic face.
I fear no censure, nor what thou canst say,
Nor shall my spirit one jot of vigor lose
Think'st thou my wit shall keep the pack-horse way
That ev'ry dudgeon low invention goes?
Since sonnets thus in bundles are impressed,
And ev'ry drudge doth dull our satiate ear,
Think'st thou my love shall in those rags be dressed
That ev'ry dowdy, ev'ry trull doth wear?
   Up to my pitch no common judgment flies,
   I scorn all earthly dung-bred scarabies.[1]

[1] scarabies/beetles

37. "Dear, why should you command me to my rest"

Dear, why should you command me to my rest,
When now the night doth summon all to sleep?
Methinks this time becometh lovers best;
Night was ordained together friends to keep.
How happy are all other living things,
Which though the day disjoin by sev'ral flight,
The quiet evening yet together brings,
And each returns unto his love at night!
O thou that art so courteous else to all,
Why shouldst thou, Night, abuse me only thus,
That ev'ry creature to his kind dost call,
And yet 'tis thou dost only sever us?
   Well could I wish it would be ever day,
   If when night comes you bid me go away.

44. "Whilst thus my pen strives to eternize thee"

Whilst thus my pen strives to eternize thee,
Age rules my lines with wrinkles in my face,
Where, in the map of all my misery,

Is modeled out the world of my disgrace;
Whilst in despite of tyrannizing times,
Medea-like I make thee young again.
Proudly thou scorn'st my world-outwearing rhymes,
And murther'st virtue with thy coy disdain;
And though in youth my youth untimely perish
To keep thee from oblivion and the grave,
Ensuing ages yet my rhymes shall cherish,
Where I, entombed, my better part shall save;
   And though this earthly body fade and die,
   My name shall mount upon eternity.

61. "Since there's no help . . ."

Since there's no help, come let us kiss and part;
Nay, I have done, you get no more of me,
And I am glad, yea glad with all my heart
That thus so cleanly I myself can free;
Shake hands forever, cancel all our vows,
And when we meet at any time again,
Be it not seen in either of our brows
That we one jot of former love retain.
Now at the last gasp of love's latest breath,
When, his pulse failing, passion speechless lies,
When faith is kneeling by his bed of death,
And innocence is closing up his eyes,
   Now if thou wouldst, when all have given him over,
   From death to life thou mightst him yet recover.

E. C.

The sequence *Emaricdulfe* appeared in 1595 with the letters
"E. C." on the title page. The author has never been identified.

————————

6. *"Within her hair . . ."*

Within her hair Venus and Cupid sport them;
　　Some time they twist it, amber-like, in gold,
To which the whistling winds do oft resort them,
　　As if they strove to have the knots unrolled;
Some time they let their golden tresses dangle,
　　And therewith nets and amorous gins[1] they make
Wherewith the hearts of lovers to entangle,
　　Which once enthralled, no ransom they will take.
But as two tyrants sitting in their thrones
　　Look on their slaves with tyrannizing eyes;
So they, no whit regarding lovers' moans,
　　Doom worlds of hearts to endless slaveries
Unless they subject-like swear to adore
And serve Emaricdulfe forevermore.

[1] gins/snares

29. *"My heart is like a ship . . ."*

My heart is like a ship on Neptune's back;
　　Thy beauty is the sea where my ship saileth;
Thy frowns the surges are that threat my wrack,
　　Thy smiles the winds that on my sails soft galeth.
Long tossed betwixt fair hope and foul despair,
　　My sea-sick heart, arrived on thy shore—
Thy love, I mean—begs that he may repair
　　His broken vessel with thy bounteous store.
Dido relieved Æneas in distress,
　　And lent him love, and gave to him her heart;
If half such bounty thou to me express,

From thy fair shore I never will depart,
But thank kind fortune that my course did sort
To suffer shipwreck on so sweet a port.

EDMUND SPENSER
(c.1552–1599)

Educated at Cambridge, Spenser spent most of his adult life in
Ireland as a civil servant. His most famous work, of course, is
The Fairy Queen. Spenser wrote in a variety of verse forms,
developing his interest in the sonnet while still at school. In his
sequence *Amoretti* (1595) Spenser developed his own system of
interlocking rhyme. He was regarded by most of his contempo-
raries as England's greatest living poet.

Early Unrhymed Sonnets*

"It was the time . . ."

It was the time when rest, the gift of Gods,
Sweetly sliding into the eyes of men,
Doth drown in the forgetfulness of sleep,
The careful travails of the painful day;
Then did a ghost appear before mine eyes
On that great river bank that runs by Rome,
And calling me then by my proper name,
He bade me upward unto heaven look.

---

*These two poems, written in blank verse but titled sonnets, ap-
peared with thirteen similar poems in a volume called *A Theater* . . .
[*for*] *Voluptuous Worldlings* published in 1569. They are interesting
because they show Spenser's early work in the form. Though his
name does not appear in the volume, he is generally recognized as
the translator of these poems by the French poet Du Bellay; these
same poems appear later, rewritten with rhymes, in Spenser's *Com-
plaints.* The rhymed versions immediately follow.

He cried to me, and lo (quoth he) behold,
What under this great Temple is contained,
Lo all is nought but flying vanity.
So I knowing the world's unstedfastness,
Sith only God surmounts the force of time,
In God alone do stay my confidence.

"I saw the bird that dares behold the sun"

I saw the bird that dares behold the sun,
With feeble flight venture to mount to heaven.
By more and more she gan to trust her wings,
Still following th' example of her dame.
I saw her rise, and with a larger flight
Surmount the tops even of the highest hills,
And pierce the clouds, and with her wings to reach
The place where is the Temple of the Gods.
There was she lost, and suddenly I saw
Where tumbling through the air in lompe[1] of fire,
All flaming down she fell upon the plain.
I saw her body turned all to dust,
And saw the fowl that shuns the cheerful light
Out of her ashes as a worm arise.

[1] lompe/mass

The Visions of Bellay

1. "It was the time . . ."

It was the time, when rest, soft sliding down
From heaven's height into men's heavy eyes,
In the forgetfulness of sleep doth drown
The careful thoughts of mortal miseries;
Then did a ghost before mine eyes appear,
On that great river's bank, that runs by Rome;
Which, calling me by name, bad me to rear
My looks to heaven whence all good gifts do come,
And crying loud, Lo! now behold (quoth he)
What under this great temple placed is:
Lo, all is nought but flying vanity!

So I, that know this world's inconstancies,
　Sith only God surmounts all Time's decay,
　In God alone my confidence do stay.

7. *"I saw the bird that can the sun endure"*

I saw the bird that can the sun endure,
With feeble wings essay to mount on hight[1];
By more and more she gan her wings t' assure,
Following th' ensample[2] of her mother's sight:
I saw her rise, and with a larger flight
To pierce the clouds, and with wide pinions
To measure the most haughty mountain's height,
Until she raught the gods' own mansions:
There was she lost; when sudden I beheld,
Where, tumbling through the air in fiery fold,
All flaming down she on the plain was felled,
And soon her body turned to ashes cold.
　I saw the fowl, that doth the light despise,
　Out of her dust like to a worm arise.

[1] on hight/aloft　　[2] ensample/example

FROM AMORETTI

1. *"Happy ye leaves . . ."*

Happy ye leaves! whenas those lily hands,
Which hold my life in their dead-doing might,
Shall handle you, and hold in love's soft bands,
Like captives trembling at the victor's sight.
And happy lines! on which, with starry light,
Those lamping eyes will deign sometimes to look,
And read the sorrows of my dying sprite,[1]
Written with tears in heart's close-bleeding book.
And happy rhymes! bathed in the sacred brook
Of Helicon, whence she derived is;
When ye behold that angel's blessed look,
My soul's long-lacked food, heaven's bliss;
　Leaves, lines, and rhymes, seek her to please alone,
　Whom if ye please, I care for other none!

[1] sprite/spirit

8. *"More than most fair . . ."*[1]

More than most fair, full of the living fire,
Kindled above unto the Maker near;
No eyes but joys, in which all powers conspire,
That to the world nought else be counted dear;
Through your bright beams doth not the blinded guest
Shoot out his darts to base affections wound;
But angels come to lead frail minds to rest
In chaste desires, on heavenly beauty bound.
You frame my thoughts, and fashion me within;
You stop my tongue, and teach my heart to speak;
You calm the storm that passion did begin,
Strong through your cause, but by your virtue weak.
　　Dark is the world, where your light shined never;
　　Well is he born, that may behold you ever.

[1] Spenser here departs from his usual interlocking rhymes.

13. *"In that proud port . . ."*

In that proud port,[1] which her so goodly graceth,
Whiles her face she rears up to the sky,
And to the ground her eyelids low embaseth,[2]
Most goodly temperature ye may descry;
Mild humblesse,[3] mixt with awful majesty.
For, looking on the earth whence she was born,
Her mind rememb'reth her mortality,
Whatso is fairest shall to earth return.
But that same lofty countenance seems to scorn
Base thing, and think how she to heaven may climb;
Treading down earth as loathsome and forlorn,
That hinders heavenly thoughts with drossy slime.
　　Yet lowly still vouchsafe to look on me;
　　Such lowliness shall make you lofty be.

[1] port/bearing　[2] embaseth/lowers　[3] humblesse/humility

15. "Ye tradeful merchants . . ."

Ye tradeful merchants, that with weary toil
Do seek most precious things to make your gain;
And both the Indias of their treasure spoil;
What needeth you to seek so far in vain?
For lo, my love doth in herself contain
All this world's riches that may far be found:
If sapphires, lo, her eyes be sapphires plain;
If rubies, lo, her lips be rubies sound;
If pearls, her teeth be pearls, both pure and round;
If ivory, her forehead ivory ween;
If gold, her locks are finest gold on ground;
If silver, her fair hands are silver sheen:
 But that which fairest is, but few behold,
 Her mind adorned with virtues manifold.

27. "Fair proud, now tell me, why should fair be proud"

Fair proud, now tell me, why should fair be proud,
Sith all world's glory is but dross unclean,
And in the shade of death itself shall shroud,
However now thereof ye little ween!
That goodly idol, now so gay beseen,
Shall doff her flesh's borrowed fair attire,
And be forgot as it had never been;
That many now much worship and admire!
Ne any then shall after it inquire,
Ne any mention shall thereof remain,
But what this verse, that never shall expire,
Shall to you purchase with her thankless pain!
 Fair, be no longer proud of that shall perish;
 But that, which shall you make immortal, cherish.

37. "What guile is this . . ."

What guile is this, that those her golden tresses
She doth attire under a net of gold;
And with sly skill so cunningly them dresses,
That which is gold, or hair, may scarce be told?

Is it that men's frail eyes, which gaze too bold,
She may entangle in that golden snare;
And, being caught, may craftily enfold
Their weaker hearts, which are not well aware?
Take heed, therefore, mine eyes, how ye do stare
Henceforth too rashly on that guileful net,
In which, if ever ye entrapped are,
Out of her bands ye by no means shall get.
    Fondness it were for any, being free,
    To covet fetters, though they golden be!

55. *"So oft as I her beauty do behold"*

So oft as I her beauty do behold,
And therewith do her cruelty compare,
I marvel of what substance was the mold,
The which her made at once so cruel fair.
Not earth, for her high thoughts more heavenly are:
Not water, for her love doth burn like fire:
Not air, for she is not so light or rare:
Not fire, for she doth freeze with faint desire.
Then needs another element inquire
Whereof she mote[1] be made; that is, the sky.
For to the heaven her haughty looks aspire:
And eke her mind is pure immortal high.
    Then, sith to heaven ye likened are the best,
    Be like in mercy as in all the rest.

[1] mote/might

56. *"Fair ye be sure . . ."*

Fair ye be sure, but cruel and unkind,
As is a tiger, that with greediness
Hunts after blood; when he by chance doth find
A feeble beast, doth felly[1] him oppress.
Fair be ye sure, but proud and pitiless,
As is a storm, that all things doth prostrate;
Finding a tree alone all comfortless,
Beats on it strongly, it to ruinate.
Fair be ye sure, but hard and obstinate,
As is a rock amidst the raging floods:

'Gainst which, a ship, of succor desolate,
Doth suffer wreck both of herself and goods.
   That ship, that tree, and that same beast, am I,
   Whom ye do wreck, do ruin, and destroy.

¹ felly/fiercely

61. "The glorious image of the Maker's beauty"

The glorious image of the Maker's beauty,
My sovereign saint, the idol of my thought,
Dare not henceforth, above the bounds of duty,
T' accuse of pride, or rashly blame for aught.
For being as she is, divinely wrought,
And of the brood of angels heavenly born;
And with the crew of blessed saints upbrought,
Each of which did her with their gifts adorn;
The bud of joy, the blossom of the morn,
The beam of light, whom mortal eyes admire;
What reason is it then but she should scorn
Base things, that to her love too bold aspire!
   Such heavenly forms ought rather worshipt be
   Than dare be loved by men of mean degree.

64. "Coming to kiss her lips . . ."

Coming to kiss her lips (such grace I found),
Meseemed, I smelt a garden of sweet flowers,
That dainty odors from them threw around,
For damsels fit to deck their lovers' bowers.
Her lips did smell like unto gillyflowers;
Her ruddy cheeks like unto roses red;
Her snowy brows like budded bellamoures;
Her lovely eyes like pinks but newly spread;
Her goodly bosom like a strawberry bed;
Her neck like to a bunch of columbines;
Her breast like lilies, ere their leaves be shed;
Her nipples like young blossomed jessamines:
   Such fragrant flowers do give most odorous smell;
   But her sweet odor did them all excel.

67. "Like as a huntsman . . ."

Like as a huntsman, after weary chase,
Seeing the game from him escaped away,
Sits down to rest him in some shady place,
With panting hounds beguiled of their prey—
So after long pursuit and vain assay,
When I all weary had the chase forsook,
The gentle deer returned the selfsame way,
Thinking to quench her thirst at the next brook.
There she, beholding me with milder look,
Sought not to fly, but fearless still did bide:
Till I in hand her yet half trembling took,
And with her own good will her firmly tied.
    Strange thing, me seemed, to see a beast so wild,
    So goodly won, with her own will beguiled.

68. "Most glorious Lord of life . . ."

Most glorious Lord of life, that on this day,
Didst make thy triumph over death and sin;
And, having harrowed hell, didst bring away
Captivity thence captive, us to win:
This joyous day, dear Lord, with joy begin;
And grant that we, for whom thou didest die,
Being with thy dear blood clean washed from sin,
May live for ever in felicity!
And that thy love we weighing worthily,
May likewise love thee for the same again;
And for thy sake, that all like dear didst buy,
With love may one another entertain:
    So let us love, dear Love, like as we ought;
    Love is the lesson which the Lord us taught.

70. "Fresh spring, the herald of love's mighty king"

Fresh spring, the herald of love's mighty king,
In whose coat-armor richly are displayed
All sorts of flowers, the which on earth do spring,
In goodly colors gloriously arrayed;

Go to my love, where she is careless laid,
Yet in her winter's bower not well awake;
Tell her the joyous time will not be stayed,
Unless she do him by the forelock take;
Bid her therefore herself soon ready make,
To wait on Love amongst his lovely crew;
Where every one, that misseth then her make,
Shall be by him amerced[1] with penance due.
  Make haste, therefore, sweet love, whilst it is prime;
  For none can call again the passed time.

[1] amerced/punished

72. "Oft, when my spirit doth spread her bolder wings"

Oft, when my spirit doth spread her bolder wings,
In mind to mount up to the purest sky,
It down is weighed with thought of earthly things,
And clogged with burden of mortality;
Where, when that sovereign beauty it doth spy,
Resembling heaven's glory in her light,
Drawn with sweet pleasure's bait, it back doth fly,
And unto heaven forgets her former flight.
There my frail fancy, fed with full delight,
Both bathe in bliss, and mantleth[1] most at ease;
Ne thinks of other heaven, but how it might
Her heart's desire with most contentment please.
  Heart need not wish none other happiness,
  But here on earth to have such heaven's bliss.

[1] mantleth/to stretch the wings for exercise

75. "One day I wrote her name upon the strand"

One day I wrote her name upon the strand;
But came the waves, and washed it away:
Again, I wrote it with a second hand;
But came the tide, and made my pains his prey.

Vain man, said she, that dost in vain assay
A mortal thing so to immortalize;
For I myself shall like to this decay,
And eke my name be wiped out likewise.
Not so, quoth I; let baser things devise
To die in dust, but you shall live by fame:
My verse your virtues rare shall eternize,
And in the heavens write your glorious name.
　Where, whenas death shall all the world subdue,
　Our love shall live, and later life renew.

79. *"Men call you fair . . ."*

Men call you fair, and you do credit it,
For that yourself ye daily such do see:
But the true fair, that is the gentle wit,
And virtuous mind, is much more praised of me:
For all the rest, however fair it be,
Shall turn to nought and lose that glorious hue;
But only that is permanent and free
From frail corruption, that doth flesh ensue.
That is true beauty: that doth argue you
To be divine, and born of heavenly seed;
Derived from that fair Spirit, from whom all true
And perfect beauty did at first proceed:
　He only fair, and what he fair hath made;
　All other fair, like flowers, untimely fade.

81. *"Fair is my love . . ."*

Fair is my love, when her fair golden hairs
With the loose wind ye waving chance to mark;
Fair, when the rose in her red cheeks appears;
Or in her eyes the fire of love does spark.
Fair, when her breast, like a rich-laden bark,
With precious merchandise she forth doth lay;
Fair, when that cloud of pride, which oft doth dark
Her goodly light, with smiles she drives away.
But fairest she, when so she doth display
The gate with pearls and rubies richly dight,[1]
Through which her words so wise do make their way

To bear the message of her gentle sprite.
 The rest be works of nature's wonderment:
 But this the work of heart's astonishment.

¹dight/ordered, arranged

GEORGE CHAPMAN
(c.1559–1634)

Little is known of Chapman's life. By 1598 he was an established dramatist. He had a good deal of classical learning and produced excellent translations of Homer's *Iliad* and *Odyssey*, for which later generations have praised him (see p. 192). In his short sequence, *A Coronet for his Mistress Philosophy*, which appeared with *Ovid's Banquet of Sense* (1595), he put the sonnet to "higher" use than the poets who sang of their more earthly mistresses.

FROM A CORONET FOR HIS MISTRESS PHILOSOPHY

1. *"Muses that sing love's sensual empery"*

Muses that sing love's sensual empery,¹
 And lovers kindling your enraged fires
 At Cupid's bonfires burning in the eye,
 Blown with the empty breath of vain desires;
You that prefer the painted cabinet
 Before the wealthy jewels it doth store ye,
 That all your joys in dying figures set,
 And stain the living substance of your glory:
Abjure those joys, abhor their memory,
 And let my love the honored subject be
 Of love, and honor's complete history;
 Your eyes were never yet let in to see
The majesty and riches of the mind,
But dwell in darkness; for your god is blind.

¹empery/dominion

2. *"But dwell in darkness . . ."*

But dwell in darkness, for your god is blind,
   Humour pours down such torrents on his eyes;
   Which, as from mountains, fall on his base kind,
   And eat your entrails out with ecstasies.
Color, whose hands for faintness are not felt,
   Can bind your waxen thoughts in adamant;[1]
   And with her painted fires your heart doth melt,
   Which beat your souls in pieces with a pant.
But my love is the cordial of souls,
   Teaching by passion what perfection is,
   In whose fixed beauties shine the sacred scroll,
   And long-lost records of your human bliss,
Spirit to flesh, and soul to spirit giving,
Love flows not from my liver[2] but her living.

[1] adamant/a legendary stone, magnetic and impregnable
[2] liver/Elizabethan convention held that love struck through the
liver instead of the heart.

3. *"Love flows not from my liver . . ."*

Love flows not from my liver but her living,
   From whence all stings to perfect love are darted
   All power, and thought of prideful lust depriving
   Her life so pure and she so spotless hearted.
In whom sits beauty with so firm a brow,
   That age, nor care, nor torment can contract it;
   Heaven's glories shining there, do stuff allow,
   And virtue's constant graces do compact it.
Her mind—the beam of God—draws in the fires
   Of her chaste eyes, from all earth's tempting fuel;
   Which upward lifts the looks of her desires,
   And makes each precious thought in her a jewel.
And as huge fires compressed more proudly flame,
So her close beauties further blaze her fame.

SIR JOHN DAVIES
(1569–1626)

Davies was born in Wiltshire and educated at Oxford. He held a number of government positions in Ireland and was finally appointed Lord Chief Justice of England, but died before he could take office. His poetry contrasts sharply with the prevailingly mellifluous verse of his time. The *Gulling Sonnets* (1595) effectively satirize the poetic abuses of the great sonnet vogue.

THE GULLING[1] SONNETS

To His Good Friend, Sir Anthony Cooke

Here my chameleon muse herself doth change
To divers shapes of gross absurdities,
And like an antic mocks with fashion strange
The fond admirers of lewd gulleries.
Your judgment sees with pity and with scorn
The bastard sonnets of these rhymers base,
Which in this whisking age are daily born,
To their own shames and poetry's disgrace.
Yet some praise those—and some perhaps will praise
Even these of mine; and therefore these I send
To you, that pass in court your glorious days;
That if some rich rash gull[2] these rhymes commend,
Thus you may set this formal wit to school,
Use your own grace, and beg him for a fool.

[1]Gulling/cheating, tricking   [2]gull/dupe

1. "The lover, under burthen of his mistress' love"

The lover, under burthen of his mistress' love
Which like to Ætna did his heart oppress,
Did give such piteous groans that he did move
The heavens at length to pity his distress.
But for the Fates, in their high court above,

Forbade to make the grievous burthen less,
The gracious powers did all conspire to prove
If miracle this mischief might redress.
Therefore, regarding that the load was such
As no man might with one man's might sustain,
And that mild patience imported much
To him that should endure an endless pain,
By their decree he soon transformed was
Into a patient burden-bearing ass.

2. "As when the bright cerulean firmament"

As when the bright cerulean firmament
Hath not his glory with black clouds defaced,
So were my thoughts void of all discontent,
And with no mist of passions overcast.
They all were pure and clear, till at the last
An idle careless thought forth wandering went,
And of that poisonous beauty took a taste
Which do the hearts of lovers so torment.
Then as it chanceth in a flock of sheep,
When some contagious ill breeds first in one,
Daily it spreads and secretly doth creep,
Till all the silly troupe be overgone.
So by close neighborhood within my breast,
One scurvy thought infecteth all the rest.

3. "What eagle can behold her sunbright eye"

What eagle can behold her sunbright eye,
Her sunbright eye that lights the world with love,
The world of love wherein I live and die,
I live and die and divers changes prove.
I changes prove, yet still the same am I,
The same am I and never will remove,
Never remove until my soul doth fly,
My soul doth fly, and I surcease to move.
I cease to move which now am moved by you,
Am moved by you that move all mortal hearts,
All mortal hearts whose eyes your eyes doth view,
Your eyes doth view whence Cupid shoots his darts.

Whence Cupid shoots his darts and woundeth those
That honor you and never were his foes.

4. *"The hardness of her heart and truth of mine"*

The hardness of her heart and truth of mine
When the all-seeing eyes of heaven did see,
They straight concluded that by power divine
To other forms our hearts should turned be.
Then hers, as hard as flint, a flint became,
And mine, as true as steel, to steel was turned;
And then between our hearts sprang forth the flame
Of kindest love, which unextinguished burned.
And long the sacred lamp of mutual love
Incessantly did burn in glory bright,
Until my folly did her fury move
To recompense my service with despite;
And to put out with snuffers of her pride
The lamp of love which else had never died.

5. *"Mine eye, mine ear, my will, my wit, my heart"*

Mine eye, mine ear, my will, my wit, my heart
Did see, did hear, did like, discern, did love
Her face, her speech, her fashion, judgment, art,
Which did charm, please, delight, confound, and move.
Then fancy, humor, love, conceit, and thought
Did so draw, force, entice, persuade, devise,
That she was won, moved, carried, compassed, wrought
To think me kind, true, comely, valiant, wise;
That heaven, earth, hell, my folly, and her pride
Did work, contrive, labor, conspire, and swear
To make me scorned, vile, cast off, base, defied
With her my love, my light, my life, my dear;
So that my heart, my wit, will, ear, and eye
Doth grieve, lament, sorrow, despair, and die.

6. "The sacred muse that first made love divine"

The sacred muse that first made love divine
Hath made him naked and without attire;
But I will clothe him with this pen of mine,
That all the world his fashion shall admire:
His hat of hope, his band of beauty fine,
His cloak of craft, his doublet of desire,
Grief, for a girdle, shall about him twine,
His points[1] of pride, his eyelet holes of ire,
His hose[2] of hate, his codpiece of conceit,
His stockings of stern strife, his shirt of shame,
His garters of vainglory gay and slight,
His pantofles[3] of passions I will frame;
Pumps of presumption shall adorn his feet,
And socks of sullenness exceeding sweet.

[1] points/laces used for attaching the doublet to the hose
[2] hose/breeches or trunks
[3] pantofles/overshoes

7. "Into the middle Temple of my heart"

Into the middle Temple[1] of my heart
The wanton Cupid did himself admit,
And gave for pledge your eagle-sighted wit
That he would play no rude uncivil part;
Long time he cloaked his nature with his art,
And sad and grave and sober he did sit,
But at the last he gan to revel it,
To break good rules and orders to pervert;
Then love and his young pledge were both convented
Before sad reason, that old Bencher[2] grave,
Who this sad sentence unto him presented;
By diligence, that sly and secret knave,
That love and wit, for ever should depart
Out of the middle Temple of my heart.

[1] middle Temple/A play on the Middle Temple, one of the Inns of
Court
[2] Bencher/judge

8. *"My case is this . . ."*[1]

My case is this: I love Zepheria bright;
Of her I hold my heart by fealty,
Which I discharge to her perpetually;
Yet she thereof will never me acquite.
For now, supposing I withhold her right,
She hath distrained my heart to satisfy
The duty which I never did deny,
And far away impounds it with despite.
I labor therefore justly to repleve
My heart, which she unjustly doth impound;
But quick conceit, which now is love's high shrieve[2]
Returns; it is esloigned,[3] not to be found.
Then, which the law affords, I only crave
Her heart for mine in withernam[4] to have.

[1] Davies is here parodying the author of the sequence to *Zepheria;* see p. 39.
[2] shrieve/sheriff
[3] esloigned/removed from the jurisdiction of the court
[4] withernam/a legal term meaning the taking of other goods in place of those seized

9. *"To Love, my lord, I do knight's service owe"*

To Love, my lord, I do knight's service owe,
And therefore now he hath my wit in ward,
But while it is in his tuition so,
Methinks he doth entreat it passing hard;
For though he hath it married long ago
To Vanity, a wench of no regard,
And now to full and perfect age doth grow,
Yet now of freedom it is most debarred.
But why should Love after minority,
When I am past the one and twentieth year,
Preclude my wit of his sweet liberty,
And make it still the yoke of hardship bear.
I fear he hath an other title got,
And holds my wit now for an idiot!

Richard Barnfield
(1574–1627)

After receiving a degree at Oxford, Barnfield went to London
where he became friendly with Watson, Drayton, and other
poets. His poetic fame stems solely from three books of poetry,
all published before he was twenty-five. His sonnets included in
Cynthia (1595), addressed to a young man, are quite openly
homoerotic.

To His Friend Master R. L., In Praise of Music and Poetry

If music and sweet poetry agree,
As they must needs (the sister and the brother),
Then must the love be great 'twixt thee and me,
  Because thou lov'st the one, and I the other.
  Dowland to thee is dear, whose heavenly touch
Upon the lute doth ravish human sense;
Spenser to me, whose deep conceit is such
  As, passing all conceit, needs no defence.
  Thou lov'st to hear the sweet melodious sound
That Phœbus' lute (the queen of music) makes;
And I in deep delight am chiefly drowned
  Whenas himself to singing he betakes.
    One god is god of both (as poets feign),
    One knight loves both, and both in thee remain.

FROM CYNTHIA

11. "Sighing, and sadly sitting by my love"

Sighing, and sadly sitting by my love,
  He asked the cause of my heart's sorrowing,
  Conjuring me by heaven's eternal King
To tell the cause which me so much did move.
Compelled (quoth I), to thee will I confess,
  Love is the cause, and only love it is
  That doth deprive me of my heavenly bliss.

Love is the pain that doth my heart oppress.
And what is she (quoth he) whom thou dost love?
    Look in this glass (quoth I), there shalt thou see
    The perfect form of my felicity.
When, thinking that it would strange magic prove,
    He opened it, and taking off the cover,
    He straight perceived himself to be my lover.

17. "Cherry-lipped Adonis . . ."

Cherry-lipped Adonis in his snowy shape,
    Might not compare with his pure ivory white,
    On whose fair front a poet's pen might write,
Whose rosiate red excels the crimson grape.
His love-enticing delicate soft limbs,
    Arc rarely framed t' intrap poor gazing eyes;
    His cheeks, the lily and carnation dyes,
With lovely tincture which Apollo's dims.
His lips ripe strawberries in nectar wet,
    His mouth a hive, his tongue a honeycomb,
    Where muses (like bees) make their mansion.
His teeth pure pearl in blushing coral set.
    Oh how can such a body sin-procuring,
    Be slow to love, and quick to hate, enduring?

RICHARD LYNCHE
(fl.1596–1601)

Diella appeared in 1596 as written by "R. L., Gentleman."
Richard Lynche, author of a few other works, about whom
almost nothing is known, is generally assumed to be the author
of this sequence. It is obvious from the sonnets included in
Diella that the sequence vogue is running dry.

FROM DIELLA

2. *"Soon as the azure-colored gates . . ."*

Soon as the azure-colored gates of th' east
   Were set wide open by the watchful morn,
I walked abroad, as having took no rest
   (For nights are tedious to a man forlorn);
And viewing well each pearl-bedewed flower,
   Then waxing dry by splendor of the sun,
All scarlet-hued I saw him 'gin to lour
   And blush, as though some heinous act were done.
At this amazed, I hied me home amain,
   Thinking that I his anger caused had.
And at his set, abroad I walked again;
   When lo, the moon looked wondrous pale and sad:
Anger the one, and envy moved the other,
To see my love more fair than Love's fair mother.

4. *"What sugared terms . . ."*

What sugared terms, what all-persuading art,
   What sweet mellifluous words, what wounding looks
Love used for his admittance to my heart!
   Such eloquence was never read in books.
He promised pleasure, rest, and endless joy,
   Fruition of the fairest she alive.
His pleasure, pain; rest, trouble; joy, annoy,
   Have I since found, which me of bliss deprive.

The Trojan horse thus have I now let in,
    Wherein enclosed these armed men were placed—
Bright eyes, fair cheeks, sweet lips, and milk-white skin;
    These foes my life have overthrown and razed.
Fair outward shows prove inwardly the worst,
Love looketh fair, but lovers are accurst.

WILLIAM SMITH
(fl.1596)

All that is known of Smith derives from his sequence *Chloris*
(1596). Like Richard Lynche and Bartholomew Griffin, he wrote
his sonnet sequence when the vogue was already past its prime.

FROM CHLORIS

To the Most Excellent and Learned Shepherd, Colin Clout[1]

Colin, my dear and most entire beloved,
    My muse audacious stoops her pitch to thee,
    Desiring that thy patience be not moved
    By these rude lines, written here you see;
Fain would my muse, whom cruel love hath wronged,
    Shroud her love-labors under thy protection,
    And I myself with ardent zeal have longed
    That thou mightst know to thee my true affection.
Therefore, good Colin, graciously accept
    A few sad sonnets which my muse hath framed;
    Though they but newly from the shell are crept,
    Suffer them not by envy to be blamed.
But underneath the shadow of thy wings
Give warmth to these young-hatched orphan things.

[1]Colin Clout/Edmund Spenser used this name in *The Shepherd's
Calendar* and in *Colin Clout's Come Home Again*.

3. *"Feed, silly sheep . . ."*

Feed, silly sheep, although your keeper pineth,
   Yet like to Tantalus doth see his food.
   Skip you and leap, no bright Apollo shineth,
   Whilst I bewail my sorrows in yon wood
Where woeful Philomela[1] doth record,
   And sings with notes of sad and dire lament
   The tragedy wrought by her sister's lord;
   I'll bear a part in her black discontent.
That pipe which erst was wont to make you glee,
   Upon these downs whereon you careless graze,
   Shall to her mournful music tuned be.
   Let not my plaints, poor lambkins, you amaze;
There underneath that dark and dusky bower
Whole showers of tears to Chloris I will pour.

[1] Philomela/In the Greek myth Philomela was raped by Tereus and later transformed into a nightingale.

BARTHOLOMEW GRIFFIN
(fl.1596)

Fidessa (1596) is the only volume Griffin is known to have published. Of his life nothing is known.

FROM FIDESSA

5. *"Arraigned, poor captive . . ."*

Arraigned, poor captive at the bar I stand,
   The bar of beauty, bar to all my joys;
   And up I hold my ever-trembling hand,
   Wishing or life or death to end annoys.
And when the judge doth question of the guilt
   And bids me speak, then sorrow shuts up words.
   Yea, though he say, Speak boldly what thou wilt,
   Yet my confused affects no speech affords.

For why, alas, my passions have no bound,
  For fear of death that penetrates so near;
  And still one grief another doth confound,
  Yet doth at length a way to speech appear.
Then, for I speak too late, the judge doth give
His sentence that in prison I shall live.

15. *"Care-charmer sleep, sweet ease in restless misery"*

Care-charmer sleep, sweet ease in restless misery,
  The captive's liberty, and his freedom's song,
  Balm of the bruised heart, man's chief felicity,
  Brother of quiet death, when life is too, too long!
A comedy it is, and now an history—
  What is not sleep unto the feeble mind!
  It easeth him that toils and him that's sorry,
  It makes the deaf to hear, to see the blind.
Ungentle sleep, thou helpest all but me,
  For when I sleep my soul is vexed most.
  It is Fidessa that doth master thee;
  If she approach, alas, thy power is lost.
But here she is. See, how he runs amain!
I fear at night he will not come again.

Robert Tofte
(d.1620)

Tofte was the author of two volumes of poetry and of several translations. None of the poems included in *Laura* (1597) are of fourteen lines. The ten- and twelve-line poems found here are examples of the kinds of verse that often went to make up "sonnet" sequences.

———————————

FROM LAURA

Part One, 30. *"Unto thy favor . . ."*

Unto thy favor, which when nature formed
She went beyond herself with cunning hand,
I may compare what is in world adorned
With beauty most and with most grace doth stand.
By every mortal whiteness ne'er so white
The ivory white of thy white hand exceeds,
So that my soul, which doth fair whiteness like,
Rests on fair whiteness and on whiteness feeds.
 For this is thought and hoped of from thee:
 White as thy hands, so white thy faith shall be.

Part Three, 7. *"When she was born . . ."*

When she was born she came with smiling eye
Laughing into the world, a sign of glee;
When I was born, to her quite contrary,
Wailing I came into the world to see.
 Then mark this wonder strange: what nature gave,
 From first to th' last this fashion kept we have.
She in my sad laments doth take great joy;
I through her laughing die, and languish must
Unless that love, to save me from this 'noy,
Do unto me, unworthy, show so just
 As for to change her laughter into pain,
 And my complaints into her joy again.

HENRY LOK
(c.1553–1608)

Chiefly a writer of religious poetry, Lok was a prolific though uninspired sonneteer. One of the first Elizabethans to use the form for religious poetry, he wrote nearly four hundred sonnets. *Sundry Christian Passions* appeared in 1597.

FROM SUNDRY CHRISTIAN PASSIONS
CONTAINED IN TWO HUNDRED SONNETS

Preface: "It is not, Lord, the sound of many words"

It is not, Lord, the sound of many words,
  The bowed knee, or abstinence of man,
  The filed phrase that eloquence affords,
  Or poet's pen, that heavens do pierce, or can;
By heavy cheer of color pale and wan,
  By pined body of the Pharisay,
  A mortal eye repentance oft doth scan,
  Whose judgment doth on outward shadows stay.
But thou, O God, dost heart's intent bewray[1]
  For from thy sight, Lord, nothing is concealed,
  Thou formedst the frame fro out the very clay,
  To thee the thoughts of hearts are all revealed.
    To thee, therefore, with heart and mind prostrate,
    With tears I thus deplore my sinful state.

[1] bewray/expose

Conclusion: "Words may well want . . ."

Words may well want, both ink and paper fail,
  Wits may grow dull, and will may weary grow,
  And world's affairs may make my pen more slow,
  But yet my heart and courage shall not quail.
Though cares and troubles do my peace assail
  And drive me to delay thy praise awhile,
  Yet all the world shall not from thoughts exile
  Thy mercies, Lord, by which my plaints prevail.

And though the world with face should grateful smile
   And me her peddler's pack of pleasures show,
   No hearty love on her I would bestow,
   Because I know she seeks me to beguile;
     Ne will defile my happy peace of mind
     For all the solace I in earth may find.

MARK ALEXANDER BOYD
(1563–1601)

Born in Scotland, Boyd led an eccentric life as a soldier and a
Latin scholar. Most of his writing, including a good deal of verse,
is in Latin. Boyd's "Fra bank to bank" is the finest sonnet in
Scots.

"Fra bank to bank . . ."

Fra[1] bank to bank, fra wood to wood I rin,[2]
   Ourhailit[3] with my feeble fantasie;
   Like til a leaf that fallis from a tree,
Or til a reed ourblawin[4] with the win.

Twa[5] gods guides me: the ane[6] of tham is blin,[7]
   Yea and a bairn[8] brocht up in vanitie;
   The next a wife ingenrit[9] of the sea,
And lichter[10] nor a dauphin with her fin.

Unhappy is the man for evermair
   That tills the sand and sawis[11] in the air;
   But twice unhappier is he, I lairn,
That feidis[12] in his hairt a mad desire,
And follows on a woman throw[13] the fire,
   Led by a blind and teachit by a bairn.

[1] fra/from   [2] rin/run   [3] ourhailit/overwhelmed
[4] ourblawin/overblown   [5] twa/two   [6] ane/one
[7] blin/blind   [8] bairn/child   [9] ingenrit/engendered
[10] lichter/lighter   [11] sawis/waves his hands
[12] feidis/feeds   [13] throw/through

WILLIAM SHAKESPEARE
(1564–1616)

England's greatest playwright, Shakespeare is also the best of the Elizabethan sonneteers. He was born in Stratford-on-Avon, came to London at an early age, and led an active life as an actor, dramatist, and poet. Whether or not Shakespeare laid bare his heart in his sonnets, as many critics have contended, they are his most personal poems. Most of his sonnets were written in the 1590s at the height of the vogue, but they were not published until 1609. The first 126 are addressed to a young man; the remainder (with the exception of the last two, which are conventional sonnets on Cupid) are addressed to an unknown "Dark Lady."

TWO SONNETS FROM THE PLAYS

"Did not the heavenly rhetoric of thine eye" [1]

Did not the heavenly rhetoric of thine eye,
'Gainst whom the world cannot hold argument,
Persuade my heart to this false perjury?
Vows for thee broke deserve not punishment.
A woman I forswore, but I will prove,
Thou being a goddess, I forswore not thee.
My vow was earthly, thou a heavenly love;
Thy grace being gained cures all disgrace in me.
Vows are but breath, and breath a vapor is.
Then thou, fair sun, which on my earth doth shine,
Exhalest this vapor-vow; in thee it is.
If broken then, it is no fault of mine.
If by me broke, what fool is not so wise
To lose an oath to win a paradise?

[1] Spoken by Longaville in *Love's Labor's Lost*, Act IV, scene 3.

"If I profane with my unworthiest hand"[1]

ROMEO. If I profane with my unworthiest hand
   This holy shrine, the gentle fine is this,
   My lips, two blushing pilgrims, ready stand
   To smooth that rough touch with a tender kiss.

JULIET. Good pilgrim, you do wrong your hand too much,
   Which mannerly devotion shows in this;
   For saints have hands that pilgrims' hands do touch,
   And palm to palm is holy palmers'[2] kiss.

ROMEO. Have not saints lips, and holy palmers too?
JULIET. Aye, pilgrim, lips that they must use in prayer.
ROMEO. Oh then, dear saint, let lips do what hands do.
   Then pray. Grant thou, lest faith turn to despair.

JULIET. Saints do not move, though grant for prayers' sake.
ROMEO. Then move not while my prayer's effect I take.

[1] From *Romeo and Juliet,* Act I, scene 5. The prologues to Acts I
and II are also written in sonnet form.
[2] palmers/pilgrims carrying palm leaves

FROM SONNETS

2. *"When forty winters shall besiege thy brow"*

When forty winters shall besiege thy brow
And dig deep trenches in thy beauty's field,
Thy youth's proud livery, so gazed on now,
Will be a tattered weed, of small worth held.
Then being asked where all thy beauty lies,
Where all the treasure of thy lusty days,
To say within thine own deep-sunken eyes
Were an all-eating shame and thriftless[1] praise.
How much more praise deserved thy beauty's use
If thou couldst answer, "This fair child of mine
Shall sum my count and make my old excuse,"
Proving his beauty by succession thine!

This were to be new-made when thou art old,
And see thy blood warm when thou feel'st it cold.

[1]thriftless/unprofitable

12. *"When I do count the clock . . ."*

When I do count the clock that tells the time
And see the brave day sunk in hideous night,
When I behold the violet past prime
And sable curls all silvered o'er with white;
When lofty trees I see barren of leaves
Which erst from heat did canopy the herd,
And summer's green all girded up in sheaves,
Borne on the bier with white and bristly beard—
Then of thy beauty do I question make,
That thou among the wastes of time must go,
Since sweets and beauties do themselves forsake
And die as fast as they see others grow.
    And nothing 'gainst Time's scythe can make defense
    Save breed, to brave him when he takes thee hence.

14. *"Not from the stars do I my judgment pluck"*

Not from the stars do I my judgment pluck,
And yet methinks I have astronomy,
But not to tell of good or evil luck,
Of plagues, of dearths, or seasons' quality.
Nor can I fortune to brief minutes tell,
Pointing to each his thunder, rain, and wind,
Or say with princes if it shall go well
By oft predict[1] that I in heaven find.
But from thine eyes my knowledge I derive,
And, constant stars, in them I read such art
As truth and beauty shall together thrive,
If from thyself to store thou wouldst convert.
    Or else of thee this I prognosticate:
    Thy end is truth's and beauty's doom and date.

[1]oft predict/frequent predictions, i.e., signs

15. "When I consider everything that grows"

When I consider everything that grows
Holds in perfection but a little moment,
That this huge stage presenteth nought but shows
Whereon the stars in secret influence comment;
When I perceive that men as plants increase,
Cheered and checked even by the self-same sky,
Vaunt in their youthful sap, at height decrease,
And wear their brave state out of memory;
Then the conceit of this inconstant stay
Sets you most rich in youth before my sight,
Where wasteful Time debateth with Decay,
To change your day of youth to sullied night;
   And all in war with Time for love of you,
    As he takes from you, I engraft you new.

18. "Shall I compare thee to a summer's day"

Shall I compare thee to a summer's day?
Thou art more lovely and more temperate.
Rough winds do shake the darling buds of May,
And summer's lease hath all too short a date.
Sometime too hot the eye of heaven shines,
And often is his gold complexion dimmed.
And every fair from fair sometime declines,
By chance or nature's changing course untrimmed.
But thy eternal summer shall not fade,
Nor lose possession of that fair thou owest;[1]
Nor shall Death brag thou wander'st in his shade
When in eternal lines to time thou grow'st.
   So long as men can breathe, or eyes can see,
    So long lives this, and this gives life to thee.

[1]owest/possess

22. "My glass shall not persuade me I am old"

My glass shall not persuade me I am old
So long as youth and thou are of one date,
But when in thee time's furrows I behold,
Then look I death my days should expiate.

For all that beauty that doth cover thee
Is but the seemly raiment of my heart,
Which in thy breast doth live, as thine in me.
How can I then be elder than thou art?
Oh, therefore, love, be of thyself so wary
As I, not for myself, but for thee will,
Bearing thy heart, which I will keep so chary
As tender nurse her babe from faring ill.
    Presume not on thy heart when mine is slain.
    Thou gavest me thine, not to give back again.

23. "As an unperfect actor on the stage"

As an unperfect actor on the stage,
Who with his fear is put besides his part,
Or some fierce thing replete with too much rage,
Whose strength's abundance weakens his own heart,
So I, for fear of trust, forget to say
The perfect ceremony of love's rite,
And in mine own love's strength seem to decay,
O'ercharged with burden of mine own love's might.
Oh, let my books be then the eloquence
And dumb presagers of my speaking breast,
Who plead for love, and look for recompense,
More than that tongue that more hath more expressed.
    Oh, learn to read what silent love hath writ.
    To hear with eyes belongs to love's fine wit.

29. "When in disgrace with fortune and men's eyes"

When in disgrace with fortune and men's eyes
I all alone beweep my outcast state,
And trouble deaf Heaven with my bootless cries,
And look upon myself and curse my fate,
Wishing me like to one more rich in hope,
Featured like him, like him with friends possessed,
Desiring this man's art and that man's scope,
With what I most enjoy contented least—
Yet in these thoughts myself almost despising,

Haply I think on thee, and then my state,
Like to the lark at break of day arising
From sullen earth, sings hymns at Heaven's gate.
  For thy sweet love remembered such wealth brings
  That then I scorn to change my state with kings.

30. "When to the sessions of sweet silent thought"

When to the sessions of sweet silent thought
I summon up remembrance of things past,
I sigh the lack of many a thing I sought,
And with old woes new wail my dear time's waste:
Then can I drown an eye, unused to flow,
For precious friends hid in death's dateless night,
And weep afresh loves' long since canceled woe,
And moan th' expense of many a vanished sight:
Then can I grieve at grievances foregone,
And heavily from woe to woe tell o'er
The sad account of fore-bemoaned moan,
Which I new pay as if not paid before.
  But if the while I think on thee, dear friend,
  All losses are restored and sorrows end.

33. "Full many a glorious morning . . ."

Full many a glorious morning have I seen
Flatter the mountaintops with sovereign eye,
Kissing with golden face the meadows green,
Gilding pale streams with heavenly alchemy,
Anon permit the basest clouds to ride
With ugly rack[1] on his celestial face
And from the forlorn world his visage hide,
Stealing unseen to west with this disgrace.
Even so my sun one early morn did shine
With all-triumphant splendor on my brow.
But out, alack! he was but one hour mine,
The region[2] cloud hath masked him from me now.
  Yet him for this my love no whit disdaineth.
  Suns of the world may stain when heaven's sun staineth.

[1] rack/clouds   [2] region/of the air

44. "If the dull substance of my flesh were thought"

If the dull substance of my flesh were thought,
Injurious distance should not stop my way.
For then, despite of space, I would be brought
From limits far remote where thou dost stay.
No matter then although my foot did stand
Upon the farthest earth removed from thee,
For nimble thought can jump both sea and land
As soon as think the place where he would be.
But, ah, thought kills me, that I am not thought,
To leap large lengths of miles when thou art gone,
But that, so much of earth and water wrought,
I must attend time's leisure with my moan,
   Receiving naught by elements so slow
   But heavy tears, badges of either's woe.

55. "Not marble, nor the gilded monuments"

Not marble, nor the gilded monuments
Of princes, shall outlive this powerful rhyme.
But you shall shine more bright in these contents
Than unswept stone, besmeared with sluttish time.
When wasteful war shall statues overturn,
And broils root out the work of masonry,
Nor Mars his sword nor war's quick fire shall burn
The living record of your memory.
'Gainst death and all-oblivious enmity
Shall you pace forth. Your praise shall still find room
Even in the eyes of all posterity
That wear this world out to the ending doom.
   So, till the judgment that yourself arise,
   You live in this, and dwell in lovers' eyes.

60. "Like as the waves . . ."

Like as the waves make toward the pebbled shore,
So do our minutes hasten to their end,
Each changing place with that which goes before,
In sequent toil all forward do contend.
Nativity, once in the main of light,
Crawls to maturity, wherewith being crowned,

Crooked eclipses 'gainst his glory fight,
And Time that gave doth now his gift confound.
Time doth transfix the flourish set on youth
And delves the parallels in beauty's brow,
Feeds on the rarities of nature's truth,
And nothing stands but for his scythe to mow.
   And yet to times in hope my verse shall stand,
    Praising thy worth, despite his cruel hand.

64. "When I have seen by Time's fell hand defaced"

When I have seen by Time's fell hand defaced
The rich-proud cost of outworn buried age;
When sometime lofty towers I see down-razed,
And brass eternal slave to mortal rage;
When I have seen the hungry ocean gain
Advantage on the kingdom of the shore,
And the firm soil win of the watery main,
Increasing store with loss and loss with store;
When I have seen such interchange of state,
Or state itself confounded to decay—
Ruin hath taught me thus to ruminate,
That Time will come and take my love away.
   This thought is as a death, which cannot choose
    But weep to have that which it fears to lose.

65. "Since brass, nor stone . . ."

Since brass, nor stone, nor earth, nor boundless sea
But sad mortality o'ersways their power,
How with this rage shall beauty hold a plea,
Whose action is no stronger than a flower?
Oh, how shall summer's honey breath hold out
Against the wreckful siege of battering days
When rocks impregnable are not so stout,
Nor gates of steel so strong, but Time decays?
O fearful meditation! Where, alack,
Shall Time's best jewel from Time's chest lie hid?
Or what strong hand can hold his swift foot back?

Or who his spoil of beauty can forbid?
  Oh, none, unless this miracle have might,
  That in black ink my love may still shine bright.

71. "No longer mourn for me . . ."

No longer mourn for me when I am dead
Than you shall hear the surly sullen bell
Give warning to the world that I am fled
From this vile world, with vilest worms to dwell.
Nay, if you read this line, remember not
The hand that writ it, for I love you so
That I in your sweet thoughts would be forgot
If thinking on me then should make you woe.
Oh, if, I say, you look upon this verse
When I perhaps compounded am with clay,
Do not so much as my poor name rehearse,
But let your love even with my life decay,
  Lest the wise world should look into your moan,
  And mock you with me after I am gone.

73. "That time of year thou mayst in me behold"

That time of year thou mayst in me behold
When yellow leaves, or none, or few, do hang
Upon those boughs which shake against the cold,
Bare ruined choirs, where late the sweet birds sang.
In me thou see'st the twilight of such day
As after sunset fadeth in the west;
Which by and by black night doth take away,
Death's second self, that seals up all the rest.
In me thou see'st the glowing of such fire,
That on the ashes of his youth doth lie,
As the deathbed whereon it must expire,
Consumed with that which it was nourished by.
  This thou perceivest, which makes thy love more strong,
  To love that well which thou must leave ere long.

74. "But he contented . . ."

But be contented. When that fell arrest
Without all bail shall carry me away,
My life hath in this line some interest,
Which for memorial still with thee shall stay.
When thou reviewest this, thou dost review
The very part was consecrate to thee.
The earth can have but earth, which is his due,
My spirit is thine, the better part of me.
So then thou hast but lost the dregs of life,
The prey of worms, my body being dead,
The coward conquest of a wretch's knife,
Too base of thee to be remembered.
    The worth of that is that which it contains,
    And that is this, and this with thee remains.

85. "My tongue-tied Muse . . ."

My tongue-tied Muse in manners holds her still,
While comments of your praise, richly compiled,
Reserve their character with golden quill,
And precious phrase by all the Muses filed.
I think good thoughts whilst other write good words,
And, like unlettered clerk, still cry "Amen"
To every hymn that able spirit affords,
In polished form of well-refined pen.
Hearing you praised, I say, " 'Tis so, 'tis true,"
And to the most of praise add something more.
But that is in my thought, whose love to you,
Though words come hindmost, holds his rank before.
    Then others for the breath of words respect,
    Me for my dumb thoughts, speaking in effect.

86. "Was it the proud full sail . . ."

Was it the proud full sail of his great verse,
Bound for the prize of all too precious you,
That did my ripe thoughts in my brain inhearse,
Making their tomb the womb wherein they grew?

Was it his spirit, by spirits taught to write
Above a mortal pitch, that struck me dead?
No, neither he, nor his compeers by night
Giving him aid, my verse astonished.
He, nor that affable familiar ghost
Which nightly gulls[1] him with intelligence,[2]
As victors, of my silence cannot boast.
I was not sick of any fear from thence.
　　But when your countenance filled up his line,
　　Then lacked I matter. That enfeebled mine.

[1]gulls/cheats　[2]intelligence/news

87. *"Farewell! Thou art too dear for my possessing"*

Farewell! Thou art too dear for my possessing,
And like enough thou know'st thy estimate.
The charter of thy worth gives thee releasing,
My bonds in thee are all determinate.
For how do I hold thee but by thy granting?
And for that riches where is my deserving?
The cause of this fair gift in me is wanting,
And so my patent back again is swerving.
Thyself thou gavest, thy own worth then not knowing,
Or me, to whom thou gavest it, else mistaking.
So thy great gift, upon misprision[1] growing,
Comes home again, on better judgment making.
　　Thus have I had thee, as a dream doth flatter,
　　In sleep a king, but waking no such matter.

[1]misprision/misunderstanding

94. *"They that have power to hurt . . ."*

They that have power to hurt and will do none,
That do not do the thing they most do show,
Who, moving others, are themselves as stone,
Unmoved, cold, and to temptation slow—
They rightly do inherit Heaven's graces
And husband nature's riches from expense.

They are the lords and owners of their faces,
Others but stewards of their excellence.
The summer's flower is to the summer sweet,
Though to itself it only live and die,
But if that flower with base infection meet,
The basest weed outbraves his dignity.
  For sweetest things turn sourest by their deeds.
  Lilies that fester smell far worse than weeds.

97. "How like a winter hath my absence been"

How like a winter hath my absence been
From thee, the pleasure of the fleeting year!
What freezings have I felt, what dark days seen!
What old December's bareness everywhere!
And yet this time removed was summer's time,
The teeming autumn, big with rich increase,
Bearing the wanton burden of the prime,
Like widowed wombs after their lords' decease.
Yet this abundant issue seemed to me
But hope of orphans and unfathered fruit,
For summer and his pleasures wait on thee,
And, thou away, the very birds are mute,
  Or if they sing, 'tis with so dull a cheer
  That leaves look pale, dreading the winter's near.

106. "When in the chronicle of wasted time"

When in the chronicle of wasted time
I see descriptions of the fairest wights,[1]
And beauty making beautiful old rhyme
In praise of ladies dead and lovely knights,
Then, in the blazon of sweet beauty's best,
Of hand, of foot, of lip, of eye, of brow,
I see their antique pen would have expressed
Even such a beauty as you master now.
So all their praises are but prophecies
Of this our time, all you prefiguring,
And, for they looked but with divining eyes,
They had not skill enough your worth to sing.

For we, which now behold these present days,
Have eyes to wonder, but lack tongues to praise.

¹ wights/men

116. *"Let me not to the marriage of true minds"*

Let me not to the marriage of true minds
Admit impediments. Love is not love
Which alters when it alteration finds,
Or bends with the remover to remove.
Oh no! It is an ever-fixed mark
That looks on tempests and is never shaken.
It is the star to every wandering bark,
Whose worth's unknown, although his height be taken.
Love's not Time's fool, though rosy lips and cheeks
Within his bending sickle's compass come.
Love alters not with his brief hours and weeks,
But bears it out even to the edge of doom.
    If this be error and upon me proved,
    I never writ, nor no man ever loved.

123. *"No, Time, thou shalt not boast that I do change"*

No, Time, thou shalt not boast that I do change.
Thy pyramids built up with newer might
To me are nothing novel, nothing strange,
They are but dressings of a former sight.
Our dates are brief, and therefore we admire
What thou dost foist upon us that is old,
And rather make them born to our desire
Than think that we before have heard them told.
Thy registers and thee I both defy,
Not wondering at the present nor the past,
For thy records and what we see doth lie,
Made more or less by thy continual haste.
    This I do now, and this shall ever be,
    I will be true, despite thy scythe and thee.

126. "O thou, my lovely boy . . ."[1]

O thou, my lovely boy, who in thy power
Dost hold Time's fickle glass, his sickle, hour,
Who hast by waning grown, and therein show'st
Thy lovers withering as thy sweet self grow'st,
If Nature, sovereign mistress over wrack,
As thou goest onwards, still will pluck thee back,
She keeps thee to this purpose, that her skill
May time disgrace and wretched minutes kill.
Yet fear her, O thou minion of her pleasure!
She may detain, but not still keep, her treasure.
Her audit, though delayed, answered must be,
And her quietus is to render thee.

[1] This is the last of the sonnets addressed to the young man; it contains only twelve lines.

129. "The expense of spirit . . ."

The expense of spirit in a waste of shame
Is lust in action, and till action, lust
Is perjured, murderous, bloody, full of blame,
Savage, extreme, rude, cruel, not to trust,
Enjoyed no sooner but despised straight,
Past reason hunted, and no sooner had,
Past reason hated, as a swallowed bait,
On purpose laid to make the taker mad.
Mad in pursuit, and in possession so,
Had, having, and in quest to have, extreme,
A bliss in proof, and proved, a very woe.
Before, a joy proposed, behind, a dream.
   All this the world well knows, yet none knows well
   To shun the Heaven that leads men to this Hell.

130. "My mistress' eyes are nothing like the sun"

My mistress' eyes are nothing like the sun,
Coral is far more red than her lips' red.
If snow be white, why then her breasts are dun,
If hairs be wires, black wires grow on her head.

I have seen roses damasked, red and white,
But no such roses see I in her cheeks.
And in some perfumes is there more delight
Than in the breath that from my mistress reeks.
I love to hear her speak, yet well I know
That music hath a far more pleasing sound.
I grant I never saw a goddess go,
My mistress, when she walks, treads on the ground.
    And yet, by Heaven, I think my love as rare
    As any she belied with false compare.

144. *"Two loves I have . . ."*

Two loves I have of comfort and despair,
Which like two spirits do suggest me still.
The better angel is a man right fair,
The worser spirit a woman colored ill.
To win me soon to Hell, my female evil
Tempteth my better angel from my side,
And would corrupt my saint to be a devil,
Wooing his purity with her foul pride.
And whether that my angel be turned fiend
Suspect I may, yet not directly tell,
But being both from me, both to each friend,
I guess one angel in another's Hell.
    Yet this shall I ne'er know, but live in doubt
    Till my bad angel fire my good one out.

145. *"Those lips that Love's own hand did make"*[1]

Those lips that Love's own hand did make
Breathed forth the sound that said "I hate,"
To me that languished for her sake.
But when she saw my woeful state,
Straight in her heart did mercy come,
Chiding that tongue that ever sweet
Was used in giving gentle doom,
And taught it thus anew to greet.

"I hate" she altered with an end
That followed it as gentle day
Doth follow night, who, like a fiend,
From Heaven to Hell is flown away.
   "I hate" from hate away she threw,
    And saved my life, saying "not you."

¹ The meter here is octosyllabic.

146. *"Poor soul, the center of my sinful earth"*

Poor soul, the center of my sinful earth,
My sinful earth, these rebel powers that thee array,
Why dost thou pine within and suffer dearth,
Painting thy outward walls so costly gay?
Why so large cost, having so short a lease,
Dost thou upon thy fading mansion spend?
Shall worms, inheritors of this excess,
Eat up thy charge? Is this thy body's end?
Then, soul, live thou upon thy servant's loss,
And let that pine to aggravate thy store.
Buy terms divine in selling hours of dross,
Within be fed, without be rich no more.
   So shalt thou feed on Death, that feeds on men,
    And Death once dead, there's no more dying then.

WILLIAM ALABASTER
(1568–1640)

Born in Hadleigh, Suffolk, educated at Cambridge, Alabaster is given a favorable mention as a Latin poet in Spenser's *Colin Clout's Come Home Again.* He served as a chaplain to the Earl of Essex on the Cadiz expedition. In 1597 he converted to Catholicism, though after several shifts seems finally to have accepted the Anglican Church. His sonnets were left in manuscript and not published until recent times.

FROM DIVINE MEDITATIONS

1. *"The night, the starless night of passion"*

The night, the starless night of passion,
From heaven began, on heaven beneath to fall,
When Christ did sound the onset martial,
A sacred hymn, upon his foes to run;
That with the fiery contemplation
Of love and joy, his soul and senses all
Surcharged might not dread the bitter thrall
Of pain and grief and torments all in one.
Then since my holy vows have undertook
To take the portrait of Christ's death in me,
Then let my love with sonnets fill this book,
With hymns to give the onset as did he,
That thoughts inflamed with such heavenly muse,
The coldest ice of fear need not refuse.

6. *"Up to Mount Olivet . . ."*

Up to Mount Olivet my soul ascend,
The mount spiritual, and there supply
Thy fainting lamp with oil of charity,
To make the light of faith the more extend.
Go by this tract which thither right doth tend,
Which Christ did first beat forth to walk thereby,
And sixteen ages of posterity
Have gone it over since from end to end.

But strike not down to any new-found balk,
Which hunters have begun of late to chalk:
For whether 'twere the glow-worm faith went out,
Or want of love did pine them in the way,
Or else the cruel devils rob or slay,
No news comes back of one of all that rout.

JOSHUA SYLVESTER
(1563–1618)

Joshua Sylvester's sonnets and lyrics have some merit, but his contemporary reputation and what fame he still has stem from his translation of the epic of the creation by the French poet Du Bartas, *The Divine Weeks and Works* (1605).

———————

"Were I as base as is the lowly plain"

Were I as base as is the lowly plain,
And you, my Love, as high as heaven above,
Yet should the thoughts of me, your humble swain,
Ascend to heaven in honor of my love.
Were I as high as heaven above the plain,
And you, my Love, as humble and as low
As are the deepest bottoms of the main,
Wheresoe'er you were, with you my love should go.
Were you the earth, dear Love, and I the skies,
My love should shine on you like to the sun,
And look upon you with ten thousand eyes
Till heaven waxed blind, and till the world were dun.
    Wheresoe'er I am, below, or else above you,
    Wheresoe'er you are, my heart shall truly love you.

"They say that shadows of deceased ghosts"

They say that shadows of deceased ghosts
Do haunt the houses and the graves about,
Of such whose life's lamp went untimely out,
Delighting still in their forsaken hosts:

So, in the place where cruel Love doth shoot
The fatal shaft that slew my love's delight,
I stalk, and walk, and wander day and night,
Even like a ghost with unperceived foot.
But those light ghosts are happier far than I,
For, at their pleasure, they can come and go
Unto the place that hides their treasure so,
And see the name with their fantastic eye:
   Where I, alas, dare not approach the cruel
   Proud monument that doth enclose my jewel.

SIR WILLIAM ALEXANDER,
EARL OF STIRLING
(c.1567–1640)

Born in Scotland, Alexander came to England along with the
Scots who followed James upon his accession to the English
throne. He was a friend of William Drummond of Hawthornden.
Alexander's verse is sometimes weighed down with Scotticisms,
but once in London, he did not hesitate to participate in the
sequence vogue even though it was no longer in full fashion.
Aurora was published in 1604. See p. 108 for King James's comment.

FROM AURORA

29. "I envy not Endymion . . ."

I envy not Endymion now no more,
Nor all the happiness his sleep did yield
While as Diana, straying through the field,
Sucked from his sleep-sealed lips balm for her sore:
Whilst I embraced the shadow of my death,
I, dreaming, did far greater pleasure prove,
And quaffed with Cupid sugared draughts of love,
Then, Jove-like, feeding on a nectared breath.
Now judge which of us two might be most proud:
He got a kiss, yet not enjoyed it right;

And I got none, yet tasted that delight
Which Venus on Adonis once bestowed:
  He only got the body of a kiss,
  And I the soul of it, which he did miss.

33. "Oh, if thou knew'st how thou thyself dost harm"

Oh, if thou knew'st how thou thyself dost harm,
And dost prejudge thy bliss, and spoil my rest;
Then thou wouldst melt the ice out of thy breast
And thy relenting heart would kindly warm.
Oh, if thy pride did not our joys control,
What world of loving wonders shouldst thou see!
For if I saw thee once transformed in me,
Then in thy bosom I would pour my soul;
Then all thy thoughts should in my visage shine,
And if that ought mischanced thou shouldst not moan
Nor bear the burden of thy griefs alone;
No, I would have my share in what were thine:
  And whilst we thus should make our sorrows one,
  This happy harmony would make them none.

68. "I hope, I fear . . ."

I hope, I fear, resolved, and yet I doubt,
I'm cold as ice, and yet I burn as fire;
I wot[1] not what, and yet much I desire,
And trembling too, am desperately stout:
Though melancholious wonders I devise,
And compass much, yet can nothing embrace;
And walk ore[2] all, yet stand still in one place,
And bound on th' earth, do soar above the skies:
I beg for life, and yet I bray for death,
And have a mighty courage, yet despair;
I ever muse, yet am without all care,
And shout aloud, yet never strain my breath:
  I change as oft as any wind can do,
  Yet for all this am ever constant too.

[1] wot/know   [2] ore/over

ALEXANDER CRAIG
(c.1567–1627)

A Scotsman, Craig, like Alexander, came to England in the train that followed James. His stay, however, was brief; he returned to Scotland shortly after receiving a pension from James. His collection of *Amorous Songs, Sonnets, and Elegies* appeared in 1606.

FROM AMOROUS SONGS, SONNETS, AND ELEGIES

To Pandora

Go you, O winds that blow from north to south,
Convey my secret sighs unto my sweet;
Deliver them from mine unto her mouth,
And make my commendations till we meet.
But if perhaps her proud aspiring sp'rit
Will not accept nor yet receive the same,
The breast and bulwark of her bosom beat,
Knock at her heart, and tell from whence you came;
Importune her, nor cease nor shrink for shame;
Sport with her curls of amber-colored hair,
And when she sighs, immix yourselves with thame,[1]
Give her her own, and thus beguile the fair.
   Blow winds, fly sighs, where as my heart doth hant,[2]
   And secretly commend me to my sanct.[3]

[1] thame/them   [2] hant/haunt   [3] sanct/saint

To his Pandora, from England

Now, while amid those dainty downs and dales
With shepherd swains I sit, unknown to me,
We sweetly sing and tell pastoral tales,
But my discourse and song's theme is of thee.
For otherways, alas, how can it be?
Let Venus leave her blest abode above
To tempt my love, yet thou, sweet soul, shalt see
That I thy man and thou shalt die my love.

No tract of time nor sad eclipse of place
Nor absence long, which sometime were due cures
To my disease, shall make thy slave to cease
From serving thee till life or breath endures;
   And till we meet, my rustic mates and I
   Through woods and plains Pandora's praise shall cry.

John Donne
(c.1572–1631)

Raised as a Catholic, Donne attended Oxford and Cambridge but took no degree. He accompanied the Earl of Essex on his expedition to Cadiz in 1596 and later traveled in Italy and Spain. Donne subsequently became secretary to Sir Thomas Egerton, the Lord Keeper of the Seal, but was dismissed in 1601 after his clandestine marriage to Egerton's niece, Anne More, became known. He spent the following years in dire poverty, and finally, after a number of disappointments, turned to a religious career, becoming Dean of St. Paul's in 1621. Donne's *Holy Sonnets*, published with the rest of his poetry after his death, are among the finest religious poems in the language. *La Corona* is a sequence of seven linked devotional sonnets.

LA CORONA

1. *"Deign at my hands this crown of prayer and praise"*

Deign at my hands this crown of prayer and praise,
Weaved in my low devout melancholy,
Thou which of good, hast, yea art treasury
All changing unchanged Ancient of days;
But do not, with a vile crown of frail bays,
Reward my muse's white sincerity,
But what thy thorny crown gained, that give me,
A crown of Glory, which doth flower always;

The ends crown our works, but thou crown'st our ends,
For, at our end begins our endless rest;
The first last end, now zealously possessed,
With a strong sober thirst, my soul attends.
'Tis time that heart and voice be lifted high,
Salvation to all that will is nigh.

2. Annunciation

Salvation to all that will is nigh;
That All, which always is All everywhere,
Which cannot sin, and yet all sins must bear,
Which cannot die, yet cannot choose but die,
Lo, faithful Virgin, yields himself to lie
In prison, in thy womb; and though he there
Can take no sin, nor thou give, yet he will wear
Taken from thence, flesh, which death's force may try.
Ere by the spheres time was created, thou
Wast in his mind, who is thy Son, and Brother;
Whom thou conceiv'st, conceived; yet thou art now
Thy Maker's maker, and thy Father's mother;
Thou hast light in dark; and shutst in little room,
Immensity cloistered in thy dear womb.

3. Nativity

Immensity cloistered in thy dear womb,
Now leaves his well-beloved imprisonment,
There he hath made himself to his intent
Weak enough, now into our world to come;
But oh, for thee, for him, hath th' Inn no room?
Yet lay him in this stall, and from the Orient,
Stars, and wisemen will travel to prevent
Th' effect of Herod's jealous general doom.
Seest thou, my Soul, with thy faith's eyes, how he
Which fills all place, yet none holds him, doth lie?
Was not his pity towards thee wondrous high,
That would have need to be pitied by thee?
Kiss him, and with him into Egypt go,
With his kind mother, who partakes thy woe.

4. Temple

With his kind mother who partakes thy woe,
Joseph turn back; see where your child doth sit,
Blowing, yea blowing out those sparks of wit,
Which himself on the Doctors did bestow;
The Word but lately could not speak, and lo,
It suddenly speaks wonders, whence comes it,
That all which was, and all which should be writ,
A shallow seeming child, should deeply know?
His Godhead was not soul to his manhood,
Nor had time mellowed him to this ripeness,
But as for one which hath a long task, 'tis good,
With the Sun to begin his business,
He in his age's morning thus began
By miracles exceeding power of man.

5. Crucifying

By miracles exceeding power of man,
He faith in some, envy in some begat,
For, what weak spirits admire, ambitious, hate;
In both affections many to him ran,
But oh! the worst are most, they will and can,
Alas, and do, unto this immaculate,
Whose creature Fate is, now prescribe a Fate,
Measuring self-life's infinity to a span,[1]
Nay to an inch. Lo, where condemned he
Bears his own cross, with pain, and yet by and by
When it bears him, he must bear more and die.
Now thou art lifted up, draw me to thee,
And at thy death giving such liberal dole,
Moist, with one drop of thy blood, my dry soul.

[1] span/the expanse of a hand; nine inches

6. Resurrection

Moist with one drop of thy blood, my dry soul
Shall (though she now be in extreme degree
Too stony hard, and yet too fleshly,) be
Freed by that drop, from being starved, hard, or foul,

And life, by this death abled, shall control
Death, whom thy death slew; nor shall to me
Fear of first or last death, bring misery,
If in thy little book my name thou enroll,
Flesh in that long sleep is not putrified,
But made that there, of which, and for which 'twas;
Nor can by other means be glorified.
May then sins sleep, and deaths soon from me pass,
That waked from both, I again risen may
Salute the last, and everlasting day.

7. Ascension

Salute the last and everlasting day,
Joy at the uprising of this Sun, and Son,
Ye whose just tears, or tribulation
Have purely washed, or burnt your drossy clay;
Behold the Highest, parting hence away,
Lightens the dark clouds, which he treads upon,
Nor doth he by ascending, show alone,
But first he, and he first enters the way.
O strong Ram, which hast battered heaven for me,
Mild Lamb, which with thy blood, hast marked the path;
Bright Torch, which shin'st, that I the way may see,
Oh, with thy own blood quench thy own just wrath,
And if thy holy Spirit, my Muse did raise,
Deign at my hands this crown of prayer and praise.

HOLY SONNETS

1. "Thou hast made me . . ."

Thou hast made me; and shall thy work decay?
Repair me now, for now mine end doth haste;
I run to death, and death meets me as fast,
And all my pleasures are like yesterday.
I dare not move my dim eyes any way;
Despair behind, and death before doth cast
Such terror, and my feeble flesh doth waste
By sin in it, which it towards hell doth weigh.

Only thou art above, and when towards thee
By thy leave I can look, I rise again;
But our old subtle foe so tempteth me
That not one hour myself I can sustain.
Thy Grace may wing me to prevent his art,
And thou like Adamant[1] draw mine iron heart.

[1] Adamant/a legendary stone, impregnable and magnetic

4. *"Oh my black Soul . . ."*

Oh my black Soul! now thou art summoned
By sickness, death's herald, and champion;
Thou art like a pilgrim, which abroad hath done
Treason, and durst not turn to whence he is fled,
Or like a thief, which till death's doom be read,
Wisheth himself delivered from prison;
But damned and haled to execution,
Wisheth that still he might be imprisoned.
Yet grace, if thou repent, thou canst not lack;
But who shall give thee that grace to begin?
Oh make thy self with holy mourning black,
And red with blushing, as thou art with sin;
Or wash thee in Christ's blood, which hath this might
That being red, it dyes red souls to white.

5. *"I am a little world . . ."*

I am a little world made cunningly
Of elements and an angelic sprite,
But black sin hath betrayed to endless night
My world's both parts, and, O, both parts must die.
You which beyond that heaven which was most high
Have found new spheres, and of new lands can write,
Pour new seas in mine eyes that so I might
Drown my world with my weeping earnestly,
Or wash it, if it must be drowned no more.
But, O, it must be burnt! Alas, the fire
Of lust and envy have burnt it heretofore
And made it fouler. Let their flames retire,
And burn me, O Lord, with a fiery zeal
Of thee and thy house, which doth in eating heal.

6. "This is my play's last scene . . ."

This is my play's last scene; here heavens appoint
My pilgrimage's last mile; and my race,
Idly yet quickly run, hath this last pace;
My span's last inch, my minutes' latest point;
And gluttonous death will instantly unjoint
My body and my soul, and I shall sleep a space;
But my ever-waking part shall see that face
Whose fear already shakes my every joint.
Then as my soul to heaven, her first seat, takes flight,
And earth-born body in the earth shall dwell,
So fall my sins, that all may have their right,
To where they are bred, and would press me,—to hell.
Impute me righteous, thus purged of evil,
For thus I leave the world, the flesh, the devil.

7. "At the round earth's imagined corners . . ."

At the round earth's imagined corners, blow
Your trumpets, angels; and arise, arise
From death, you numberless infinities
Of souls, and to your scattered bodies go;
All whom the flood did, and fire shall o'erthrow,
All whom war, dearth, age, agues, tyrannies,
Despair, law, chance, hath slain, and you whose eyes
Shall behold God and never taste death's woe.
But let them sleep, Lord, and me mourn a space,
For if above all these my sins abound,
'Tis late to ask abundance of thy grace
When we are there; here on this lowly ground
Teach me how to repent; for that's as good
As if thou hadst sealed my pardon with thy blood.

9. "If poisonous minerals . . ."

If poisonous minerals, and if that tree
Whose fruit threw death on else immortal us,
If lecherous goats, if serpents envious
Cannot be damned, alas! why should I be?
Why should intent or reason, born in me,
Make sins else equal, in me more heinous?

And mercy being easy and glorious
To God, in his stern wrath why threatens he?
But who am I, that dare dispute with thee,
O God? Oh, of thine only worthy blood
And my tears, make a heavenly Lethean flood,
And drown in it my sins' black memory.
That thou remember them, some claim as debt;
I think it mercy, if thou wilt forget.

10. "Death, be not proud . . ."

Death, be not proud, though some have called thee
Mighty and dreadful, for thou art not so;
For those whom thou think'st thou dost overthrow
Die not, poor Death, nor yet canst thou kill me.
From rest and sleep, which but thy pictures be,
Much pleasure; then from thee much more must flow,
And soonest our best men with thee do go,
Rest of their bones, and soul's delivery.
Thou art slave to fate, chance, kings, and desperate men,
And dost with poison, war, and sickness dwell;
And poppy or charms can make us sleep as well
And better than thy stroke; why swell'st thou then?
One short sleep past, we wake eternally,
And death shall be no more; Death, thou shalt die.

11. "Spit in my face, you Jews . . ."

Spit in my face, you Jews, and pierce my side,
Buffet, and scoff, scourge, and crucify me,
For I have sinned, and sinned, and only he,
Who could do no iniquity, hath died:
But by my death can not be satisfied
My sins, which pass the Jews' impiety:
They killed once an inglorious man, but I
Crucify him daily, being now glorified.
Oh let me then, his strange love still admire:
Kings pardon, but he bore our punishment.
And Jacob came clothed in vile harsh attire
But to supplant, and with gainful intent:
God clothed himself in vile man's flesh, that so
He might be weak enough to suffer woe.

13. "What if this present were the world's last night"

What if this present were the world's last night?
Mark in my heart, O soul, where thou dost dwell,
The picture of Christ crucified, and tell
Whether his countenance can thee affright:
Tears in his eyes quench the amazing light,
Blood fills his frowns, which from his pierced head fell.
And can that tongue adjudge thee unto hell,
Which prayed forgiveness for his foes' fierce spite?
No, no; but as in my idolatry
I said to all my profane mistresses,
Beauty, of pity, foulness only is
A sign of rigor; so I say to thee:
To wicked spirits are horrid shapes assigned;
This beauteous form assumes a piteous mind.

14. "Batter my heart . . ."

Batter my heart, three-personed God, for you
As yet but knock, breathe, shine, and seek to mend;
That I may rise and stand, o'erthrow me; and bend
Your force to break, blow, burn, and make me new.
I, like an usurped town to another due,
Labor to admit you, but oh, to no end.
Reason, your viceroy in me, me should defend,
But is captived, and proves weak or untrue.
Yet dearly I love you, and would be loved fain,
But am betrothed unto your enemy;
Divorce me, untie or break that knot again;
Take me to you, imprison me, for I,
Except you enthrall me, never shall be free,
Nor ever chaste, except you ravish me.

16. "Father, part of his double interest"

Father, part of his double interest
Unto his kingdom, thy Son gives to me,
His jointure in the knotty Trinity
He keeps, and gives to me his death's conquest.

This Lamb, whose death, with life the world hath blest,
Was from the world's beginning slain, and He
Hath made two wills, which with the legacy
Of his and thy kingdom, do thy sons invest.
Yet such are thy laws, that men argue yet
Whether a man those statutes can fulfill;
None doth; but all-healing grace and spirit
Revive again what law and letter kill.
Thy law's abridgment, and thy last command
Is all but love; Oh let this last will stand.

17. "Since she whom I loved hath paid her last debt"

Since she whom I loved hath paid her last debt
To Nature, and to hers, and my good is dead,
And her soul early into heaven ravished,
Wholly on heavenly things my mind is set.
Here the admiring her my mind did whet
To seek thee God; so streams do show their head;
But though I have found thee, and thou my thirst hast fed,
A holy thirsty dropsy melts me yet.
But why should I beg more love, when as thou
Dost woo my soul for hers; offering all thine:
And dost not only fear lest I allow
My love to saints and angels, things divine,
But in thy tender jealousy dost doubt
Lest the world, flesh, yea devil put thee out.

18. "Show me, dear Christ . . ."

Show me, dear Christ, thy spouse[1] so bright and clear.
What! is it she which on the other shore
Goes richly painted?[2] or which, robbed and tore,
Laments and mourns in Germany and here?[3]
Sleeps she a thousand, then peeps up one year?
If she self-truth, and errs? now new, now outwore?
Doth she, and did she, and shall she evermore
On one, on seven, or on no hill[4] appear?
Dwells she with us, or like adventuring knights
First travel we to seek, and then make love?

Betray, kind husband, thy spouse to our sights,
And let mine amorous soul court thy mild dove,
Who is most true and pleasing to thee then
When she is embraced and open to most men.

[1]spouse/i.e., the Church
[2]painted/the Church of Rome
[3]here/Protestant church in Germany and England
[4]hill/Mount of Olives, the seven hills of Rome, and possibly in
Canterbury or by Lake Geneva

19. "Oh, to vex me . . ."

Oh, to vex me, contraries meet in one:
Inconstancy unnaturally hath begot
A constant habit; that when I would not
I change in vows, and in devotion.
As humorous[1] is my contrition
As my profane love, and as soon forgot:
As riddlingly distempered, cold and hot,
As praying, as mute as infinite, as none.
I durst not view heaven yesterday; and today
In prayers, and flattering speeches I court God:
Tomorrow I quake with true fear of his rod.
So my devout fits come and go away
Like a fantastic ague[2]: save that here
Those are my best days, when I shake with fear.

[1]humorous/capricious   [2]ague/fever

Ben Jonson
(c.1572–1637)

Born just a month after his father died, Jonson received a good classical education at Westminster School, after which he worked for a short time at his stepfather's trade of bricklaying. To escape this trade, he volunteered for military service and fought with the English forces at Flanders. After he returned to London, Jonson joined a company of actors and began writing plays. Among the dramatists of his age, he is second only to Shakespeare. His taste in poetry was classical, and he cared little for .the flowery sonnet writing of the Elizabethans. The few sonnets he wrote serve as epigrams.

On Poet-Ape

Poor Poet-Ape, that would be thought our chief,
  Whose works are e'en[1] the frippery of wit,
From brokage[2] is become so bold a thief,
  As we, the robbed, leave rage, and pity it.
At first he made low shifts, would pick and glean,
  Buy the reversion of old plays; now grown
To a little wealth, and credit in the scene,
  He takes up all, makes each man's wit his own.
And, told of this, he slights it. Tut, such crimes
  The sluggish gaping auditor devours;
He marks not whose 'twas first, and after-times
  May judge it to be his, as well as ours.
Fool, as if half eyes will not know a fleece
  From locks of wool, or shreds from the whole piece.

[1]e'en/even [2]brokage/brokerage, acting as a broker

An Epigram, to the Household, 1630[1]

What can the cause be, when the K. hath given
  His poet sack, the Household will not pay?
Are they so scanted in their store? or driven
  For want of knowing the poet, to say him nay?

Well, they should know him, would the K. but grant
    His poet leave to sing his Household true;
He'd frame such ditties of their store, and want,
    Would make the very Green-cloth[2] to look blue;
And rather wish, in their expense of sack,
    So, the allowance from the King to use,
As the old Bard, should Canary[3] lack;
    'T were better spare a butt, then spill his muse.
For in the genius of a poet's verse
    The King's fame lies. Go now, deny his tierce.[4]

[1]The King's Household
[2]Green-cloth/The Board of Green Cloth controlled domestic
expenditures of the Royal household.
[3]Canary/a Spanish wine
[4]tierce/a wine keg holding forty-two gallons

JAMES I
(1566–1625)

King James VI of Scotland, James I of England, fancied himself
a writer and produced works on such varied subjects as tobacco,
witchcraft, poetry, and religion. He wrote most of his verse
before he acceded to the English throne in 1603.

An Epitaph on Sir Philip Sidney

Thou mighty Mars, the god of soldiers brave,
And thou, Minerva, that does in wit excel,
And thou, Apollo, that does knowledge have
Of every art that from Parnassus fell,
With all the sisters that thereon do dwell,
Lament for him who duly served you all,
Whom-in you wisely all your arts did mell,[1]—
Bewail, I say, his unexpected fall.
I need not in remembrance for to call
His youth, his race, the hope had of him aye,

Since that in him doth cruel death appall
Both manhood, wit, and learning every way.
    Now in the bed of honor doth he rest,
    And evermore of him shall live the best.

[1]mell/mix

A Sonnet on Sir William Alexander's Harsh Verses After the English Fashion

Hold, hold your hand, hold; mercy, mercy, spare
Those sacred Nine that nursed you many a year.
Full oft, alas, with comfort and with care
We bathed you in Castalia's fountain clear.
Then on our wings aloft we did you bear,
And set you on our stately forked hill
Where you our heavenly harmonies did hear,
The rocks resounding with their echoes still.
Although your neighbors have conspired to spill
That art which did the laurel crown obtain,
And borrowing from the raven their ragg'd quill,
Bewray their harsh, hard, trotting, tumbling wain;
    Such hammering hard the metals hard require;
    Our songs are filed with smoothly flowing fire.

JOHN DAVIES OF HEREFORD
(c.1563–1618)

An expert penman, a writing master, and a poet, John Davies wrote large quantities of religious and moral verse. He incorporated a number of sonnets into several of his books. *The Holy Rood* appeared in 1609. *Wit's Pilgrimage* and *The Scourge of Folly,* which contained most of his epigrams, are uncertainly dated 1605 and 1611.

FROM THE HOLY ROOD

"Although we do not all the good we love"

Although we do not all the good we love,
But still, in love, desire to do the same;
Nor leave the sins we hate, but hating move
Our soul and body's powers their powers to tame;
The good we do God takes as done aright,
That we desire to do he takes as done;
The sin we shun he will with grace requite,
And not impute the sin we seek to shun.
But good desires produce no worser deeds,
For God doth both together lightly give,
Because he knows a righteous man must needs
By faith, that works by love, forever live.
    Then to do nought but only in desire
    Is love that burns, but burns like painted fire.

FROM THE SCOURGE OF FOLLY

The Author Loving These Homely Meats Specially, Viz.: Cream, Pancakes, Buttered Pippin-Pies (Laugh, Good People), and Tobacco; Writ to That Worthy And Virtuous Gentlewoman, Whom He Calleth Mistress, As Followeth

If there were, oh! an Hellespont of cream
Between us, milk-white mistress, I would swim
To you, to show to both my love's extreme,
Leander-like,—yea! dive from brim to brim.
But met I with a buttered pippin-pie
Floating upon 't, that would I make my boat
To waft me to you without jeopardy,
Though seasick I might be while it did float.
Yet if a storm should rise, by night or day,
Of sugar-snows and hail of caraways,
Then, if I found a pancake in my way,
It like a plank should bring me to your kays;[1]
    Which having found, if they tobacco kept,
    The smoke should dry me well before I slept.

[1] kays/quays

FROM WIT'S PILGRIMAGE

"Some blaze the precious beauties of their loves"

Some blaze the precious beauties of their loves
By precious stones, and other some by flowers,
Some by the planets and celestial powers,
Or by what else their fancy best approves;
Yet I by none of these will blazon mine,
But only say her self herself is like,
For those similitudes I much mislike
That are much used, though they be divine.
In saying she is like herself, I say
She hath no like, for she is past compare.

Then who aright commends this creature rare
Must say, "She is"; and there of force must stay,
　Because by words she cannot be expressed;
　So say, "She is," and wond'ring owe the rest.

WILLIAM DRUMMOND OF
HAWTHORNDEN
(1585–1649)

Drummond was educated at the University of Edinburgh, traveled for a time in France, and then settled on his hereditary estate in Scotland. He was friendly with a number of poets, among them Alexander, Drayton, and Ben Jonson. Drummond wrote numerous sonnets throughout his life, many of which are of high quality.

FROM POEMS

"I know that all beneath the moon decays"

I know that all beneath the moon decays,
And what by mortals in this world is brought
In time's great periods shall return to nought;
That fairest states have fatal nights and days.
I know how all the muses' heavenly lays,
With toil of sprite which are so dearly bought,
As idle sounds of few or none are sought,
And that nought lighter is than airy praise.
I know frail beauty, like the purple flower
To which one morn oft birth and death affords;
That love a jarring is of minds' accords,
Where sense and will invassal[1] reason's power;
　Know what I list, this all can not me move,
　But that, oh me, I both must write and love!

[1] invassal/make a vassal of, enslave

"Sleep, silence' child . . ."

Sleep, silence' child, sweet father of soft rest,
Prince whose approach peace to all mortals brings,
Indifferent host to shepherds and to kings,
Sole comforter of minds with grief oppressed,
Lo, by thy charming rod all breathing things
Lie slumb'ring, with forgetfulness possessed;
And yet o'er me to spread thy drowsy wings
Thou spares, alas, who cannot be thy guest.
Since I am thine, O come, but with that face
To inward light which thou art wont to show,
With feigned solace ease a true-felt woe;
Or if, deaf god, thou do deny that grace,
   Come as thou wilt, and what thou wilt bequeath;
   I long to kiss the image of my death.

"My lute, be as thou wast . . ."

My lute, be as thou wast when thou didst grow
With thy green mother in some shady grove,
When immelodious winds but made thee move,
And birds on thee their ramage[1] did bestow.
Sith that dear voice, which did thy sounds approve,
Which used in such harmonious strains to flow,
Is reft from earth to tune those spheres above,
What art thou but a harbinger of woe?
Thy pleasing notes be pleasing notes no more,
But orphan wailings to the fainting ear;
Each stop a sigh, each sound draws forth a tear,
Be therefore silent as in woods before:
   Or, if that any hand to touch thee deign,
   Like widowed turtle still her loss complain.

[1] ramage/songs or cries

"Sweet Spring . . ."

Sweet Spring, thou turn'st with all thy goodly train,
Thy head with flames, thy mantle bright with flowers:
The zephyrs curl the green locks of the plain,
The clouds for joy in pearls weep down their showers.

Thou turn'st, sweet youth, but, ah! my pleasant hours
And happy days with thee come not again;
The sad memorials only of my pain
Do with thee turn, which turn my sweets in sours.
Thou art the same which still thou wast before,
Delicious, wanton, amiable, fair;
But she, whose breath embalmed thy wholesome air,
Is gone; nor gold, nor gems, her can restore.
   Neglected virtue, seasons go and come,
   While thine forgot lie closed in a tomb.

FROM URANIA, OR SPIRITUAL POEMS

"Too long I followed . . ."

Too long I followed have my fond desire,
And too long painted on the ocean streams;
Too long refreshment sought amidst the fire,
And hunted joys, which to my soul were blames.
Ah! when I had what most I did admire,
And seen of life's delights the last extremes,
I found all but a rose hedged with a briar,
A nought, a thought, a show of mocking dreams.
Henceforth on thee mine only good I'll think,
For only thou canst grant what I do crave;
Thy nail my pen shall be, thy blood mine ink,
Thy winding sheet my paper, study grave;
   And till that soul forth of this body fly,
   No hope I'll have but only onely thee.

LADY MARY WROTH
(c.1586–1640)

Niece of Sir Philip Sidney, Lady Mary Wroth was a member of a famous family of writers. Her single published work, *Urania* (1621), is a prose romance that follows in the tradition of her uncle's *Arcadia*. *Pamphilia to Amphilanthus*, a sequence consisting of 83 sonnets and 19 songs, appears in this volume. It is interesting in that, while following the Petrarchan mode of the Elizabethans, the sonnets are addressed by a woman, Pamphilia, to a man. Praised in her own time by Ben Jonson, it is only recently that her poems have been published in a modern edition.

————————

FROM PAMPHILIA TO AMPHILANTHUS

1. *"When night's black mantle . . ."*

When night's black mantle could most darkness prove,
    And sleep (death's image) did my senses hire
    From knowledge of myself, then thoughts did move
    Swifter than those, most switness[1] need require.

In sleep, a chariot drawn by wing'd Desire,
    I saw, where sate[2] bright Venus, Queen of love,
    And at her feet her son, still adding fire
    To burning hearts, which she did hold above.

But one heart flaming more than all the rest,
    The goddess held, and put it to my breast.
    Dear Son, now shoot, she said, this must we win.

He her obeyed, and martyr'd my poor heart.
    I waking hop'd as dreams it would depart,
    Yet since, O me, a lover have I been.

[1] switness/sweetness   [2] sate/sat

7. *"Love leave to urge . . ."*

Love leave to urge, thou knowest thou hast the hand.
  'Tis cowardice to strive where none resist.
  Pray thee, leave off, I yield unto thy band,
  Do not still in thine own power persist.

Behold, I yield, let forces be dismissed,
  I am thy subject conquer'd bound to stand,
  Never thy foe, but did thy claim assist,
  Seeking thy due of those who did withstand.

But now it seems thou would'st I should thee love,
  I do confess, 'twas thy will made me choose,
  And thy fair shows made me a lover prove
  When I my freedom did for pain refuse.

Yet this, Sir god, your Boyship I despise,
Your charms I obey, but love not want of eyes.

WILLIAM BROWNE
(c.1591–1643)

Browne was born in Devonshire and was educated at Oxford. His pastoralism is established in *The Shepherd's Pipe* (1614), to which George Wither also contributed, and reaches its fullest development in *Britannia's Pastorals* (1613 and 1616). He admired Drayton but reserved his highest admiration for Spenser.

FROM CÆLIA

1. *"Lo, I the man . . ."*

Lo, I the man that whilom[1] loved and lost,
Not dreading loss, do sing again of love,
And like a man but lately tempest-tossed,
Try if my stars still inauspicious prove;

Not to make good that poets never can
Long time without a chosen mistress be,
Do I sing thus, or my affections ran
Within the maze of mutability.
What last I loved was beauty of the mind,
And that lodged in a temple truly fair,
Which ruined now by death, if I can find
The saint that lived therein some otherwhere,
I may adore it there and love the cell
For entertaining what I loved so well.

[1] whilom/once

4. "So sat the Muses . . ."

So sat the Muses on the banks of Thames,
And pleased to sing our heavenly Spenser's wit,
Inspiring almost trees with powerful flames,
As Cælia, when she sings what I have writ;
Methinks there is a spirit more divine,
An elegance more rare when aught is sung
By her sweet voice, in every verse of mine,
Than I conceive by any other tongue;
So a musician sets what some one plays
With better relish, sweeter stroke, than he
That first composed; nay, oft the maker weighs
If what he hears his own or other's be.
　　Such are my lines: the highest, best of choice,
　　Become more gracious by her sweetest voice.

GEORGE HERBERT
(1593–1633)

A member of a prominent family, Herbert was educated at Westminster School and Cambridge. His mother, Magdalen Herbert, was friendly with John Donne. In 1620 Herbert was appointed Public Orator at Cambridge, and seemed for a time to consider a career in public life. Eventually he entered the church, and in 1630 he was ordained and became rector at Bemerton. Although Herbert began writing religious poetry while still at Cambridge, it was not published until after his death.

FROM THE TEMPLE

Redemption

Having been tenant long to a rich Lord,
   Not thriving, I resolved to be bold,
   And make a suit unto him to afford
A new small-rented lease and cancel th' old.
In heaven at his manor I him sought.
   They told me there that he was lately gone
   About some land which he had dearly bought
Long since on earth, to take possession.
I straight returned, and knowing his great birth,
   Sought him accordingly in great resorts,
   In cities, theaters, gardens, parks, and courts.
At length I heard a ragged noise and mirth
   Of thieves and murderers; there I him espied,
   Who straight, "Your suit is granted," said, and died.

Prayer

Prayer the church's banquet, Angel's age,
   God's breath in man returning to his birth,
   The soul in paraphrase, heart in pilgrimage,
The Christian plummet sounding heaven and earth;

Engine against th' Almighty, sinner's tower,
   Reversed thunder, Christ-side-piercing spear,
   The six-day's world transposing in an hour,
A kind of tune, which all things hear and fear;
Softness, and peace, and joy, and love, and bliss,
   Exalted Manna, gladness of the best,
   Heaven in ordinary, man well drest,
The milky way, the bird of Paradise,
   Church-bells beyond the stars heard, the soul's bloud,[1]
   The land of spices; something understood.

[1] bloud/blood

Love (1)

Immortal Love, author of this great frame,
   Sprung from that beauty which can never fade;
   How hath man parceled out thy glorious name,
And thrown it on that dust which thou hast made,
While mortal love doth all the title gain!
   Which siding with invention, they together
   Bear all the sway, possessing heart and brain,
(Thy workmanship) and give thee share in neither.
Wit fancies beauty, beauty raiseth wit:
   The world is theirs; they two play out the game,
   Thou standing by: and though thy glorious name
Wrought our deliverance from th' infernal pit,
   Who sings thy praise? only a scarf or glove
   Doth warm our hands, and make them write of love.

Love (2)

Immortal Heat, O let thy greater flame
   Attract the lesser to it: let those fires,
   Which shall consume the world, first make it tame;
And kindle in our hearts such true desires,
As may consume our lusts, and make thee way.
   Then shall our hearts pant thee; then shall our brain
   All her invention on thine altar lay,
And there in hymns send back thy fire again:

Our eyes shall see thee, which before saw dust;
   Dust blown by wit, till that they both were blind:
   Thou shalt never recover all thy goods in kind,
Who wert diseased by usurping lust:
   All knees shall bow to thee; all wits shall rise,
   And praise him who did make and mend our eyes.

The Son

Let foreign nations of their language boast,
What fine variety each tongue affords;
I like our language, as our men and coast;
Who cannot dress it well, want wit, not words.
How neatly do we give one only name
To parents' issue and the sun's bright star!
A son is light and fruit, a fruitful flame
Chasing the father's dimness, carried far
From the first man in th' East to fresh and new
Western discov'ries of posterity.
So in one word our Lord's humility
We turn upon him in a sense most true;
   For what Christ once in humbleness began,
   We him in glory call, The Son of Man.

JOHN MILTON
(1608–1674)

John Milton was born in London and educated at St. Paul's and Christ's College, Cambridge. Instead of entering the church as might have been expected after receiving the Master of Arts degree in 1632, he retired to his father's house in Horton, Buckinghamshire, where for a number of years he read voraciously in preparation for his poetic vocation. He served as Secretary for Foreign Tongues to the Council of State under Oliver Cromwell. Milton wrote only twenty-four sonnets, including five in Italian, but he wrote sonnets throughout his life. Milton's influence on the later development of the sonnet cannot be overestimated, nor can the greatness of his sonnets be overstated.

"How soon hath Time . . ."

How soon hath Time, the subtle thief of youth,
    Stolen on his wing my three-and-twentieth year!
    My hasting days fly on with full career,
    But my late spring no bud or blossom shew'th.
Perhaps my semblance might deceive the truth
    That I to manhood am arrived so near;
    And inward ripeness doth much less appear,
    That some more timely-happy spirits endu'th.
Yet, be it less or more, or soon or slow,
    It shall be still[1] in strictest measure even
    To that same lot, however mean or high,
Toward which Time leads me, and the will of Heaven,
    All is, if I have grace to use it so,
    As ever in my great Taskmaster's eye.

[1] still/always

When the Assault Was Intended to the City[1]

Captain or Colonel, or Knight in Arms,
    Whose chance on these defenseless doors may seize,
    If deed of honor did thee ever please,
    Guard them, and him within protect from harms.

He can requite thee; for he knows the charms
 That call fame on such gentle acts as these,
 And he can spread thy name o'er lands and seas,
Whatever clime the sun's bright circle warms.
Lift not thy spear against the Muses' bower:
 The great Emathian conqueror[2] bid spare
 The house of Pindarus, when temple and tower
Went to the ground; and the repeated air
 Of sad Electra's poet had the power
 To save th' Athenian walls from ruin bare.

[1] An unsuccessful assault on London was part of the Royalist
campaign of 1642.
[2] Emathian conqueror/Alexander the Great

"Lady that in the prime . . ."

Lady that in the prime of earliest youth,
 Wisely hast shunned the broad way and the green,
 And with those few art eminently seen
That labor up the Hill of Heavenly Truth,
The better part with Mary and with Ruth
 Chosen thou hast; and they that overween,
 And at thy growing virtues fret their spleen,
No anger find in thee, but pity and ruth.
Thy care is fixt and zealously attends
 To fill thy odorous lamp with deeds of light,
 And hope that reaps not shame. Therefore be sure
Thou, when the Bridegroom with his feastful friends
 Passes to bliss at the mid-hour of night,
 Hast gained thy entrance, Virgin wise and pure.

On the Detraction Which Followed upon My Writing Certain Treatises[1]

A book was writ of late called Tetrachordon,
 And woven close, both matter, form, and style;
 The subject new: it walked the town a while,
Numbering good intellects; now seldom pored on.

Cries the stall-reader, "Bless us! what a word on
    A title-page is this!"; and some in file
    Stand spelling false,[2] while one might walk to Mile-
End Green. Why is it harder, sirs, than Gordon,
Colkitto, or Macdonnel, or Galasp?
    Those rugged names to our like mouths grow sleek,
    That would have made Quintilian stare and gasp.
Thy age, like ours, O soul of Sir John Cheke,[3]
    Hated not learning worse than toad or asp,
    When thou taught'st Cambridge and King Edward Greek.

[1] Certain Treatises/Milton's divorce pamphlets, of which
Tetrachordon was the third
[2] spelling false/misinterpreting
[3] Sir John Cheke/the first Professor of Greek at Cambridge

On the Same[1]

I did but prompt the age to quit their clogs
    By the known rules of ancient liberty,
    When straight a barbarous noise environs me
Of owls and cuckoos, asses, apes, and dogs;
As when those hinds that were transformed to frogs
    Railed at Latona's[2] twin-born progeny,
    Which after held the Sun and Moon in fee.
But this is got by casting pearl to hogs,
That bawl for freedom in their senseless mood,
    And still revolt when truth would set them free.
    License they mean when they cry liberty;
For who loves that must first be wise and good:
    But from that mark how far they rove we see,
    For all this waste of wealth and loss of blood.

[1] This is the second of Milton's sonnets against his detractors.
[2] Latona/The mother of Apollo and Diana prayed to Zeus, their
father, to turn her tormentors into frogs.

On the New Forcers of Conscience Under the Long Parliament[1]

Because you have thrown off your prelate lord,
  And with stiff vows renounced his liturgy,
  To seize the widowed whore Plurality
From them whose sin ye envied, not abhorred,
Dare ye for this adjure the civil sword
  To force our consciences that Christ set free,
  And ride us with a classic hierarchy
Taught ye by mere A. S. and Rutherford?[2]
Men whose life, learning, faith and pure intent
  Would have been held in high esteem with Paul
  Must now be named and printed heretics
By shallow Edwards and Scotch what d'ye call:[3]
  But we do hope to find out all your tricks,
  Your plots and packings worse than those of Trent,
                    That so the Parliament
May with their wholesome and preventive shears
Clip your phylacteries, though balk your ears,
                    And succor our just fears
When they shall read this clearly in your charge
New presbyter is but old priest writ large.

[1] This form of the sonnet, containing two three-line "tails," was popular in Italy. The "new forcers" are the Presbyterians.
[2] A. S. and Rutherford/Presbyterian pamphleteers
[3] Edwards and Scotch what d'ye call/Thomas Edwards, a Presbyterian controversialist and Scottish religionists in general.

To the Lord General Cromwell, on the Proposals of Certain Ministers at the Committee for Propagation of the Gospel

Cromwell, our chief of men, who through a cloud
  Not of war only, but detractions rude,
  Guided by faith and matchless fortitude,
  To peace and truth thy glorious way hast ploughed,
And on the neck of crowned Fortune proud
  Hast reared God's trophies, and his work pursued,
  While Darwen stream, with blood of Scots imbrued,
  And Dunbar field, resounds thy praises loud,

And Worcester's laureate wreath: yet much remains
    To conquer still; Peace hath her victories
    No less renowned than War: new foes arise,
Threatening to bind our souls with secular chains.
    Help us to save free conscience from the paw
    Of hireling wolves, whose Gospel is their maw.

To Sir Henry Vane[1] the Younger

Vane, young in years, but in sage counsel old,
    Than whom a better senator ne'er held
    The helm of Rome, when gowns, not arms, repelled
    The fierce Epirot,[2] and the African bold,[3]
Whether to settle peace, or to unfold
    The drift of hollow states, hard to be spelled;
    Then to advise how war may best, upheld,
    Move by her two main nerves, iron and gold,
In all her equipage; besides, to know
    Both spiritual power and civil, what each means,
    What severs each, thou hast learned, which few have done.
The bounds of either sword to thee we owe:
    Therefore on thy firm hand Religion leans
    In peace, and reckons thee her eldest son.

[1] Sir Henry Vane/Governor of Massachusetts Bay Colony, 1636–1637; Parliamentarian and diplomat
[2] Epirot/Pyrrhus, King of Epirus, invaded Italy in the 3rd century B.C.
[3] African bold/Hannibal

On the Late Massacre in Piedmont[1]

Avenge, O Lord, thy slaughtered saints, whose bones
    Lie scattered on the Alpine mountains cold;
    Even them who kept thy truth so pure of old,
    When all our fathers worshipped stocks and stones,
Forget not: in thy book record their groans
    Who were thy sheep, and in their ancient fold
    Slain by the bloody Piedmontese, that rolled
    Mother with infant down the rocks. Their moans

The vales redoubled to the hills, and they
    To Heaven. Their martyred blood and ashes sow
    O'er all th' Italian fields, where still doth sway
The triple Tyrant[2]; that from these may grow
    A hundredfold, who, having learnt thy way,
    Early may fly the Babylonian[3] woe.

[1] Late Massacre in Piedmont/Persecution of the Waldensians, a.
Protestant religious sect, by the Duke of Savoy in 1655.
[2] Tyrant/the Pope
[3] Babylonian/The Church of Rome is identified here with the
"whore of Babylon" (Revelation xvii, xviii).

"When I consider . . ."

When I consider how my light is spent
    Ere half my days in this dark world and wide,
    And that one talent which is death to hide
    Lodged with me useless, though my soul more bent
To serve therewith my Maker, and present
    My true account, lest he returning chide,
    "Doth God exact day-labor, light denied?"
    I fondly ask. But Patience, to prevent
That murmur, soon replies, "God doth not need
    Either man's work or his own gifts. Who best
    Bear his mild yoke, they serve him best. His state
Is kingly: thousands at his bidding speed,
    And post o'er land and ocean without rest;
    They also serve who only stand and wait."

"Cyriack,[1] whose grandsire . . ."

Cyriack, whose grandsire on the royal bench
    Of British Themis, with no mean applause,
    Pronounced, and in his volumes taught, our laws,
    Which others at their bar so often wrench,
Today deep thoughts resolve with me to drench
    In mirth that after no repenting draws;
    Let Euclid rest, and Archimedes pause,
    And what the Swede intend, and what the French.

To measure life learn thou betimes, and know
    Towards solid good what leads the nearest way;
    For other things mild Heaven a time ordains,
And disapproves that care, though wise in show.
    That with superfluous burden loads the day,
    And, when God sends a cheerful hour, refrains.

[1] Cyriack/Cyriack Skinner, a former pupil of Milton's and a lifelong friend

To Mr. Cyriack Skinner upon His Blindness

Cyriack, this three years' day these eyes, though clear,
    To outward view, of blemish or of spot,
    Bereft of light, their seeing have forgot;
    Nor to their idle orbs doth sight appear
Of sun, or moon, or star, throughout the year,
    Or man, or woman. Yet I argue not
    Against Heaven's hand or will, nor bate a jot
    Of heart or hope, but still bear up and steer
Right onward. What supports me, dost thou ask?
    The conscience, friend, to have lost them overplied
    In liberty's defense, my noble task,
Of which all Europe rings from side to side.
    This thought might lead me through the world's vain mask
    Content, though blind, had I no better guide.

"Methought I saw . . ."

Methought I saw my late espoused saint[1]
    Brought to me like Alcestis from the grave,
    Whom Jove's great son to her glad husband gave,
    Rescued from Death by force, though pale and faint.
Mine, as whom washed from spot of childbed taint
    Purification in the Old Law did save,
    And such as yet once more I trust to have
    Full sight of her in Heaven without restraint,
Came vested all in white, pure as her mind.
    Her face was veiled; yet to my fancied sight
    Love, sweetness, goodness, in her person shined

So clear, as in no face with more delight.
  But, oh! as to embrace me she inclined,
  I waked, she fled, and day brought back my night.

[1] saint/Milton's second wife, Katherine Woodcock, died in 1658.

PART TWO

The Seventeenth and Eighteenth Centuries

CHARLES COTTON
(1630–1687)

Charles Cotton of Beresford, Staffordshire, is best remembered today for his friendship with Izaak Walton and for his authorship of Part II of *The Compleat Angler,* "Being Instructions how to angle for a Trout or Grayling in a clear stream" (1676). He is also known for his translation of Montaigne's *Essays* in 1685.

Resolution in Four Sonnets, of a Poetical Question Put to Me by a Friend, Concerning Four Rural Sisters

1. "Alice is tall and upright as a pine"

Alice is tall and upright as a pine,
White as blanched almonds, or the falling snow,
Sweet as are damask roses when they blow,
And doubtless fruitful as the swelling vine.

Ripe to be cut, and ready to be pressed,
Her full cheeked beauties very well appear,
And a year's fruit she loses every year,
Wanting a man t' improve her to the best.

Full fain she would be husbanded, and yet,
Alas! she cannot a fit laborer get
To cultivate her to her own content:

Fain would she be (God wot) about her task,
And yet (forsooth) she is too proud to ask,
And (which is worse) too modest to consent.

2. *"Marg'ret of humbler stature by the head"*

Marg'ret of humbler stature by the head
Is (as it oft falls out with yellow hair)
Than her fair sister, yet so much more fair,
As her pure white is better mixed with red.

This, hotter than the other ten to one,
Longs to be put unto her mother's trade,
And loud proclaims she lives too long a maid,
Wishing for one t' untie her virgin zone.

She finds virginity a kind of ware,
That's very very troublesome to bear,
And being gone, she thinks will ne'er be mist:

And yet withal, the girl has so much grace,
To call for help I know she wants the face,
Though asked, I know not how she would resist.

3. *"Mary is black . . ."*

Mary is black, and taller than the last,
Yet equal in perfection and desire,
To the one's melting snow, and t' other's fire,
As with whose black their fairness is defaced.

She pants as much for love as th' other two,
But she so virtuous is, or else so wise,
That she will win or will not love a prize,
And upon but good terms will never do:

Therefore, who her will conquer ought to be
At least as full of love and wit as she,
Or he shall ne'er gain favor at her hands:

Nay, though he have a pretty store of brains,
Shall only have his labor for his pains,
Unless he offer more than she demands.

4. "Martha is not so tall . . ."

Martha is not so tall, nor yet so fair
As any of the other lovely three,
Her chiefest grace is poor simplicity,
Yet were the rest away, she were a star.

She's fair enough, only she wants the art
To set her beauties off as they can do,
And that's the cause she ne'er heard any woo,
Nor ever yet made conquest of a heart:

And yet her blood's as boiling as the best,
Which, pretty soul, does so disturb her rest,
And makes her languish so, she's fit to die.

Poor thing, I doubt she still must lie alone,
For being like to be attacked by none,
She's no more wit to ask than to deny.

PHILIP AYRES
(1638–1712)

Ayres was educated at Winchester and at St. John's College,
Oxford. A friend of John Dryden, he appears to have spent most
of his life as a tutor in a nobleman's family. Little more is known
of his life. His major work, *Lyric Poems Made in Imitation of the
Italians*, was published in 1687. Like those of Cotton, his son-
nets represent the close of the older sonnet tradition.

Invites Poets and Historians to Write in Cynthia's Praise

Come all ye Wits, that with immortal rhymes,
    Glory to others, and yourselves, create:
And you that gratify the future times,
    Whilst tales of Love, and battles ye relate;

Come, turn your studies, and your eyes this way,
　　This theme will crown your heads with lasting bays,
　　'Tis Cynthia's beauty, Heavenly Cynthia;
　　Come swell your volumes all with Cynthia's praise.

Posterity will then your works admire,
　　And for her sake shall them as jewels prize,
All things to Cynthia's glory must conspire,
　　She shall be worshiped with the deities.

　　To her make foreign lands pay honors due,
　　Thus shall you live by her, and she by you.

On Lydia Distracted

With hairs, which for the wind to play with, hung,
　　With her torn garments, and with naked feet,
　　Fair Lydia dancing went from street to street,
Singing with pleasant voice her foolish song.

On her she drew all eyes in every place,
　　And them to pity by her pranks did move,
　　Which turned with gazing longer into Love
By the rare beauty of her charming face.

In all her frenzies, and her mimicries,
While she did Nature's richest gifts despise,
　　There active Love did subtly play his part.

Her antic postures made her look more gay,
Her ragged clothes her treasures did display,
　　And with each motion she ensnared a heart.

THOMAS EDWARDS
(1699–1757)

The Canons of Criticism (1748), Edwards's vigorous assault on William Warburton's edition of Shakespeare, provoked Dr. Johnson to remark, "A fly, sir, may sting a stately horse and make him wince; but one is but an insect, and the other is a horse still." Of the fourteen sonnets printed in the second volume of Dodsley's *Collection of Poems, by Several Hands* (1748), thirteen were by Edwards; his importance in the history of the revival of the sonnet is considerable.

To the Author of Clarissa[1]

O Master of the heart, whose magic skill
The close recesses of the Soul can find,
Can rouse, becalm, and terrify the mind,
Now melt with pity, now with anguish thrill,
Thy moral page with virtuous precepts fill,
Warm from the heart, to mend the Age designed,
Wit, strength, truth, decency are all conjoined
To lead our Youth to Good, and guard from Ill:
O long enjoy, what thou so well hast won,
The grateful tribute of each honest heart
Sincere, nor hackneyed in the ways of men;
At each distressful stroke their true tears run,
And Nature, unsophisticate by Art,
Owns and applauds the labors of thy pen.

[1] *Clarissa*/a novel by Samuel Richardson (1689–1761)

"Tongue-doughty Pedant[1] *. . ."*

Tongue-doughty Pedant; whose ambitious mind
Prompts thee beyond thy native pitch to soar;
And, imped[2] with borrowed plumes of index-lore,
Range through the Vast of Science unconfined!
Not for thy wings was such a flight designed:
Know thy own strength, and wise attempt no more;

But lowly skim round Error's winding shore,
In quest of Paradox from Sense refined.
Much hast thou written—more than will be read;
Then cease from Shakespeare thy unhallowed rage;
Nor by a fond o'erweening pride misled,
Hope fame by injuring the sacred dead:
Know, who would comment well his godlike page,
Critic, must have a heart as well as head.

[1] Pedant/William Warburton (1698–1779) published editions of
Shakespeare in 1747 and of Alexander Pope in 1751.
[2] imped/furnished, engrafted

To the Editor of Mr. Pope's Works

O, born in luckless hour, with every Muse
And every Grace to foe! what wayward fate
Drives thee with fell and unrelenting hate
Each choicest work of genius to abuse?
Sufficed it not with sacrilegious views
Great Shakespeare's awful shade to violate:
And *His* fair Paradise contaminate,
Whom impious Lauder[1] blushes to accuse.
Must Pope, thy friend, mistaken hapless bard!
(To prove no sprig of laurel e'er can grow
Unblasted by thy venom) must he groan,
Now daubed with flattery, now by censure scarred,
Disguised, deformed, and made the public show
In motley weeds, and colors not his own?

[1] William Lauder (d.1771) was a Scottish scholar who asserted that
Milton had plagiarized much of *Paradise Lost* and who supported
his accusations with forgeries.

To Shakespeare

Shakespeare, whose heartfelt scenes shall ever give
Instructive pleasure to the listening age;
And shine unrivaled on the British stage
By native worth and high prerogative;

When full of fame thou didst retire to live
In studious leisure, had thy judgment sage
Cleared off the rubbish cast on thy fair page
By players or ignorant or forgetive—
O what a sea of idly squandered ink,
What heaps of notes by blundering critics penned
(The dreams of ignorance in wisdom's guise)
Had then been spared! nor *Knapton*[1] then, I think,
And honest *Draper*[1] had been forced to send
Their dear-bought reams to cover plums and spice.

[1] Knapton and Draper were well-known London booksellers and publishers.

THOMAS GRAY
(1716–1771)

Gray was born in London and educated at Eton (where his friendships with Horace Walpole and Richard West were formed) and Cambridge. After a brief stay in Stoke Poges, Buckinghamshire, he settled in Cambridge in 1742. Here, according to Samuel Johnson, he lived quietly, "very little solicitous of what others did or thought, and cultivated his mind and enlarged his views. . . ." His most famous poem is, of course, the "Elegy Written in a Country Churchyard." His only sonnet, written in 1742 but not published until 1775, is chiefly interesting as the object of Wordsworth's criticism in the *Preface* of 1800.

On the Death of Mr. Richard West

In vain to me the smiling mornings shine,
　And redd'ning Phœbus lifts his golden fire;
The birds in vain their amorous descant join,
　Or cheerful fields resume their green attire:
These ears, alas! for other notes repine,
　A different object do these eyes require:
My lonely anguish melts no heart but mine;
　And in my breast the imperfect joys expire.

Yet morning smiles the busy race to cheer,
   And newborn pleasure brings to happier men:
The fields to all their wonted tribute bear;
   To warm their little loves the birds complain:
I fruitless mourn to him that cannot hear,
   And weep the more, because I weep in vain.

THOMAS WARTON, THE YOUNGER
(1728–1790)

Thomas Warton, the Younger, belonged to a distinguished literary family. His father, Thomas Warton, was a minor poet and professor of poetry at Oxford from 1718 to 1728. Joseph Warton, his elder brother, was a poet and critic. Like his father, Thomas Warton, the Younger, was professor of poetry at Oxford for ten years. He was the author of a three-volume *History of English Poetry* (1774–1781) in addition to a small but influential amount of poetry. He was appointed Poet Laureate in 1785.

Written in a Blank Leaf of Dugdale's Monasticon[1]

Deem not devoid of elegance the Sage,
By Fancy's genuine feelings unbeguiled,
Of painful Pedantry the poring child;
Who turns, of these proud domes, the historic page,
Now sunk by Time, and Henry's[2] fiercer rage.
Thinkst thou the warbling Muses never smiled
On his lone hours? Ingenuous views engage
His thoughts, on themes, unclassic falsely styled,
Intent. While cloistered Piety displays
Her moldering roll, the piercing eye explores
New manners, and the pomp of elder days,
Whence culls the pensive bard his pictured stores.
Nor rough, nor barren, are the winding ways
Of hoar Antiquity, but strewn with flowers.

[1] Monasticon/*Monasticon Anglicanum,* a scholarly study of English monasteries by Sir William Dugdale (1605–1686)
[2] King Henry VIII

Written at Stonehenge

Thou noblest monument of Albion's isle!
Whether by Merlin's aid from Scythia's shore,
To Amber's fatal plain Pendragon[1] bore,
Huge frame of giant hands, the mighty pile,
To entomb his Britons slain by Hengist's[2] guile:
Or Druid priests, sprinkled with human gore,
Taught mid thy massy maze their mystic lore:
Or Danish chiefs, enriched with savage spoil,
To Victory's idol vast, an unhewn shrine,
Reared the rude heap: or, in thy hallowed round,
Repose the kings of Brutus'[3] genuine line;
Or here those kings in solemn state were crowned:
Studious to trace thy wondrous origin,
We muse on many an ancient tale renowned.

[1] Pendragon/King Arthur's father, Uther Pendragon
[2] Hengist's/Invaded Britain from Jutland about 449
[3] Brutus was the great-grandson of Aeneas and according to a popular tradition was the founder of the British race.

To Mr. Gray

Not that her blooms are marked with beauty's hue,
My rustic Muse her votive chaplet brings;
Unseen, unheard, O Gray, to thee she sings!—
While slowly pacing through the churchyard dew,
At curfew-time, beneath the dark-green yew,
Thy pensive genius strikes the moral strings;
Or borne sublime on Inspiration's wings,
Hears Cambria's bards devote the dreadful clue
Of Edward's race, with murders foul defiled;
Can aught my pipe to reach thine ear essay?
No, bard divine! For many a care beguiled
By the sweet magic of thy soothing lay,
For many a raptured thought, and vision wild,
To thee this strain of gratitude I pay.

On King Arthur's Round Table, at Winchester

Where Venta's Norman castle still uprears
Its raftered hall, that o'er the grassy fosse,
And scattered flinty fragments clad in moss,
On yonder steep in naked state appears;
High-hung remains, the pride of warlike years,
Old Arthur's board: on the capacious round
Some British pen has sketched the names renowned,
In marks obscure, of his immortal peers.
Though joined by magic skill, with many a rhyme,
The Druid frame, unhonored falls a prey
To the slow vengeance of the wizard Time,
And fade the British characters away;
Yet Spenser's page, that chants in verse sublime
Those chiefs, shall live, unconscious of decay.

WILLIAM COWPER
(1731–1800)

Cowper read law and was called to the bar in 1754, but recurrent attacks of madness forced him to lead a retired life, primarily at Olney in the home of Mary Unwin. He contributed a number of still remembered hymns to the *Olney Hymns* (1779) and published what is to many his most enjoyable work, *The Task,* in 1785. His death released him from the spiritual anguish expressed in "The Castaway."

To William Wilberforce,[1] Esq.

Thy country, Wilberforce, with just disdain,
Hears thee, by cruel men and impious, called
Fanatic, for thy zeal to loose the enthralled
From exile, public sale, and slavery's chain.
Friend of the poor, the wronged, the fetter-galled,
Fear not lest labor such as thine be vain!
Thou hast achieved a part; hast gained the ear
Of Britain's senate to thy glorious cause;

Hope smiles, joy springs, and tho' cold caution pause
And weave delay, the better hour is near,
That shall remunerate thy toils severe
By peace for Afric, fenced with British laws.
　Enjoy what thou hast won, esteem and love
　From all the just on earth, and all the blest above!

1 William Wilberforce (1759–1833) was prominent in the abolition of
slavery in the British Empire.

To William Hayley, Esq.: In Reply to His Solicitation to Write with Him in a Literary Work

Dear architect of fine *Chateaux en l'air*,
Worthier to stand forever, if they could,
Than any built with stone, or yet with wood
For back of royal elephant to bear!—
Oh for my youth again, that I might share,
Much to my own, tho' little to thy good,
With thee, not subject to the jealous mood,
A partnership of literary ware!
But I am bankrupt now, and doomed henceforth
To drudge, in descant dry, on others' lays,
Bards, I acknowledge, of unequaled worth,
But what is commentator's happiest praise?
That he has furnished lights for others' eyes,
Which they who need them use, and then despise.

WILLIAM HAYLEY
(1745–1820)

Robert Southey wrote of Hayley, "Everything about that man is good except his poetry." Time has not brought this judgment into question. His most popular poem, *The Triumphs of Temper,* was published in 1781. Byron ridiculed Hayley's *Triumphs of Music* (1804), but Anna Seward, Charlotte Smith, and Cowper dedicated poems to him.

To Mrs. Smith, Occasioned by the First of Her Sonnets

Thou whose chaste song simplicity inspires,
    Attractive poetess of plaintive strain!
Speak not unjustly of poetic fires,
    Nor the pure bounty of thy Muse arraign:
    No, not the source, the soother she of pain.
If thy soft breast the thorns of anguish knew,
    Ah! think what myriads with thy truth complain
Of fortune's thorny paths! and think how few
    Of all those myriads know thy magic art,
The fiercer pangs of sorrow to subdue,
    By those melodious tears that ease thy heart,
And bid the breath of fame thy life renew;
Sure to excite, till nature's self decays,
Her lasting sympathy, her endless praise!

To Mr. William Long, On His Recovery from a Dangerous Illness, 1785

Blessed be the day which bids my grief subside,
    Raised by the sickness of my distant friend!
Blessed the dear lines, so long to hope denied,
    By languor's aching fingers kindly penned!
    How keen the fear to feel his letters end,
Whose wit was my delight, whose truth my guide!
    But how did joy that painful fear transcend,
When I again his well-known hand descried!

Such was the dread of new-created man,
When first he missed the setting orb of day;
  Such the delight that through his bosom ran,
When he perceived the re-ascending ray.
Ah no! his thoughts endured less anxious strife;
Thou, friendship! art the sun of mental life.

ANNA SEWARD
(1747–1809)

Though Sir Walter Scott published her poetical works in three posthumous volumes in 1810 and despite W. C. Oulton's selection of *The Beauties of Anna Seward,* the "Swan of Lichfield" is now remembered chiefly as an arch bluestocking and for her association with such worthies as Dr. Johnson, Boswell, Erasmus Darwin, and Scott. The sonnets of the author of *Louisa, a Poetical Novel* (1782) are more notable for their abundance than for their quality.

On the Use of New and Old Words in Poetry

While with false pride, and narrow jealousy,
  Numbers reject each new expression, won,
  Perchance, from language richer than our own,
  O! with glad welcome may the Poet see
Extension's golden vantage! The decree
  Each way exclusive, scorn, and re-enthrone
  The obsolete, if strength, or grace or tone
  Or imagery await it, with a free,
And liberal daring!—For the critic train,
  Whose eyes severe our verbal stores review,
  Let the firm bard require that they explain
Their cause of censure; then in balance true
  Weigh it; but smile at the objections vain
  Of sickly spirits, hating for they do!

On Catania and Syracuse Swallowed Up by an Earthquake, From the Italian of Filicaja[1]

Here, from laborious art, proud towns, ye rose!
　Here, in an instant, sunk!—nor aught remains
　Of all ye were!—on the wide, lonely plains
Not e'en a stone, that might these words disclose,
"Here stood Catania;"—or whose surface shows
　That this was Syracuse:—but louring reigns
　A trackless desolation.—Dim domains!
Pale, mournful strand! how oft, with anxious throes,
Seek I sad relics, which no spot supplies!—
　A silence—a fixed horror sears my soul—
　Inexplicable doom of human crimes,
What art thou?—Ye o'erwhelmed cities, rise!
　That your terrific skeletons may scowl
　Portentous warning to succeeding times!

[1] Vincenzo da Filicaja (1642–1707), Italian poet whose sonnets were once admired.

Written December 1790

Lyre of the sonnet, that full many a time
　Amused my lassitude, and soothed my pains,
　When graver cares forbade the lengthened strains,
To thy brief bound, and oft-returning chime
A long farewell!—the splendid forms of rhyme
　When grief in lonely orphanism reigns,
　Oppress the drooping soul.—Death's dark domains
Throw mournful shadows o'er the Æonian clime;
For in their silent bourne my filial bands
　Lie all dissolved;—and swiftly-wasting pour
　From my frail glass of life, health's sparkling sands.
Sleep, then, my Lyre, thy tuneful tasks are o'er;
　Sleep! for my heart bereaved, and listless hands,
　Wake with rapt touch thy glowing strings no more!

CHARLOTTE SMITH
(1749–1806)

Charlotte Smith married early and unfortunately, and literary activity became a financial necessity. Her first book of poetry, *Elegiac Sonnets and Other Essays,* was dedicated to William Hayley and published through his intervention in 1784. By 1789 it had been through five editions. In 1797 more poems were added, and a two-volume edition was published with Cowper, Horace Walpole, Mrs. Siddons, and Joseph and Thomas Warton among the subscribers. Mrs. Smith also produced numerous novels.

To the Moon

Queen of the silver bow!—by thy pale beam,
Alone and pensive, I delight to stray,
And watch thy shadow trembling in the stream,
Or mark the floating clouds that cross thy way.
And while I gaze, thy mild and placid light
Sheds a soft calm upon my troubled breast;
And oft I think—fair planet of the night—
That in thy orb, the wretched may have rest:
The sufferers of the earth perhaps may go,
Released by Death—to thy benignant sphere,
And the sad children of Despair and Woe
Forget, in thee, their cup of sorrow here.
Oh! that I soon may reach thy world serene,
Poor wearied pilgrim—in this toiling scene!

To Sleep

Come balmy Sleep! tired Nature's soft resort!
On these sad temples all thy poppies shed;
And bid gay dreams from Morpheus' airy court,
Float in light vision round my aching head!
Secure of all thy blessings, partial Power!
On his hard bed the peasant throws him down;
And the poor sea boy, in the rudest hour,
Enjoys thee more than he who wears a crown.

Clasped in her faithful shepherd's guardian arms,
Well may the village girl sweet slumbers prove,
And they, O gentle Sleep! still taste thy charms,
Who wake to labor, liberty and love.
But still thy opiate aid dost thou deny
To calm the anxious breast; to close the streaming eye.

The Captive Escaped in the Wilds of America
Addressed to the Honorable Mrs. O'Neill

If by his torturing, savage foes untraced,
The breathless captive gain some trackless glade,
Yet hears the warwhoop howl along the waste,
And dreads the reptile monsters of the shade;
The giant reeds that murmur round the flood,
Seem to conceal some hideous form beneath;
And every hollow blast that shakes the wood,
Speaks to his trembling heart, of woe and death.
With horror fraught, and desolate dismay,
On such a wanderer falls the starless night;
But if, far streaming, a propitious ray
Leads to some amicable fort his sight,
He hails the beam benign that guides his way,
As I, my Harriet, bless thy friendship's cheering light.

ROBERT BURNS
(1759–1796)

Born in Ayrshire, the son of an ambitious farmer, Burns spent his youth working with his father on a number of unsuccessful farms. With the publication of his first book of poetry in 1786, he was lionized as a plowman-poet by Edinburgh society. He well deserves his reputation as Scotland's greatest poet for his poems in Scots, but those deserts are admittedly less clearly discernible in his English poems.

A Sonnet upon Sonnets

Fourteen, a sonneteer thy praises sings;
What magic myst'ries in that number lie!
Your hen hath fourteen eggs beneath her wings
That fourteen chickens to the roost may fly.
Fourteen full pounds the jockey's stone must be;
His age fourteen—a horse's prime is past.
Fourteen long hours too oft the Bard must fast;
Fourteen bright bumpers—bliss he ne'er must see!
Before fourteen, a dozen yields the strife;
Before fourteen—e'en thirteen's strength is vain.
Fourteen good years—a woman gives us life;
Fourteen good men—we lose that life again.
What lucubrations can be more upon it?
Fourteen good measur'd verses make a sonnet.

John Bampfylde
(1754–1796)

Bampfylde's *Sixteen Sonnets,* published in 1778, was dedicated to a niece of Sir Joshua Reynolds. When Sir Joshua discouraged Bampfylde's attentions and forbade a marriage, the poet responded by breaking Sir Joshua's windows. Bampfylde spent many years "in a private madhouse."

To the Redbreast

When that the fields put on their gay attire,
  Thou silent sitt'st near brake or river's brim,
  Whilst the gay thrush sings loud from covert dim;
But when pale Winter lights the social fire,
And meads with slime are sprent,[1] and ways with mire,
  Thou charm'st us with thy soft and solemn hymn
  From battlement, or barn, or haystack trim;
And now not seldom tunest, as if for hire,
Thy thrilling pipe to me, waiting to catch
  The pittance due to thy well-warbled song:
Sweet bird! sing on; for oft near lonely hatch,
  Like thee, myself have pleased the rustic throng,
And oft for entrance, 'neath the peaceful thatch,
  Full many a tale have told, and ditty long.

[1] sprent/splashed

On Hearing That Torture Was Suppressed Throughout the Austrian Dominions, in Consequence of Beccaria's Treatise on Crimes and Punishments[1]

Hail to the sage divine of Milan's plains!
  Whose labors reached the horrors of the cell,
  Brought Mercy down from heaven with man to dwell,
And curbed the biting laws, and checked the reins
Of Justice too severe.—And, lo! the chains,

At thy command, from off the convict fell,
  The wheel appeared no more, nor scaffold bell
Bade him prepare for more than mortal pains.
Oh! may thy voice pervade the nations round,
  And monarchs of their subjects' woes remind;
So shall thy praise o'er earth and seas resound,
Nor shall thy own Italia boast a name
To be compared with thine in future fame,
  So loved by all the good, so dear to humankind.

[1] The Marquis di Beccaria (1735–1794) was an Italian humanitarian.

THOMAS RUSSELL
(1762–1788)

Born in Beaminster in Dorset, Thomas Russell distinguished himself at Winchester and at New College, Oxford. He was ordained in 1786. Russell's poems were published posthumously in 1789, and his sonnets gained the praise of Wordsworth, Coleridge, and Bowles, with whom he shares a place in the history of the rejuvenation of the sonnet.

To Oxford

Oxford, since late I left thy peaceful shore,
  Much I regret thy domes with turrets crowned,
  Thy crested walls with twining ivy bound,
  Thy Gothic fanes, dim isles, and cloisters hoar,
And treasured rolls of Wisdom's ancient lore;
  Nor less thy varying bells, which hourly sound
  In pensive chime, or ring in lively round,
  Or toll in the slow Curfew's solemn roar;
Much too thy moonlight walks, and musings grave
  Mid silent shades of high-embowering trees,
  And much thy Sister-Streams, whose willows wave
In whispering cadence to the evening breeze;
  But most those Friends, whose much-loved converse gave
  Thy gentle charms a tenfold power to please.

To the Spider

Ingenious insect, but of ruthless mold,
　Whose savage craft, as Nature taught, designs
　A mazy web of death, the filmy lines,
That form thy circling labyrinth, enfold
Each thoughtless fly that wanders near thy hold,
　Sad victim of thy guile; nor aught avail
　His silken wings, nor coat of glossy mail,
Nor varying hues of azure, jet, or gold:
Yet though thus ill the fluttering captive fares
　Whom, heedless of the fraud, thy toils trepan[1];
Thy tyrant fang, that slays the stranger, spares
　The bloody brothers of thy cruel clan;
While man against his fellows spreads his snares,
　Then most delighted, when his prey is man.

[1] trepan/ensnare

SIR SAMUEL EGERTON BRYDGES
(1762–1837)

Brydges studied at Queen's College, Cambridge, and then entered the Middle Temple. In 1787 he was called to the bar, but never practiced, devoting himself instead to literary activities. Despite the assertions of his *Autobiography* (1834), he was not much of a poet and still less of a genius. His first collection of poems appeared in 1782; his major work was the ten-volume *Censura Literaria, Containing Titles, Abstracts, and Opinions of Old English Books . . .* (1805–1809). Brydges devoted much of his spare time to an unsuccessful attempt to claim the barony of Chandos for his family.

To Miss M——, Written by Moonlight, July 18, 1782

Sweet gentle angel, not that I aspire
  To win thy favor, though ambition raise
  My wishes high, I wake anew my lays;
  But that thine image may adorn my lyre
With beauty, more than fancy could inspire!
  As, when behind the silver clouds she strays,
  The moon peeps through, and sheds a mellow blaze,
  Till woods, hills, valleys, with enchantment fire;
So does thy soul, though pent in mortal mold,
  Break through the brightened veil; illume thy form;
With softened lights each varied feature warm;
  And in thine eyes such fairy radiance hold,
That on each object round they beam a magic charm.

On Dreams, October 15, 1782

O gentle Sleep, come, wave thine opiate wing,
  And with thy dewy fingers close mine eyes!
  Then shall freed Fancy from her cell arise,
  And elves, and fairies dance in airy ring
Before her sight, and melting visions bring
  Of virgin love, pure faith, and lonely sighs;
  While on the passing gale soft music dies,
  And hands unseen awake the aerial string.
Ye dreams, to me than waking bliss more dear;
  Love-breathing forms, before my view displayed;
  And fairy songs, that charm my ravished ear;
Let blackening cares my day with darkness shade,
  In smiling patience every wrong I'll bear,
  While ye relume me with your nightly aid!

William Lisle Bowles
(1762–1850)

The son of the vicar of King's Sutton in Northamptonshire, Bowles attended Winchester and Trinity College, Oxford, and followed his father into the church. His sonnets, he tells us, were composed ". . . when, in youth a wanderer among distant scenes, I sought forgetfulness of the first disappointment in early affections." *Fourteen Sonnets* was published in 1789 and met with immediate success, gaining in particular the admiration of Coleridge and Wordsworth. Bowles also published an edition of Pope in 1806.

At Tynemouth Priory, After a Tempestuous Voyage

As slow I climb the cliff's ascending side,
  Much musing on the track of terror past,
  When o'er the dark wave rode the howling blast,
Pleased I look back, and view the tranquil tide
That laves the pebbled shore: and now the beam
  Of evening smiles on the gray battlement,
  And yon forsaken tower that time has rent:—
The lifted oar far off with transient gleam
Is touched, and hushed is all the billowy deep!
  Soothed by the scene, thus on tired Nature's breast
  A stillness slowly steals, and kindred rest;
While sea-sounds lull her, as she sinks to sleep,
Like melodies that mourn upon the lyre,
Waked by the breeze, and, as they mourn, expire!

The Tweed Visited

O Tweed! a stranger, that with wandering feet
  O'er hill and dale has journeyed many a mile,
  (If so his weary thoughts he might beguile),
Delighted turns thy stranger-stream to greet.
The waving branches that romantic bend
  O'er thy tall banks a soothing charm bestow;
  The murmurs of thy wandering wave below

Seem like the converse of some long-lost friend.
Delightful stream! though now along thy shore,
  When spring returns in all her wonted pride,
The distant pastoral pipe is heard no more;
  Yet here while laverocks[1] sing could I abide,
Far from the stormy world's contentious roar,
  To muse upon thy banks at eventide.

[1] laverocks/larks

To a Friend

Go, then, and join the murmuring city's throng!
  Me thou dost leave to solitude and tears;
  To busy phantasies, and boding fears,
Lest ill betide thee; but 't will not be long
Ere the hard season shall be past; till then
  Live happy; sometimes the forsaken shade
  Remembering, and these trees now left to fade;
Nor, mid the busy scenes and hum of men,
Wilt thou my cares forget: in heaviness
  To me the hours shall roll, weary and slow,
  Till mournful autumn past, and all the snow
Of winter pale, the glad hour I shall bless
That shall restore thee from the crowd again,
To the green hamlet on the peaceful plain.

Netley Abbey

Fallen pile! I ask not what has been thy fate;
  But when the winds, slow wafted from the main,
  Through each rent arch, like spirits that complain,
Come hollow to my ear, I meditate
On this world's passing pageant, and the lot
  Of those who once majestic in their prime
  Stood smiling at decay, till bowed by time
Or injury, their early boast forgot,
They may have fallen like thee! Pale and forlorn,
  Their brow, besprent with thin hairs, white as snow,
They lift, still unsubdued, as they would scorn
  This short-lived scene of vanity and woe;

Whilst on their sad looks smilingly they bear
The trace of creeping age, and the pale hue of care!

Milton: On the Busts of Milton, in Youth and Age, at Stourhead

In Youth

Milton, our noblest poet, in the grace
    Of youth, in those fair eyes and clustering hair,
    That brow untouched by one faint line of care,
To mar its openness, we seem to trace
The front of the first lord of human race,
    Mid thine own Paradise portrayed so fair,
    Ere Sin or Sorrow scathed it: such the air
That characters thy youth. Shall time efface
    These lineaments as crowding cares assail!
It is the lot of fallen humanity.
    What boots it! armed in adamantine mail,
The unconquerable mind, and genius high,
Right onward hold their way through weal and woe,
Or whether life's brief lot be high or low!

In Age

And art thou he, now "fallen on evil days,"
    And changed indeed! Yet what do this sunk cheek,
    These thinner locks, and that calm forehead speak!
A spirit reckless of man's blame or praise,—
A spirit, when thine eyes to the noon's blaze
    Their dark orbs roll in vain, in suffering meek,
    As in the sight of God intent to seek,
Mid solitude or age, or through the ways
    Of hard adversity, the approving look
Of its great Master; whilst the conscious pride
    Of wisdom, patient and content to brook
All ills to that sole Master's task applied,
Shall show before high heaven the unaltered mind,
Milton, though thou art poor, and old, and blind!

The Nineteenth Century

PART THREE

The Nineteenth Century

WILLIAM WORDSWORTH
(1770–1850)

Wordsworth was born in Cockermouth, Cumberland, the son of a lawyer; he was educated at Hawkshead Grammar School and St. John's College, Cambridge. After the publication of *Lyrical Ballads* in 1798, he settled at Dover Cottage, Grasmere. He was appointed Distributor of Stamps for Westmorland and Cumberland in 1813 and poet laureate in 1843. Any accounting of the history of the English sonnet must place Wordsworth among the greatest of sonneteers. The fervidly patriotic *Sonnets Dedicated to National Independence and Liberty* are certainly among his finest; but his range was wide, and he was capable of delicacy as well as militancy. After *Poems in Two Volumes* (1807) Wordsworth's poetry underwent a decline. The sequential sonnets of *The River Duddon* (1820) and the *Ecclesiastical Sonnets* (1822) are too didactic and cold for most tastes, but even they confirm the truth of Wordsworth's absolute mastery of the form he celebrates in "Nuns fret not . . ."

"Nuns fret not . . ."

Nuns fret not at their convent's narrow room;
And hermits are contented with their cells;
And students with their pensive citadels;
Maids at the wheel, the weaver at his loom,
Sit blithe and happy; bees that soar for bloom,
High as the highest Peak of Furness-fells,
Will murmur by the hour in foxglove bells:
In truth the prison, unto which we doom
Ourselves, no prison is: and hence for me,
In sundry moods, 'twas pastime to be bound
Within the Sonnet's scanty plot of ground;
Pleased if some Souls (for such there needs must be)
Who have felt the weight of too much liberty,
Should find brief solace there, as I have found.

157

To Sleep (I)

O Gentle Sleep! do they belong to thee,
These twinklings of oblivion? Thou dost love
To sit in meekness, like the brooding Dove,
A captive never wishing to be free.
This tiresome night, O Sleep! thou art to me
A Fly, that up and down himself doth shove
Upon a fretful rivulet, now above,
Now on the water vexed with mockery.
I have no pain that calls for patience, no;
Hence am I cross and peevish as a child:
Am pleased by fits to have thee for my foe,
Yet ever willing to be reconciled:
O gentle Creature! do not use me so,
But once and deeply let me be beguiled.

To Sleep (II)

Fond words have oft been spoken to thee, Sleep!
And thou hast had thy store of tenderest names;
The very sweetest Fancy culls or frames,
When thankfulness of heart is strong and deep!
Dear Bosom-child we call thee, that dost steep
In rich reward all suffering; Balm that tames
All anguish; Saint that evil thoughts and aims
Takest away, and into souls dost creep,
Like to a breeze from heaven. Shall I alone,
I surely not a man ungently made,
Call thee worst Tyrant by which Flesh is crossed?
Perverse, self-willed to own and to disown,
Mere slave of them who never for thee prayed,
Still last to come where thou art wanted most!

1801

I grieved for Buonaparté, with a vain
And an unthinking grief! The tenderest mood
Of that Man's mind—what can it be? what food
Fed his first hopes? what knowledge could *he* gain?
'Tis not in battles that from youth we train
The Governor who must be wise and good,

And temper with the sternness of the brain
Thoughts motherly, and meek as womanhood.
Wisdom doth live with children round her knees:
Books, leisure, perfect freedom, and the talk
Man holds with week-day man in the hourly walk
Of the mind's business: these are the degrees
By which true Sway doth mount; this is the stalk
True Power doth grow on; and her rights are these.

"It is a beauteous evening . . ."

It is a beauteous evening, calm and free,
The holy time is quiet as a Nun
Breathless with adoration; the broad sun
Is sinking down in its tranquillity;
The gentleness of heaven broods o'er the Sea:
Listen! the mighty Being is awake,
And doth with his eternal motion make
A sound like thunder—everlastingly.
Dear Child[1]! dear Girl! that walkest with me here,
If thou appear untouched by solemn thought,
Thy nature is not therefore less divine:
Thou liest in Abraham's bosom all the year;
And worshipp'st at the Temple's inner shrine,
God being with thee when we know it not.

[1] Child/Wordsworth's daughter by Annette Vallon, Caroline

Composed by the Seaside, near Calais, August, 1802

Fair Star of evening, Splendor of the west,
Star of my Country!—on the horizon's brink
Thou hangest, stooping, as might seem, to sink
On England's bosom; yet well pleased to rest,
Meanwhile, and be to her a glorious crest
Conspicuous to the Nations. Thou, I think,
Shouldst be my Country's emblem; and shouldst wink,
Bright Star! with laughter on her banners, drest
In thy fresh beauty. There! that dusky spot
Beneath thee, that is England; there she lies.

Blessings be on you both! one hope, one lot,
One life, one glory!—I, with many a fear
For my dear Country, many heartfelt sighs,
Among men who do not love her, linger here.

London, 1802

Milton! thou shouldst be living at this hour:
England hath need of thee: she is a fen
Of stagnant waters: altar, sword, and pen,
Fireside, the heroic wealth of hall and bower,
Have forfeited their ancient English dower
Of inward happiness. We are selfish men;
Oh! raise us up, return to us again;
And give us manners, virtue, freedom, power.
Thy soul was like a Star, and dwelt apart;
Thou hadst a voice whose sound was like the sea:
Pure as the naked heavens, majestic, free,
So didst thou travel on life's common way,
In cheerful godliness; and yet thy heart
The lowliest duties on herself did lay.

Composed upon Westminster Bridge, September 3, 1802

Earth has not anything to show more fair:
Dull would he be of soul who could pass by
A sight so touching in its majesty:
This City now doth, like a garment, wear
The beauty of the morning; silent, bare,
Ships, towers, domes, theaters, and temples lie
Open unto the fields, and to the sky;
All bright and glittering in the smokeless air.
Never did sun more beautifully steep
In his first splendor, valley, rock, or hill;
Ne'er saw I, never felt, a calm so deep!
The river glideth at his own sweet will:
Dear God! the very houses seem asleep;
And all that mighty heart is lying still!

"Great men have been among us . . ."

Great men have been among us; hands that penned
And tongues that uttered wisdom—better none:
The later Sidney, Marvel, Harrington,
Young Vane, and others who called Milton friend.
These moralists could act and comprehend:
They knew how genuine glory was put on;
Taught us how rightfully a nation shone
In splendor: what strength was, that would not bend
But in magnanimous meekness. France, 'tis strange,
Hath brought forth no such souls as we had then.
Perpetual emptiness! unceasing change!
No single volume paramount, no code,
No master spirit, no determined road;
But equally a want of books and men!

"England! the time is come . . ."

England! the time is come when thou shouldst wean
Thy heart from its emasculating food;
The truth should now be better understood;
Old things have been unsettled; we have seen
Fair seedtime, better harvest might have been
But for thy trespasses; and at this day,
If for Greece, Egypt, India, Africa,
Aught good were destined, thou wouldst step between.
England! all nations in this charge agree:
But worse, more ignorant in love and hate,
Far—far more abject, is thine Enemy:
Therefore the wise pray for thee, though the freight
Of thy offences be a heavy weight:
Oh grief that Earth's best hopes rest all with thee!

"The world is too much with us . . ."

The world is too much with us; late and soon,
Getting and spending, we lay waste our powers:
Little we see in Nature that is ours;
We have given our hearts away, a sordid boon!
This Sea that bares her bosom to the moon;

The winds that will be howling at all hours,
And are up-gathered now like sleeping flowers;
For this, for everything, we are out of tune;
It moves us not.—Great God! I'd rather be
A Pagan suckled in a creed outworn;
So might I, standing on this pleasant lea,
Have glimpses that would make me less forlorn;
Have sight of Proteus rising from the sea;
Or hear old Triton blow his wreathed horn.

" 'With how sad steps, O Moon . . .' "

"With how sad steps, O Moon, thou climb'st the sky,
How silently, and with how wan a face!"
Where art thou? Thou so often seen on high
Running among the clouds a Wood-nymph's race!
Unhappy Nuns, whose common breath's a sigh
Which they would stifle, move at such a pace!
The northern Wind, to call thee to the chase,
Must blow tonight his bugle horn. Had I
The power of Merlin, Goddess! this should be:
And all the stars, fast as the clouds were riven,
Should sally forth, to keep thee company,
Hurrying and sparkling through the clear blue heaven;
But, Cynthia! should to thee the palm be given,
Queen both for beauty and for majesty.

"Surprised by joy . . ."

Surprised by joy—impatient as the Wind
I turned to share the transport—Oh! with whom
But thee, deep buried in the silent tomb,
That spot which no vicissitude can find?
Love, faithful love, recalled thee to my mind—
But how could I forget thee? Through what power,
Even for the least division of an hour,
Have I been so beguiled as to be blind
To my most grievous loss!—That thought's return
Was the worst pang that sorrow ever bore,
Save one, one only, when I stood forlorn,
Knowing my heart's best treasure was no more;

That neither present time, nor years unborn
Could to my sight that heavenly face restore.

"I watch, and long have watched . . ."

I watch, and long have watched, with calm regret
Yon slowly-sinking star—immortal Sire
(So might he seem) of all the glittering quire!
Blue ether still surrounds him—yet—and yet;
But now the horizon's rocky parapet
Is reached, where, forfeiting his bright attire,
He burns—transmuted to a dusky fire—
Then pays submissively the appointed debt
To the flying moments, and is seen no more.
Angels and gods! We struggle with our fate,
While health, power, glory, from their height decline,
Depressed; and then extinguished: and our state,
In this, how different, lost Star, from thine,
That no tomorrow shall our beams restore!

"Scorn not the Sonnet . . ."

Scorn not the Sonnet; Critic, you have frowned,
Mindless of its just honors; with this key
Shakspeare unlocked his heart; the melody
Of this small lute gave ease to Petrarch's wound;
A thousand times this pipe did Tasso sound;
With it Camöens soothed an exile's grief;
The Sonnet glittered a gay myrtle leaf
Amid the cypress with which Dante crowned
His visionary brow: a glowworm lamp,
It cheered mild Spenser, called from Faerie-land
To struggle through dark ways; and when a damp
Fell round the path of Milton, in his hand
The Thing became a trumpet; whence he blew
Soul-animating strains—alas, too few!

" 'Change me, some God, into that breathing rose!' "

"Change me, some God, into that breathing rose!"
The love-sick Stripling fancifully sighs,
The envied flower beholding, as it lies
On Laura's breast, in exquisite repose;
Or he would pass into her bird, that throws
The darts of song from out its wiry cage;
Enraptured,—could he for himself engage
The thousandth part of what the Nymph bestows;
And what the little careless innocent
Ungraciously receives. Too daring choice!
There are whose calmer mind it would content
To be an unculled floweret of the glen,
Fearless of plow and scythe; or darling wren
That tunes on Duddon's banks her slender voice.

Trepidation of the Druids

Screams round the Arch-druid's brow the sea-mew—white
As Menai's foam; and toward the mystic ring
Where Augurs stand, the Future questioning,
Slowly the cormorant aims her heavy flight,
Portending ruin to each baleful rite
That, in the lapse of ages, hath crept o'er
Diluvian truths, and patriarchal lore.
Haughty the Bard: can these meek doctrines blight
His transports? wither his heroic strains?
But all shall be fulfilled;—the Julian spear
A way first opened; and, with Roman chains,
The tidings come of Jesus crucified;
They come—they spread—the weak, the suffering hear;
Receive the faith, and in the hope abide.

SAMUEL TAYLOR COLERIDGE
(1772–1834)

The son of the vicar of Ottery St. Mary, Devon, Coleridge attended Christ's Hospital and Jesus College, Cambridge. His friendship with Wordsworth began in 1795; "The Rime of the Ancient Mariner" was first published in their *Lyrical Ballads* in 1798. Many of Coleridge's poems were published in the *Morning Post* between 1798 and 1802. His *Biographia Literaria* appeared in 1817.

To the River Otter

Dear native Brook! wild Streamlet of the West!
  How many various-fated years have past,
  What happy and what mournful hours, since last
  I skimmed the smooth thin stone along thy breast,
  Numbering its light leaps! yet so deep imprest
Sink the sweet scenes of childhood, that mine eyes
  I never shut amid the sunny ray,
But straight with all their tints thy waters rise,
  Thy crossing plank, thy marge with willows gray,
And bedded sand that veined with various dyes
Gleamed through thy bright transparence! On my way,
  Visions of Childhood! oft have ye beguiled
Lone manhood's cares, yet waking fondest sighs:
  Ah! that once more I were a careless Child!

On a Discovery Made Too Late

Thou bleedest, my poor Heart! and thy distress
Reasoning I ponder with a scornful smile
And probe thy sore wound sternly, though the while
Swollen be mine eye and dim with heaviness.
Why didst thou listen to Hope's whisper bland?
Or, listening, why forget the healing tale,
When Jealousy with feverish fancies pale
Jarred thy fine fibers with a maniac's hand?

Faint was that Hope, and rayless!—Yet 'twas fair
And soothed with many a dream the hour of rest:
Thou should'st have loved it most, when most opprest,
And nursed it with an agony of care,
Even as a mother her sweet infant heir
That wan and sickly droops upon her breast!

To the Rev. W. L. Bowles

My heart has thanked thee, Bowles! for those soft strains,
   That, on the still air floating, tremblingly
   Waked in me Fancy, Love, and Sympathy!
For hence, not callous to a Brother's pains
Through Youth's gay prime and thornless paths I went;
   And, when the *darker* day of life began,
   And I did roam, a thought-bewildered man!
Thy kindred Lays an healing solace lent,
Each lonely pang with dreamy joys combined,
   And stole from vain Regret her scorpion stings;
   While shadowy Pleasure, with mysterious wings,
Brooded the wavy and tumultuous mind,
   Like that great Spirit, who with plastic sweep
   Moved on the darkness of the formless Deep!

Composed on a Journey Homeward; the Author Having Received Intelligence of the Birth of a Son[1], Sept. 20, 1796

Oft o'er my brain does that strange fancy roll
   Which makes the present (while the flash doth last)
   Seem a mere semblance of some unknown past,
Mixed with such feelings, as perplex the soul
Self-questioned in her sleep; and some have said
   We lived, ere yet this robe of flesh we wore.
   O my sweet baby! when I reach my door,
If heavy looks should tell me thou art dead,
(As sometimes, through excess of hope, I fear)
I think that I should struggle to believe
   Thou wert a spirit, to this nether sphere
Sentenced for some more venial crime to grieve;

Did'st scream, then spring to meet Heaven's quick reprieve,
   While we wept idly o'er thy little bier!

[1] son/Hartley Coleridge

Sonnets Attempted in the Manner of Contemporary Writers[1]

1. "Pensive at eve . . ."

Pensive at eve on the hard world I mused,
And my poor heart was sad: so at the moon
I gazed—and sighed, and sighed!—for, ah! how soon
Eve darkens into night. Mine eye perused
With tearful vacancy the *dampy* grass
Which wept and glittered in the paly ray;
And I did pause me on my lonely way,
And mused me on those wretched ones who pass
O'er the black heath of Sorrow. But, alas!
Most of Myself I thought: when it befell
That the sooth Spirit of the breezy wood
Breathed in mine ear—"All this is very well;
But much of *one* thing is for *no* thing good."
Ah! my poor heart's inexplicable swell!

[1] Writers/These poems, which parodied contemporary abuses of the sonnet, were signed "Nehemiah Higginbottom."

2. To Simplicity

O! I do love thee, meek *Simplicity*!
For of thy lays the lulling simpleness
Goes to my heart and soothes each small distress,
Distress though small, yet haply great to me!
'Tis true on Lady Fortune's gentlest pad
I amble on; yet, though I know not why,
So sad I am!—but should a friend and I
Grow cool and *miff*. O! I am *very* sad!

And then with sonnets and with sympathy
My dreamy bosom's mystic woes I pall;
Now of my false friend plaining plaintively,
Now raving at mankind in general;
But, whether sad or fierce, 'tis simple all,
All very simple, meek Simplicity!

3. On a Ruined House in a Romantic Country

And this reft house is that the which he built,
Lamented Jack! And here his malt he piled,
Cautious in vain! These rats that squeak so wild,
Squeak, not unconscious of their father's guilt.
Did ye not see her gleaming through the glade?
Belike, 'twas she, the maiden all forlorn.
What though she milk no cow with crumpled horn,
Yet *aye* she haunts the dale where *erst* she strayed;
And *aye* beside her stalks her amorous knight!
Still on his thighs their wonted brogues are worn,
And through those brogues, still tattered and betorn,
His hindward charms gleam an unearthly white;
As when through broken clouds at night's high noon
Peeps in fair fragments forth the full-orbed harvest moon!

Work Without Hope: Lines Composed 21st February 1827

All Nature seems at work. Slugs leave their lair—
The bees are stirring—birds are on the wing—
And Winter slumbering in the open air,
Wears on his smiling face a dream of Spring!
And I the while, the sole unbusy thing,
Nor honey make, nor pair, nor build, nor sing.

Yet well I ken the banks where amaranths blow,
Have traced the fount whence streams of nectar flow.
Bloom, O ye amaranths! bloom for whom ye may,
For me ye bloom not! Glide, rich streams, away!
With lips unbrightened, wreathless brow, I stroll:
And would you learn the spells that drowse my soul?
Work without Hope draws nectar in a sieve,
And Hope without an object cannot live.

ROBERT SOUTHEY
(1774–1843)

If industry were a true gauge of poetic merit, Southey would stand in the first rank of English poets. Unfortunately, his vast poetic output is largely unread today. Southey was educated at Westminster School and at Oxford, where he met Coleridge. The French Revolution inspired one of a number of epics, *Joan of Arc* (1796); but his revolutionary fervor was not sustained, and in 1813 he succeeded H. J. Pye as poet laureate.

TWO POEMS CONCERNING THE SLAVE TRADE

"Hold your mad hands . . ."

Hold your mad hands! for ever on your plain
Must the gorged vulture clog his beak with blood?
For ever must your Niger's tainted flood,
Roll to the ravenous shark his banquet slain?
Hold your mad hands! and learn at length to know,
And turn your vengeance on the common foe,
Yon treacherous vessel and her godless crew!
Let never traders with false pretext fair
Set on your shores again their wicked feet:
With interdict and indignation meet
Repel them, and with fire and sword pursue!
Avarice, the white cadaverous fiend, is there,
Who spreads his toils accursed wide and far,
And for his purveyor calls the demon War.

"High in the air exposed . . ."

High in the air exposed the slave is hung,
To all the birds of heaven, their living food!
He groans not, though awaked by that fierce sun
New torturers live to drink their parent blood;
He groans not, though the gorging vulture tear
The quivering fiber. Hither look, O ye
Who tore this man from peace and liberty!

Look hither, ye who weigh with politic care
The gain against the guilt! Beyond the grave
There is another world: bear ye in mind,
Ere your decree proclaims to all mankind
The gain is worth the guilt, that there the Slave,
Before the Eternal, "thunder-tongued shall plead
Against the deep damnation of your deed."

"Go, Valentine . . ."

Go, Valentine, and tell that lovely maid
Whom fancy still will portray to my sight,
How here I linger in this sullen shade,
This dreary gloom of dull monastic night;
Say, that from every joy of life remote
At evening's closing hour I quit the throng,
Listening in solitude the ring-dove's note,
Who pours like me her solitary song;
Say, that her absence calls the sorrowing sigh;
Say, that of all her charms I love to speak,
In fancy feel the magic of her eye,
In fancy view the smile illume her cheek,
Court the lone hour when silence stills the grove,
And heave the sigh of memory and of love.

To a Goose

If thou didst feed on western plains of yore;
Or waddle wide with flat and flabby feet
Over some Cambrian mountain's plashy moor;
Or find in farmer's yard a safe retreat
From gypsy thieves, and foxes sly and fleet;
If thy gray quills, by lawyer guided, trace
Deeds big with ruin to some wretched race,
Or love-sick poet's sonnet, sad and sweet,
Wailing the rigor of his lady fair;
Or if, the drudge of housemaid's daily toil,
Cobwebs and dust thy pinions white besoil,
Departed Goose! I neither know nor care.
But this I know, that we pronounced thee fine,
Seasoned with sage and onions, and port wine.

CHARLES LAMB
(1775–1834)

Lamb was educated at Christ's Hospital, where his friendship with Coleridge began. From 1792 until his retirement in 1825, Lamb was employed by the East India Company. He is best remembered for his letters and the *Essays of Elia*, which first appeared in the *London Magazine*, 1820–1825.

"As when a child . . ."

As when a child on some long winter's night
Affrighted clinging to its Grandam's knees
With eager wond'ring and perturbed delight
Listens strange tales of fearful dark decrees
Muttered to wretch by necromantic spell;
Or of those hags, who at the witching time
Of murky midnight ride the air sublime,
And mingle foul embrace with fiends of Hell:
Cold Horror drinks its blood! Anon the tear
More gentle starts, to hear the Beldame tell
Of pretty babes, that loved each other dear,
Murdered by cruel Uncle's mandate fell:
Ev'n such the shiv'ring joys thy tones impart,
Ev'n so thou, Siddons![1] meltest my sad heart!

[1] Siddons/Mrs. Sarah Siddons (1755–1831), a famous tragic actress

"Methinks how dainty sweet it were . . ."

Methinks how dainty sweet it were, reclined
Beneath the vast out-stretching branches high
Of some old wood, in careless sort to lie,
Nor of the busier scenes we left behind
Aught envying. And, O Anna! mild-eyed maid!
Beloved! I were well content to play
With thy free tresses all a summer's day,
Losing the time beneath the greenwood shade.

Or we might sit and tell some tender tale
Of faithful vows repaid by cruel scorn,
A tale of true love, or of friend forgot;
And I would teach thee, lady, how to rail
In gentle sort, on those who practice not
Or love or pity, though of woman born.

"We were two pretty babes . . ."

We were two pretty babes, the youngest she,
The youngest, and the loveliest far, I ween,
And Innocence her name. The time has been,
We two did love each other's company;
Time was, we two had wept to have been apart.
But when, by show of seeming good beguiled,
I left the garb and manners of a child,
And my first love for man's society,
Defiling with the world my virgin heart—
My loved companion dropped a tear, and fled,
And hid in deepest shades her awful head.
Beloved, who shall tell me where thou art—
In what delicious Eden to be found—
That I may seek thee, the wide world around?

The Family Name

What reason first imposed thee, gentle name,
Name that my father bore, and his sire's sire,
Without reproach? we trace our stream no higher;
And I, a childless man, may end the same.
Perchance some shepherd on Lincolnian plains,
In manners guileless as his own sweet flocks,
Received thee first amid the merry mocks
And arch allusions of his fellow swains.
Perchance from Salem's holier fields returned,
With glory gotten on the heads abhorred
Of faithless Saracens, some martial lord
Took His meek title, in whose zeal he burned.
Whate'er the fount whence thy beginnings came,
No deed of mine shall shame thee, gentle name.

To John Lamb, Esq.: Of the South-Sea House

John, you were figuring in the gay career
Of blooming manhood with a young man's joy,
When I was yet a little peevish boy—
Though time has made the difference disappear
Betwixt our ages, which *then* seemed so great—
And still by rightful custom you retain
Much of the old authoritative strain,
And keep the elder brother up in state.
O! you do well in this. 'Tis man's worst deed
To let the "things that have been" run to waste,
And in the unmeaning present sink the past:
In whose dim glass even now I faintly read
Old buried forms, and faces long ago,
Which you, and I, and one more, only know.

JOSEPH BLANCO WHITE
(1775–1841)

White was born in Seville, where he was ordained a priest in
1800; later he left the priesthood, came to England, and studied
at Oxford. He wrote little poetry, but his sonnet "To Night" was
praised by Coleridge as the finest sonnet in the language and
enjoyed many years of popularity.

To Night

Mysterious Night! when our first parent knew
Thee from report divine, and heard thy name,
Did he not tremble for this lovely frame,
This glorious canopy of light and blue?
Yet 'neath a curtain of translucent dew,
Bathed in the rays of the great setting flame,
Hesperus with the host of heaven came,
And lo! Creation widened in man's view.

Who could have thought such darkness lay concealed
Within thy beams, O sun! or who could find,
Whilst fly and leaf and insect stood revealed,
That to such countless orbs thou mad'st us blind!
Why do we then shun death with anxious strife?
If Light can thus deceive, wherefore not Life?

EBENEZER ELLIOTT
(1781–1849)

Elliott, the self-educated "Corn Law Rhymer," was a Sheffield
iron foundry master for many years. His verse is propagandistic
and owes its power to the strength of his moral indignation over
social conditions. His particular concern about the regulations
that limited the importation of grain and kept domestic prices
high was expressed in his *Corn Law Rhymes* (1831). *The Year of
Seeds* (1848) Elliot described as a "cycle of revolutionary son-
nets."

_____

"In these days . . ."

In these days, every mother's son or daughter
Writes verse, which no one reads except the writer,
Although, uninked, the paper would be whiter,
And worth, per ream, a hare, when you have caught her.
Hundreds of unstaunched Shelleys daily water
Unanswering dust; a thousand Wordsworths scribble;
And twice a thousand Corn Law Rhymers dribble
Rhymed prose, unread. Hymners of fraud and slaughter,
By cant called other names, alone find buyers—
Who buy, but read not. "What a loss in paper,"
Groans each immortal of the host of sighers!
"What profanation of the midnight taper
In expirations vile! But I write well,
And wisely print. Why don't my poems sell?"

"John . . ."

John. In the sound of that rebellious word
There is brave music. Jack, and Jacobin,
Are vulgar terms; law-linked to shame and sin,
They have a twang of Jack the Hangman's cord:
Yet John hath merit which can well afford
To be called Jack's. By life's strange offs and ons!
Glory hath had great dealings with the Johns,
Since history first awaked where fable snored.
John Cade, John Huss, John Hampden, and John Knox!
Ay, these were names of fellows who had will.
John Wilson's name, far sounded, sounds not ill;
But how unlike John Milton's or John Locke's!
John Bright, like Locke and Milton, scorns paid sloth;
And Johnson might have liked to gibbet both.

Poet vs. Parson

A hireling's wages to the priest are paid;
While lives and dies, in want and rags, the bard!
But preaching ought to be its own reward,
And not a sordid, if an honest trade.
Paul, laboring proudly with his hands, arrayed
Regenerated hearts in peace and love;
And when, with power, they preached the mystic dove,
Penn, Barclay, Clarkson, asked not Mammon's aid.
As, for its own sake, poetry is sweet
To poets—so, on tasks of mercy bound,
Religion travels with unsandaled feet,
Making the flinty desert holy ground;
And never will her triumph be complete
While one paid pilgrim upon earth is found.

"Toy of the Titans! . . ."

Toy of the Titans! Tiny Harp! again
I quarrel with the order of thy strings,
Established by the law of sonnet-kings,
And used by giants who do nought in vain.
Was Petrarch, then mistaken in the strain
That charms Italia? Were they tasteless things
That Milton wrought? And are they mutterings
Untuneful, that pay Wordsworth with pleased pain?
No. But I see that tyrants come of slaves;
That states are won by rush of robbers' steel;
And millions starved and tortured to their graves,
Because as they are taught men think and feel;
Therefore, I change the sonnet's slavish notes
For cheaper music, suited to my thoughts.

"Give not our blankets, tax-fed Squire . . ."

Give not our blankets, tax-fed Squire, to him,
Thy willing pauper, with the dangerous brow!
He is not worthier, generous Squire, than thou,
But stronger far, and sound in wind and limb.
Know'st thou yon widow? She is wise and chaste;
And comely, though her famished eyes wax dim.
Her husband built a house upon the waste,
And lost it: they who found it should make haste
With help for her who, else, will die today.
She hath no blankets! and no parish-pay:
But she hath frosted feet, a fireless grate,
A well-swept floor—by neighbor's feet untrod!
Tears, which are ice; a starved dog, a clean plate,
Her wedding ring, her bible—and her God!

"Ralph Leech believes . . ."

Ralph Leech believes (and he can read and write),
That Conference Sunday schools have saved the nation.
He would compel the dark to seek his light,
Yet hates, for freedom's sake, state education.

That corn laws are "Man's wisdom, and God's mercy";
That Prairie is the Book of Common Prayer;
And that one Shakspeare is a fat old Player;
He doubts no more than that Canton's in Jersey.
Though cold the night, how fast his chapel fills!
Why? Sir De Suckem hath a message sent,
Urging the Suckems of the People's Cause
To prop Saint Suckem's Navigation Laws;
Therefore, our friends petition Parliament
Against cheap sugar, slavery, and steam mills!

JAMES HENRY LEIGH HUNT
(1784–1859)

Like Coleridge and Lamb, Leigh Hunt was educated at Christ's
Hospital. In 1808 he founded *The Examiner*, in which he intro-
duced both Keats and Shelley to the public. In 1813 Hunt was
imprisoned for comments about the Prince Regent made in *The
Examiner;* he was later associated with Byron and *The Liberal*.
Hunt's poetry is overshadowed by his associations with the
major poets of his time.

To the Grasshopper and the Cricket[1]

Green little vaulter in the sunny grass,
   Catching your heart up at the feel of June,
   Sole voice that's heard amidst the lazy noon,
When even the bees lag at the summoning brass;—
And you, warm little housekeeper, who class
   With those who think the candles come too soon,
   Loving the fire, and with your tricksome tune
Nick the glad silent moments as they pass;—

Oh sweet and tiny cousins, that belong,
   One to the fields, the other to the hearth,
Both have your sunshine; both, though small, are strong
   At your clear hearts; and both were sent on earth

To sing in thoughtful ears this natural song—
　　In doors and out,—summer and winter—Mirth.

[1] written in competition with Keats, see p. 192.

To Percy Shelley: On the Degrading Notions of Deity

What wonder, Percy, that with jealous rage
　　Men should defame the kindly and the wise,
　　When in the midst of the all-beauteous skies,
And all this lovely world, that should engage
Their mutual search for the old golden age,
　　They seat a phantom, swell into grim size
　　Out of their own passions and bigotries,
And then, for fear, proclaim it meek and sage!

And this they call a light and a revealing!
　　Wise as the clown, who plodding home at night
　　In autumn, turns at call of fancied elf,
And sees upon the fog, with ghastly feeling,
　　A giant shadow in its imminent might,
　　Which his own lantern throws up from himself.

To John Keats

'Tis well you think me truly one of those,
　　Whose sense discerns the loveliness of things;
　　For surely as I feel the bird that sings
Behind the leaves, or dawn as it up grows,
Or the rich bee rejoicing as he goes,
　　Or the glad issue of emerging springs,
　　Or overhead the glide of a dove's wings,
Or turf, or trees, or, midst of all, repose:

And surely as I feel things lovelier still,
　　The human look, and the harmonious form
Containing woman, and the smile in ill,
　　And such a heart as Charles'[1] wise and warm,—

As surely as all this, I see, ev'n now,
Young Keats, a flowering laurel on your brow.

[1]Charles/Charles Cowden Clarke (1787–1877), a friend of both
Keats and Hunt

On Receiving a Crown of Ivy from the Same[1]

A crown of ivy! I submit my head
   To the young hand that gives it,—young, 'tis true,
   But with a right, for 'tis a poet's too.
How pleasant the leaves feel! and how they spread
With their broad angles, like a nodding shed
   Over both eyes! and how complete and new,
   As on my hand I lean, to feel them strew
My sense with freshness,—Fancy's rustling bed!

Tress-tossing girls, with smell of flowers and grapes
   Come dancing by and downward piping cheeks,
   And up-thrown cymbals, and Silenus old
Lumpishly borne, and many trampling shapes,—
   And lastly, with his bright eyes on her bent,
   Bacchus,—whose bride has of his hand fast hold.

[1]same/Keats

George Noel Gordon, Lord Byron
(1788–1824)

Byron's first book of verse was printed while he was still at Trinity College, Cambridge. He replied to the *Edinburgh Review*'s criticism of it with *English Bards and Scotch Reviewers* (1809). In 1812 the first two cantos of *Childe Harold* were published. In 1816 Byron exiled himself from England; his epic satire *Don Juan* began to appear in 1819. The epitome of one aspect of the romantic movement, Byron died in Greece, where he had gone to fight for Greek independence.

Sonnet on Chillon[1]

Eternal Spirit of the chainless Mind!
  Brightest in dungeons, Liberty! thou art,
  For there thy habitation is the heart—
The heart which love of thee alone can bind;
And when thy sons to fetters are consigned—
  To fetters, and the damp vault's dayless gloom,
  Their country conquers with their martyrdom,
And Freedom's fame finds wings on every wind.
Chillon! thy prison is a holy place,
  And thy sad floor an altar—for 'twas trod,
Until his very steps have left a trace
  Worn, as if thy cold pavement were a sod,
By Bonnivard!—May none those marks efface!
  For they appeal from tyranny to God.

[1] Chillon/the Castle of Chillon, on Lake Geneva, where the Swiss patriot François de Bonnivard was imprisoned, 1530–1536

Sonnet to Lake Leman

Rousseau—Voltaire—our Gibbon—and De Staël—
  Leman! these names are worthy of thy shore,
  Thy shore of names like these! wert thou no more,
Their memory thy remembrance would recall:
  But they have made them lovelier, for the lore
  Of mighty minds doth hallow in the core

Of human hearts the ruin of a wall
   Where dwelt the wise and wondrous; but by *thee*
How much more, Lake of Beauty! do we feel,
   In sweetly gliding o'er thy crystal sea,
The wild glow of that not ungentle zeal,
   Which of the Heirs of Immortality
Is proud, and makes the breath of Glory real!

PERCY BYSSHE SHELLEY
(1792–1822)

Sent down from Oxford in 1811 for his pamphlet *The Necessity of Atheism,* Shelley married in the same year; but in 1815 he went to Italy with Mary Godwin, whom he married in 1816 after his wife drowned herself. Shelley formed friendships with Leigh Hunt, Thomas Love Peacock, and Lord Byron. *Prometheus Bound* was published in 1820; the following year saw the composition of the *Defense of Poetry* and the publication of *Adonais,* the elegy on the death of Keats. Shelley was not quite thirty when he drowned while sailing.

To Wordsworth

Poet of Nature, thou hast wept to know
That things depart which never may return:
Childhood and youth, friendship and love's first glow,
Have fled like sweet dreams, leaving thee to mourn.
These common woes I feel. One loss is mine
Which thou too feel'st, yet I alone deplore.
Thou wert as a lone star, whose light did shine
On some frail bark in winter's midnight roar:
Thou hast like to a rock-built refuge stood
Above the blind and battling multitude:
In honored poverty thy voice did weave
Songs consecrate to truth and liberty,—
Deserting these, thou leavest me to grieve,
Thus having been, that thou shouldst cease to be.

Feelings of a Republican on the Fall of Bonaparte

I hated thee, fallen tyrant! I did groan
To think that a most unambitious slave,
Like thou, shouldst dance and revel on the grave
Of Liberty. Thou mightst have built thy throne
Where it had stood even now: thou didst prefer
A frail and bloody pomp which Time has swept
In fragments towards Oblivion. Massacre,
For this I prayed, would on thy sleep have crept,
Treason and Slavery, Rapine, Fear, and Lust,
And stifled thee, their minister. I know
Too late, since thou and France are in the dust,
That Virtue owns a more eternal foe
Than Force or Fraud: old Custom, legal Crime,
And bloody Faith the foulest birth of Time.

Ozymandias

I met a traveler from an antique land
Who said: Two vast and trunkless legs of stone
Stand in the desert. Near them, on the sand,
Half sunk, a shattered visage lies, whose frown,
And wrinkled lip, and sneer of cold command,
Tell that its sculptor well those passions read
Which yet survive, stamped on these lifeless things,
The hand that mocked them and the heart that fed;
And on the pedestal these words appear:
"My name is Ozymandias, king of kings;
Look on my works, ye Mighty, and despair!"
Nothing beside remains. Round the decay
Of that colossal wreck, boundless and bare
The lone and level sands stretch far away.

"Lift not the painted veil . . ."

Lift not the painted veil which those who live
Call Life: though unreal shapes be pictured there,
And it but mimic all we would believe
With colors idly spread,—behind, lurk Fear

And Hope, twin Destinies; who ever weave
Their shadows, o'er the chasm, sightless and drear.
I knew one who had lifted it—he sought,
For his lost heart was tender, things to love,
But found them not, alas! nor was there aught
The world contains, the which he could approve.
Through the unheeding many he did move,
A splendor among shadows, a bright blot
Upon this gloomy scene, a Spirit that strove
For truth, and like the Preacher found it not.

England in 1819

An old, mad, blind, despised, and dying king,—
Princes, the dregs of their dull race, who flow
Through public scorn,—mud from a muddy spring,—
Rulers who neither see, nor feel, nor know,
But leechlike to their fainting country cling,
Till they drop, blind in blood, without a blow,—
A people starved and stabbed in the untilled field,—
An army, which liberticide and prey
Makes as a two-edged sword to all who wield,—
Golden and sanguine laws which tempt and slay;
Religion Christless, Godless—a book sealed;
A Senate,—Time's worst statute unrepealed,—
Are graves, from which a glorious Phantom may
Burst, to illumine our tempestuous day.

JOHN CLARE
(1793–1864)

The "Thresher Poet" was born in the village of Helpstone, Northamptonshire, the son of a laborer. He was self-educated and showed an early interest in poetry. Despite the immediate success of *Poems, Descriptive of Rural Life and Scenery* (1820), Clare was always poor. His mind gave way in 1837, and he spent the remainder of his life in the private asylum of Dr. Allen and in the Northampton County Lunatic Asylum. *The Shepherd's Calendar* (1827) is probably his finest work.

To Wordsworth

Wordsworth I love, his books are like the fields,
  Not filled with flowers, but works of human kind;
The pleasant weed a fragrant pleasure yields,
  The briar and broomwood shaken by the wind,
The thorn and bramble o'er the water shoot
  A finer flower than gardens e'er gave birth,
The aged huntsman grubbing up the root—
  I love them all as tenants of the earth:
Where genius is, there often die the seeds;
  What critics throw away I love the more;
I love to stoop and look among the weeds,
  To find a flower I never knew before;
Wordsworth, go on—a greater poet be;
Merit will live, though parties disagree!

Hen's Nest

Among the orchard weeds, from every search,
Snugly and sure, the old hen's nest is made,
Who cackles every morning from her perch
To tell the servant girl new eggs are laid;
Who lays her washing by; and far and near
Goes seeking all about from day to day,
And stung with nettles tramples everywhere;
But still the cackling pullet lays away.

The boy on Sundays goes the stack to pull
In hopes to find her there, but naught is seen,
And takes his hat and thinks to find it full,
She's laid so long so many might have been.
But naught is found and all is given o'er
Till the young brood come chirping to the door.

To John Clare

Well, honest John, how fare you now at home?
The spring is come, and birds are building nests;
The old cock-robin to the sty is come,
With olive feathers and its ruddy breast;
And the old cock, with wattles and red comb,
Struts with the hens, and seems to like some best,
Then crows, and looks about for little crumbs,
Swept out by little folks an hour ago;
The pigs sleep in the sty; the bookman[1] comes—
The little boy lets home-close[2] nesting go,
And pockets tops and taws, where daisies blow,
To look at the new number just laid down,
With lots of pictures, and good stories too,
And Jack the Giant Killer's high renown.

[1] bookman/a peddlar of books and magazines
[2] home-close/the yard of the house

John Hamilton Reynolds
(1794–1852)

This friend of Keats's was the son of the head writing master of Christ's Hospital and was educated at St. Paul's School. His first volumes of poetry were published in 1814; in the *Examiner* in 1816, Leigh Hunt listed Reynolds, along with Shelley and Keats, as one of the most promising poets of the period. His later years, however, were devoted more to the practice of law than to poetry.

To Spenser

Yet that have hearts vexed with unquiet thought
Of worldly grievance, and of lost delight;
Oh! turn to Spenser's Faerie Tale,—so fraught
With all that's mild, and beautiful, and bright,—
There revel in the fancies he hath wrought,—
Fancies more fair than May,—or morning light,—
Or solitary star awake at night,—
Or breath from Lovers' lips in kisses caught.
Sweet Spenser! how I love thy faerie pages,—
Where gentle Una lives so radiantly;
Fair is thy record of romantic ages,
And calm and pure the pleasure which it yields:
While life and thought are with me,—thou shalt be
My dear companion in the silent fields.

To Keats: On Reading His Sonnet Written in Chaucer

Thy thoughts, dear Keats, are like fresh-gathered leaves,
  Or white flowers plucked from some sweet lily bed;
  They set the heart a-breathing, and they shed
The glow of meadows, mornings, and spring eves,
Over the excited soul. Thy genius weaves
  Songs that shall make the age be nature-led,
  And win that coronal for thy young head
Which Time's strange hand of freshness ne'er bereaves.

Go on! and keep thee to thine own green way,
    Singing in that same key which Chaucer sung:—
Be thou companion of the Summer day,
    Roaming the fields, and olden woods among:—
So shall thy Muse be ever in her May;
    And thy luxuriant Spirit ever young.

WILLIAM CULLEN BRYANT
(1794–1878)

Bryant was born in Cummington, Massachusetts; he attended Williams College for one year and then read for the bar. He practiced law in Great Barrington, Massachusetts, from 1816 to 1825, when he joined the New York *Evening Post,* becoming its editor-in-chief in 1829. His poetic reputation began with the publication of "Thanatopsis" in 1817. James Russell Lowell found Bryant's verse "too smooth and too polished," but admitted his "true soul for field, river, and wood. . . ."

November

Yet one smile more, departing, distant sun!
    One mellow smile through the soft vapory air,
Ere, o'er the frozen earth, the loud winds run,
    Or snows are sifted o'er the meadows bare.
One smile on the brown hills and naked trees,
    And the dark rocks whose summer wreaths are cast,
And the blue gentian flower, that, in the breeze,
    Nods lonely, of her beauteous race the last.
Yet a few sunny days, in which the bee
    Shall murmur by the hedge that skirts the way,
The cricket chirp upon the russet lea,
    And man delight to linger in thy ray.
Yet one rich smile, and we will try to bear
The piercing winter frost, and winds, and darkened air.

To ———

Ay, thou art for the grave; thy glances shine
   Too brightly to shine long; another Spring
Shall deck her for men's eyes,—but not for thine—.
   Sealed in a sleep which knows no wakening.
The fields for thee have no medicinal leaf,
   And the vexed ore no mineral of power;
And they who love thee wait in anxious grief
   Till the slow plague shall bring the fatal hour.
Glide softly to thy rest then; Death should come
   Gently, to one of gentle mold like thee,
As light winds wandering through groves of bloom
   Detach the delicate blossom from the tree.
Close thy sweet eyes, calmly, and without pain;
And we will trust in God to see thee yet again.

FELICIA DOROTHEA HEMANS
(1794–1835)

Born in Liverpool, Felicia Hemans was immensely popular in
her own day. Her lyrics are notable for their sweetness and
fluency, qualities which have prevented modern readers from
finding in them the same charm that her contemporaries enjoyed.
She is perhaps best known as the author of "The Boy Stood on
the Burning Deck."

Flight of the Spirit

Whither, oh! whither wilt thou wing thy way?
What solemn region first upon thy sight
Shall break, unveiled for terror or delight?
What hosts, magnificent in dread array,
My spirit! when thy prison-house of clay
After long strife is rent? Fond, fruitless quest!
The unfledged bird, within his narrow nest,
Sees but a few green branches o'er him play,
And through their parting leaves, by fits revealed,

A glimpse of summer sky; nor knows the field
Wherein his dormant powers must yet be tried.
Thou art that bird!—of what beyond thee lies
Far in the untracked, immeasurable skies
Knowing but this—that thou shalt find thy Guide!

Sabbath Sonnet

How many blessed groups this hour are bending,
Through England's primrose meadow-paths, their way
Towards spire and tower, 'midst shadowy elms ascending,
Whence the sweet chimes proclaim the hallowed day!
The halls from old heroic ages gray
Pour their fair children forth; and hamlets low,
With those thick orchard-blooms the soft winds play,
Send out their inmates in a happy flow,
Like a freed vernal stream. I may not tread
With them those pathways, to the feverish bed
Of sickness bound; yet, O my God! I bless
Thy mercy, that with Sabbath peace hath filled
My chastened heart, and all its throbbings stilled
To one deep calm of lowliest thankfulness.

JOHN KEATS
(1795–1821)

After attending Enfield Academy, Keats, the son of a London livery stable operator, was apprenticed to a surgeon and studied at Guy's Hospital. His *Poems* appeared in 1817, but attracted little attention. *Endymion,* however, was attacked in the *Quarterly Review* and in *Blackwood's.* For his association with Leigh Hunt, Keats was stigmatized as one of the "Cockney School," although he soon outgrew Hunt's influence. Keats died of tuberculosis in Rome.

————————————

To Leigh Hunt, Esq.

Glory and loveliness have passed away:
    For if we wander out in early morn,
    No wreathed incense do we see upborne
Into the east to meet the smiling day:
No crowd of nymphs soft voiced and young, and gay,
    In woven baskets bringing ears of corn,
    Roses, and pinks, and violets, to adorn
The shrine of Flora in her early May.
But there are left delights as high as these,
    And I shall ever bless my destiny,
    That in a time, when under pleasant trees
Pan is no longer sought, I feel a free,
    A leafy luxury, seeing I could please,
    With these poor offerings, a man like thee.

Written on the Day That Mr. Leigh Hunt Left Prison

What though, for showing truth to flattered state,
    Kind Hunt was shut in prison, yet has he,
    In his immortal spirit, been as free
As the sky-searching lark, and as elate.
Minion of grandeur! think you he did wait?
    Think you he nought but prison walls did see,
    Till, so unwilling, thou unturnedst the key?
Ah, no! far happier, nobler was his fate!

In Spenser's halls he strayed, and bowers fair,
    Culling enchanted flowers; and he flew
With daring Milton through the fields of air:
    To regions of his own his genius true
Took happy flights. Who shall his fame impair
    When thou art dead, and all thy wretched crew?

To My Brothers

Small, busy flames play through the fresh laid coals,
    And their faint cracklings o'er our silence creep
    Like whispers of the household gods that keep
A gentle empire o'er fraternal souls.
And while, for rhymes, I search around the poles,
    Your eyes are fixed, as in poetic sleep,
    Upon the lore so voluble and deep,
That aye at fall of night our care condoles.
This is your birthday, Tom, and I rejoice
    That thus it passes smoothly, quietly.
Many such eves of gently whisp'ring noise
    May we together pass, and calmly try
What are this world's true joys,—ere the great voice
    From its fair face, shall bid our spirits fly.

"Keen, fitful gusts . . ."

Keen, fitful gusts are whisp'ring here and there
    Among the bushes half leafless, and dry;
    The stars look very cold about the sky,
And I have many miles on foot to fare.
Yet feel I little of the cool bleak air,
    Or of the dead leaves rustling drearily,
    Or of those silver lamps that burn on high,
Or of the distance from home's pleasant lair:
For I am brimful of the friendliness
    That in a little cottage I have found;
Of fair-haired Milton's eloquent distress,
    And all his love for gentle Lycid drowned,
Of lovely Laura in her light green dress,
    And faithful Petrarch gloriously crowned.

On First Looking Into Chapman's Homer

Much have I traveled in the realms of gold,
    And many goodly states and kingdoms seen;
    Round many western islands have I been
Which bards in fealty to Apollo hold.
Oft of one wide expanse had I been told
    That deep-browed Homer ruled as his demesne;
    Yet did I never breathe its pure serene
Till I heard Chapman speak out loud and bold:
Then felt I like some watcher of the skies
    When a new planet swims into his ken;
Or like stout Cortez when with eagle eyes
    He stared at the Pacific—and all his men
Looked at each other with a wild surmise—
    Silent, upon a peak in Darien.

"Great spirits now on earth . . ."

Great spirits now on earth are sojourning;
    He of the cloud, the cataract, the lake,
    Who on Helvellyn's summit, wide awake,
Catches his freshness from Archangel's wing:
He of the rose, the violet, the spring,
    The social smile, the chain for Freedom's sake:
    And lo!—whose steadfastness would never take
A meaner sound than Raphael's whispering.
And other spirits there are standing apart
    Upon the forehead of the age to come;
These, these will give the world another heart,
    And other pulses. Hear ye not the hum
Of mighty workings?——
    Listen awhile ye nations, and be dumb.

On the Grasshopper and Cricket[1]

The poetry of earth is never dead:
    When all the birds are faint with the hot sun,
    And hide in cooling trees, a voice will run
From hedge to hedge about the new-mown mead;
That is the Grasshopper's—he takes the lead
    In summer luxury,—he has never done

With his delights; for when tired out with fun
He rests at east beneath some pleasant weed.
The poetry of earth is ceasing never:
On a lone winter evening, when the frost
Has wrought a silence, from the stove there shrills
The Cricket's song, in warmth increasing ever,
And seems to one in drowsiness half lost,
The Grasshopper's among some grassy hills.

¹Written in competition with Hunt, see p. 177.

"When I have fears that I may cease to be"

When I have fears that I may cease to be
Before my pen has gleaned my teeming brain,
Before high-piled books, in charact'ry,
Hold like rich garners the full-ripened grain;
When I behold, upon the night's starred face,
Huge cloudy symbols of a high romance,
And think that I may never live to trace
Their shadows, with the magic hand of chance;
And when I feel, fair creature of an hour!
That I shall never look upon thee more,
Never have relish in the fairy power
Of unreflecting love!—then on the shore
Of the wide world I stand alone, and think
Till love and fame to nothingness do sink.

To Homer

Standing aloof in giant ignorance,
Of thee I hear and of the Cyclades,
As one who sits ashore and longs perchance
To visit dolphin-coral in deep seas.
So thou wast blind;—but then the veil was rent;
For Jove uncurtained Heaven to let thee live,
And Neptune made for thee a spumy tent,
And Pan made sing for thee his forest-hive;
Ay, on the shores of darkness there is light,
And precipices show untrodden green,
There is a budding morrow in midnight,
There is a triple sight in blindness keen;

Such seeing hadst thou, as it once befell
To Dian, Queen of Earth, and Heaven, and Hell.

To Sleep

O soft embalmer of the still midnight,
    Shutting, with careful fingers and benign,
Our gloom-pleased eyes, embowered from the light,
    Enshaded in forgetfulness divine:
O soothest Sleep! if so it please thee, close
    In midst of this thine hymn my willing eyes,
Or wait the "Amen," ere thy poppy throws
    Around my bed its lulling charities.
    Then save me, or the passed day will shine
Upon my pillow, breeding many woes,—
    Save me from curious Conscience, that still lords
Its strength for darkness, burrowing like a mole;
    Turn the key deftly in the oiled wards,
And seal the hushed Casket of my soul.

To Fanny[1]

I cry your mercy—pity—love!—aye, love!—
    Merciful love that tantalizes not,
One-thoughted, never-wandering, guileless love,
    Unmasked, and being seen—without a blot!
O! let me have thee whole,—all—all—be mine!
    That shape, that fairness, that sweet minor zest
Of love, your kiss,—those hands, those eyes divine,
    That warm, white, lucent, million-pleasured breast,—
Yourself—your soul—in pity give me all,
    Withhold no atom's atom or I die,
Or living on perhaps, your wretched thrall,
    Forget, in the midst of idle misery,
    Life's purposes,—the palate of my mind
Losing its gust, and my ambition blind!

[1] Fanny Brawne, the object of Keats's hopeless love

"Bright star! would I were steadfast as thou art"

Bright star! would I were steadfast as thou art—
   Not in lone splendor hung aloft the night
And watching, with eternal lids apart,
   Like nature's patient, sleepless Eremite,
The moving waters at their priestlike task
   Of pure ablution round earth's human shores,
Or gazing on the new soft fallen mask
   Of snow upon the mountains and the moors—
No—yet still steadfast, still unchangeable,
   Pillowed upon my fair love's ripening breast,
To feel for ever its soft fall and swell,
   Awake for ever in a sweet unrest,
Still, still to hear her tender-taken breath,
And so live ever—or else swoon to death.

GEORGE DARLEY
(1795–1846)

Darley was born in Dublin and was educated at Trinity College, Dublin; he followed a career as poet and critic in London, where he wrote for the *London Magazine* and the *Athenaeum*. His long poem *Nepenthe* was privately circulated in 1835; he also published plays imitative of Jacobean drama, *Thomas à Becket* (1840) and *Ethelstan* (1841).

To Poets

You, the choice minions of the proud-lipped Nine
Who warble at the great Apollo's knee,
Why do you laugh at these rude lays of mine?
I seek not of your brotherhood to be!—
I do not play the public swan, nor try
To curve my proud neck on your vocal streams;
In my own little isle retreated, I
Lose myself in my waters and my dreams.
Forgetful of the world,—forgotten too!—

Thy cygnet of my own secluded wave,
I sing, whilst, dashing up their silver dew
For joy, the petty billows try to rave:
There is a still applause in solitude
Fitting alike my merits and my mood.

To Mie Tirante

Thou, att whose feete I waste mie soule in sighes,
  Before whose beautie mie proude hearte is meeke,
Thou who make'st dove-like mie fierce falcon-cies,
  And pale'st the rose of mie Lancastrian cheeke
With one colde smyle about this budded mouth:
  Oh! that mie harmlesse vengeaunce I could wreake,
On that pale rival bloome of thine!—the South
  Raves not more fell, prisoned an Aprill weeke,
To feede on lilie-banks, than I to prey
  Some greedie minutes on that blossome whyte,
Whose gentle ravage thou'dst too long delaie!—
  O when these Roses of our cheekes unite,
Will't not a summer-happie season be
  If not for Englande, in sweete soothe for me!

HARTLEY COLERIDGE
(1796–1849)

The eldest son of Samuel Taylor Coleridge was dismissed from
his probationary fellowship at Oriel College, Oxford, for intem-
perance. After an attempt to support himself in London, he
retired to the Lake District where he lived mostly at Grasmere.
His collected poems were published in 1851. The sonnet was
Hartley Coleridge's favorite verse form, and in it he demon-
strated something more than mere competence.

Dedicatory Sonnet to S. T. Coleridge

Father, and Bard revered! to whom I owe,
Whate'er it be, my little art of numbers,

Thou, in thy night-watch o'er my cradled slumbers,[1]
Didst meditate the verse that lives to show,
(And long shall live, when we alike are low)
Thy prayer how ardent, and thy hope how strong,
That I should learn of Nature's self the song,
The lore which none but Nature's pupils know.

The prayer was heard: I "wander'd like a breeze,"
By mountain brooks and solitary meres,
And gathered there the shapes and phantasies
Which, mixed with passions of my sadder years,
Compose this book. If good therein there be,
That good, my sire, I dedicate to thee.

[1] slumbers/a reference to S. T. Coleridge's "Frost at Midnight"

To Wordsworth

There have been poets that in verse display
The elemental forms of human passions:
Poets have been, to whom the fickle fashions
And all the willful humors of the day
Have furnished matter for a polished lay:
And many are the smooth elaborate tribe
Who, emulous of thee, the shape describe,
And fain would every shifting hue portray
Of restless Nature. But, thou mighty Seer!
'Tis thine to celebrate the thoughts that make
The life of souls, the truths for whose sweet sake
We to ourselves and to our God are dear.
Of Nature's inner shrine thou art the priest,
Where most she works when we perceive her least.

"How long I sailed . . ."

How long I sailed, and never took a thought
To what port I was bound! Secure as sleep,
I dwelt upon the bosom of the deep
And perilous sea. And though my ship was fraught
With rare and precious fancies, jewels brought
From fairyland, no course I cared to keep,

Nor changeful wind nor tide I heeded ought,
But joyed to feel the merry billows leap,
And watch the sunbeams dallying with the waves;
Or haply dream what realms beneath may lie
Where the clear ocean is an emerald sky,
And mermaids warble in their coral caves,
Yet vainly woo to me their secret home;—
And sweet it were for ever so to roam.

"Long time a child . . ."

Long time a child, and still a child, when years
Had painted manhood on my cheek, was I,—
For yet I lived like one not born to die;
A thriftless prodigal of smiles and tears,
No hope I needed, and I knew no fears.
But sleep, though sweet, is only sleep, and waking,
I waked to sleep no more, at once o'ertaking
The vanguard of my age, with all arrears
Of duty on my back. Nor child, nor man,
Nor youth, nor sage, I find my head is gray,
For I have lost the race I never ran:
A rathe December blights my lagging May;
And still I am a child, though I be old,
Time is my debtor for my years untold.

"Why should I murmur . . ."

Why should I murmur at my lot forlorn?
The selfsame Fate that doomed me to be poor
Endues me with a spirit to endure
All, and much more, than is or has been borne
By better men, of want, or worldly scorn.
My soul has faith, my body has the nerve
To brave the penance that my sins deserve.
And yet my helpless state I deeply mourn:
Well could I bear to be deserted quite,—
Less should I blame my fortune were it worse;—
But taking all, it yet hath left me friends,
For whom I needs must mourn the wayward spite
That hides my purpose in an empty purse,
Since what I grateful wish, in wishing ends.

Written on the Anniversary of Our Father's Death

Still for the world he lives, and lives in bliss,
For God and for himself. Ten years and three
Have now elapsed since he was dead to me
And all that were on earth intensely his.
Not in the dim domain of Gloomy Dis,
The death-god of the ever-guessing Greek,
Nor in the paradise of Houris sleek
I think of him whom I most sorely miss.
The sage, the poet, lives for all mankind,
As long as truth is true, or beauty fair.
The soul that ever sought its God to find
Has found Him now—no matter how, or where.
Yet can I not but mourn because he died
That was my father, should have been my guide.

"Think upon Death . . ."

Think upon Death, 'tis good to think of Death,
But better far to think upon the Dead.
Death is a specter with a bony head,
Or the mere mortal body without breath,
The state foredoomed of every son of Seth,
Decomposition—dust, or dreamless sleep.
But the dear Dead are they for whom we weep,
For whom I credit all the Bible saith.
Dead is my father, dead is my good mother,
And what on earth have I to do but die?
But if by grace I reach the blessed sky,
I fain would see the same, and not another;
The very father that I used to see,
The mother that has nursed me on her knee.

"Full well I know . . ."

Full well I know—my friends—ye look on me
A living specter of my Father dead—
Had I not borne his name, had I not fed
On him, as one leaf trembling on a tree,
A woeful waste had been my minstrelsy—
Yet have I sung of maidens newly wed
And I have wished that hearts too sharply bled

Should throb with less of pain, and heave more free
By my endeavor. Still alone I sit
Counting each thought as miser counts a penny,
Wishing to spend my pennyworth of wit
On antic wheel of fortune like a zany:
You love me for my sire, to you unknown,
Revere me for his sake, and love me for my own.

THOMAS HOOD
(1799–1845)

Hood began his literary career as an assistant sub-editor on the
London Magazine; he later served as editor of *The Gem, The
Comic Annual,* and the *New Monthly Magazine*. A sonnet like
"Silence" shows Hood's strong capabilities for serious verse; the
bulk of Hood's poetry and prose, however, was in the comic vein.

Silence

There is a silence where hath been no sound,
There is a silence where no sound may be,
In the cold grave—under the deep, deep sea,
Or in wide desert where no life is found,
Which hath been mute, and still must sleep profound:
No voice is hushed—no life treads silently,
But clouds and cloudy shadows wander free,
That never spoke, over the idle ground:
But in green ruins, in the desolate walls
Of antique palaces, where Man hath been,
Though the dun fox, or wild hyena, calls,
And owls, that flit continually between,
Shriek to the echo, and the low winds moan,
There the true Silence is, self-conscious and alone.

"The world is with me . . ."

The world is with me, and its many cares,
Its woes—its wants—the anxious hopes and fears
That wait on all terrestrial affairs—

The shades of former and of future years—
Foreboding fancies and prophetic tears,
Quelling a spirit that was once elate.
Heavens! what a wilderness the world appears,
Where youth, and mirth, and health are out of date;
But no—a laugh of innocence and joy
Resounds, like music of the fairy race,
And, gladly turning from the world's annoy,
I gaze upon a little radiant face,
And bless, internally, the merry boy
Who "makes a *son-shine* in a shady place."

THOMAS LOVELL BEDDOES
(1803–1849)

Beddoes, the son of a famous physician, was educated at Charterhouse, Oxford, and the university at Göttingen, where he studied medicine. His early play, *The Bride's Tragedy* (1822), showed his interest in things Elizabethan and Jacobean, which culminated in the Gothicism of his greatest work, *Death's Jest-Book* (1850). He took his own life in Basel, Switzerland.

To Night

So thou art come again, old black-winged Night,
  Like an huge bird, between us and the sun,
Hiding, with outstretched form, the genial light;
  And still, beneath thine icy bosom's dun
And cloudy plumage, hatching fog-breathed blight,
  And embryo storms, and crabbed frosts, that shun
Day's warm caress. The owls from ivied loop
  Are shrieking homage, as thou cowerest high,
Like sable crow pausing in eager stoop
  On the dim world thou gluttest thy clouded eye,
Silently waiting latest time's fell whoop,
    When thou shalt quit thine aerie in the sky,
      To pounce upon the world with eager claw,
      And tomb time, death, and substance in thy maw.

A Fantastic Simile

A lover is a slender, glowing urn
　On beauty's shrine, his heart is incense sweet,
Which with his eye-lit torch young love doth burn;
　Then from its ardor cloudy ringlets fleet,
That we call sighs, and they with perfume turn
　Upwards, his mistress' whisperings to meet.
The breezy whispers and the sighs embrace,
　Like pink-winged clouds mixing above the hill,
And from their lovely toyings spring a race
Of tears, which saunter down in cheek-banked rill,
Silvering with sparkling coil the fair one's face;
　Twin dewdrops which her startled senses spill
　　From violet's eyes, that hide their tender hue,
　　Deep-caverned in a fringed lake of blue.

Another

'Tis a moon-tinted primrose, with a well
　Of trembling dew; in its soft atmosphere,
A tiny whirlwind of sweet smells, doth dwell
　A ladybird; and when no sound is near
That elfin hermit fans the fairy bell
　With glazen wings (mirrors, on which appear
Atoms of colors that flizz by unseen);
　And struts about his darling flower with pride.
But, if some buzzing gnat with pettish spleen
　Comes whining by, the insect 'gins to hide,
And folds its flimsy drapery between
　His speckled buckler and soft, silken side.
　　So poets fly the critic's snappish heat,
　　And sheath their minds in scorn and self-conceit.

To Silence

Huge, viewless, ocean into which we cast
　Our passing words, and, as they sink away,
An echo bubbles up upon the blast;
　Oh! could thy waves but vomit in their play
Those unseen pearls which thou dost clasp so fast,
　And hang them at our ears washed in thy spray,

What endless stores our casket, memory,
   Would brood on, and enjoy. But wherefore now
Dost thou engulf our talk, and floodest by
   Uphurling clouds upon our moody brow?
E'en when we dumbly muse sometimes a sigh
   Of bursting blossom, or hoarse groan from bough
     Break through thy foam, like Venus, ocean sprung,
     And to our ears upon the wind are swung.

ELIZABETH BARRETT BROWNING
(1806–1861)

Elizabeth Barrett's literary activity was no doubt encouraged by her invalidism. Robert Browning's praise of her *Poems* (1844) resulted in courtship, improvement in her health, and, against the wishes of her despotic father, marriage in 1846. In *Sonnets from the Portuguese,* published at Browning's urging in 1850, she celebrated their love. Browning's assertion that these are "the finest sonnets written in any language since Shakespeare" indicates he was a better husband than critic.

FROM SONNETS FROM THE PORTUGUESE

4. *"Thou hast thy calling . . ."*

Thou hast thy calling to some palace floor,
Most gracious singer of high poems! where
The dancers will break footing, from the care
Of watching up thy pregnant lips for more.
And dost thou lift this house's latch too poor
For hand of thine? and canst thou think and bear
To let thy music drop here unaware
In folds of golden fullness at my door?
Look up and see the casement broken in,
The bats and owlets builders in the roof!
My cricket chirps against thy mandolin.
Hush, call no echo up in further proof
Of desolation! there's a voice within
That weeps . . . as thou must sing . . . alone, aloof.

9. "Can it be right to give . . ."

Can it be right to give what I can give?
To let thee sit beneath the fall of tears
As salt as mine, and hear the sighing years
Re-sighing on my lips renunciative
Through those infrequent smiles which fail to live
For all thy adjurations? O my fears,
That this can scarce be right! We are not peers,
So to be lovers; and I own, and grieve,
That givers of such gifts as mine are, must
Be counted with the ungenerous. Out, alas!
I will not soil thy purple with my dust,
Nor breathe my poison on thy Venice-glass,
Nor give thee any love—which were unjust.
Beloved, I only love thee! let it pass.

20. "Beloved, my Beloved . . ."

Beloved, my Beloved, when I think
That thou wast in the world a year ago,
What time I sat alone here in the snow
And saw no footprint, heard the silence sink
No moment at thy voice, but, link by link,
Went counting all my chains as if that so
They never could fall off at any blow
Struck by thy possible hand—why, thus I drink
Of life's great cup of wonder! Wonderful,
Never to feel thee thrill the day or night
With personal act or speech—nor ever cull
Some prescience of thee with the blossoms white
Thou sawest growing! Atheists are as dull,
Who cannot guess God's presence out of sight.

35. "If I leave all for thee . . ."

If I leave all for thee, wilt thou exchange
And be all to me? Shall I never miss
Home-talk and blessing and the common kiss
That comes to each in turn, nor count it strange,
When I look up, to drop on a new range
Of walls and floors, another home than this?

Nay, wilt thou fill that place by me which is
Filled by dead eyes too tender to know change?
That's hardest. If to conquer love, has tried,
To conquer grief, tries more, as all things prove;
For grief indeed is love and grief beside.
Alas, I have grieved so I am hard to love.
Yet love me—wilt thou? Open thine heart wide,
And fold within the wet wings of thy dove.

43. "How do I love thee? . . ."

How do I love thee? Let me count the ways.
I love thee to the depth and breadth and height
My soul can reach, when feeling out of sight
For the ends of Being and ideal Grace.
I love thee to the level of everyday's
Most quiet need, by sun and candlelight.
I love thee freely, as men strive for Right;
I love thee purely, as they turn from Praise.
I love thee with the passion put to use
In my old griefs, and with my childhood's faith.
I love thee with a love I seemed to lose
With my lost saints—I love thee with the breath,
Smiles, tears, of all my life!—and, if God choose,
I shall but love thee better after death.

William Gilmore Simms
(1806–1870)

Born in Charleston, South Carolina, Simms was at first apprenticed to a druggist but later studied law in his home city. For a time he followed a journalistic career in New York, where his most famous novel, *The Yemassee,* appeared in 1835. His marriage in 1836 brought him prosperity, and he settled down to the life of a southern planter, novelist, poet, and apologist for slavery.

The Triumph

The grave but ends the struggle!—Follows then
The triumph, which, superior to the doom,
Grows loveliest, and looks best to mortal men,
Purple in beauty, towering o'er the tomb!
O, with the stoppage of the impulsive tide
That vexed the impatient heart with needful strife,
The soul that is Hope's living leaps to life,
And shakes her fragrant plumage far and wide!
Eyes follow then in worship which but late
Frowned in defiance;—and the timorous herd
That sleekly waited for another's word
Grow bold at last to bring—obeying Fate—
The tribute of their praise but late denied,—
Tribute of homage which is sometimes—hate!

Glory and Enduring Fame

Thus Glory hath her being! thus she stands
Star-crowned,—a high divinity of woe;
Her temples fill, her columns crown all lands
Where lofty attribute is known below.
For her the smokes ascend, the waters flow,
The grave forgoes his prey, the soul goes free;
The gray rock gives out music; hearthstones grow
To temples at her word; her footprints see
On ruins, that are thus made holiest shrines,
Where Love may win devotion, and the heart
That with the fire of genius inly pines

May find the guidance of a kindred art,
And from the branch of that eternal tree
Pluck fruits at once of death and immortality!

HENRY WADSWORTH LONGFELLOW
(1807–1882)

Born in Portland, Maine, Longfellow attended Bowdoin College, where he later taught foreign languages for six years until he was given a professorship at Harvard. His first collection of poems, *Voices of the Night,* appeared in 1839, and six more volumes followed in the next ten years. His great popularity was based on such works as *The Song of Hiawatha* (1855) and *The Courtship of Miles Standish* (1858). His sonnets are a reminder of Longfellow's very real poetic gifts, too often obscured by the sentiment of his schoolroom pieces.

Chaucer

An old man in a lodge within a park;
The chamber walls depicted all around
With portraitures of huntsman, hawk, and hound,
And the hurt deer. He listeneth to the lark,
Whose song comes with the sunshine through the dark
Of painted glass in leaden lattice bound:
He listeneth and he laugheth at the sound,
Then writeth in a book like any clerk.
He is the poet of the dawn, who wrote
The Canterbury Tales, and his old age
Made beautiful with song; and as I read
I hear the crowing cock, I hear the note
Of lark and linnet, and from every page
Rise odors of ploughed field or flowery mead.

Keats

The young Endymion sleeps Endymion's sleep;
The shepherd boy whose tale was left half told!

The solemn grove uplifts its shield of gold
To the red rising moon, and loud and deep
The nightingale is singing from the steep;
It is midsummer, but the air is cold;
Can it be death? Alas, beside the fold
A shepherd's pipe lies shattered near his sheep.
Lo! in the moonlight gleams a marble white,
On which I read: "Here lieth one whose name
Was writ in water." And was this the meed
Of his sweet singing? Rather let me write:
"The smoking flax before it burst to flame
Was quenched by death, and broken the bruised reed."

FROM DIVINA COMMEDIA

1. "Oft have I seen . . ."

Oft have I seen at some cathedral door
    A laborer, pausing in the dust and heat,
    Lay down his burden, and with reverent feet
    Enter, and cross himself, and on the floor
Kneel to repeat his paternoster o'er;
    Far off the noises of the world retreat;
    The loud vociferations of the street
    Become an undistinguishable roar.
So, as I enter here from day to day,
    And leave my burden at this minster gate,
    Kneeling in prayer, and not ashamed to pray,
The tumult of the time disconsolate
    To inarticulate murmurs dies away,
    While the eternal ages watch and wait.

JOHN GREENLEAF WHITTIER
(1807–1892)

The Quaker poet Whittier was born on the family farm near Haverhill, Massachusetts. He turned from cobbling to literature under the influence of William Lloyd Garrison. At first primarily an abolitionist propagandist, Whittier won national popularity for his verse with the publication of *Snow-Bound* in 1866.

Godspeed

Outbound, your bark awaits you. Were I one
　　Whose prayer availeth much, my wish should be
　　Your favoring trade wind and consenting sea.
By sail or steed was never love outrun,
And, here or there, love follows her in whom
　　All graces and sweet charities unite,
　　The old Greek beauty set in holier light;
And her for whom New England's byways bloom,
Who walks among us welcome as the Spring,
　　Calling up blossoms where her light feet stray.
　　God keep you both, make beautiful your way,
Comfort, console, and bless; and safely bring,
Ere yet I make upon a vaster sea
The unreturning voyage, my friends to me.

Help

Dream not, O Soul, that easy is the task
　　Thus set before thee. If it proves at length,
　　As well it may, beyond thy natural strength,
Faint not, despair not. As a child may ask
A father, pray the Everlasting Good
　　For light and guidance midst the subtle snares
　　Of sin thick planted in life's thoroughfares,
For spiritual strength and moral hardihood;
Still listening, through the noise of time and sense,
　　To the still whisper of the Inward Word;
　　Bitter in blame, sweet in approval heard,

Itself its own confirming evidence:
To health of soul a voice to cheer and please,
To guilt the wrath of the Eumenides.

CHARLES TENNYSON TURNER
(1808–1879)

Charles Tennyson Turner was Alfred, Lord Tennyson's elder
brother, and collaborated with him in *Poems by Two Brothers*
(1827). He changed his name to Turner in honor of a great-uncle
who left him property. Turner spent a quiet life as a country
clergyman, but his various collections of sonnets from 1830 to
1880 won him a wide and well-deserved reputation as a son-
neteer.

_____

The Buoy Bell

How like the leper, with his own sad cry
Enforcing his own solitude, it tolls!
That lonely bell set in the rushing shoals,
To warn us from the place of jeopardy!
O friend of man! sore-vexed by ocean's power,
The changing tides wash o'er thee day by day;
Thy trembling mouth is filled with bitter spray,
Yet still thou ringest on from hour to hour;
High is thy mission, though thy lot is wild—
To be in danger's realm a guardian sound;
In seamen's dreams a pleasant part to bear,
And earn their blessing as the year goes round;
And strike the keynote of each grateful prayer,
Breathed in their distant homes by wife or child!

Old Ruralities: A Regret

With joy all relics of the past I hail;
The heath-bell, lingering in our cultured moor,
Or the dull sound of the slip-shouldered flail,
Still busy on the poor man's threshing floor:

I love this unshorn hedgerow, which survives
Its stunted neighbors, in this farming age:
The thatch and houseleek, where old Alice lives
With her old herbal, trusting every page;
I love the spinning wheel, which hums far down
In yon lone valley, though, from day to day,
The boom of Science shakes it from the town.
Ah! sweet old world! thou speedest fast away!
My boyhood's world! but all last looks are dear;
More touching is the deathbed than the bier!

Great Britain Through the Ice: Or, Premature Patriotism

Methought I lived in the icy times forlorn;
And, with a fond forecasting love and pride,
I hung o'er frozen England:—"When," I cried,
"When will the island of our hopes be born?
When will our fields be seen, our church bells heard?
And Avon, Doon, and Tweed break forth in song?
This blank unstoried ice be warmed and stirred,
And Thames, and Clyde, and Humber roll along
To a free sea-board? airs of paradise
Install our summer and our flowery springs,
And lift the larks, and land the nightingales?
And this wild alien unfamiliar Wales
Melt home among her harps? and vernal skies
Thaw out old Dover for the houseless kings?"

The Seaside: In and out of the Season

In summertime it was a paradise
Of mountain, frith, and bay, and shining sand;
Our outward rowers sang towards the land,
Followed by waving hands and happy cries:
By the full flood the groups no longer roam;
And when, at ebb, the glistening beach grows wide,
No barefoot children race into the foam,
But passive jellies wait the turn of tide.
Like some forsaken lover, lingering there,

The boatman stands; the maidens trip no more
With loosened locks; far from the billows' roar
The Mauds and Maries knot their tresses fair,
Where not a foam-flake from th' enamored shore
Comes down the sea-wind on the golden hair.

ALFRED, LORD TENNYSON
(1809–1892)

Tennyson was the fourth son of a Lincolnshire clergyman. He began writing poetry at an early age and collaborated with his brothers, Charles and Frederick, in *Poems by Two Brothers* (1827). He was educated at Trinity College, Cambridge. *Poems, Chiefly Lyrical* (1830) and *Poems* (1832) were both coolly received. Tennyson achieved great success with his 1842 *Poems,* however, and his popularity was enhanced by the publication of *In Memoriam* in 1850. He was appointed poet laureate in the same year. A partial list of Tennyson's other important works includes *Maud* (1855), *The Idylls of the King* (1859), and *Locksley Hall Sixty Years After* (1886). Tennyson wrote relatively few sonnets.

Buonaparte

He thought to quell the stubborn hearts of oak,
Madman! to chain with chains, and bind with bands
That island queen who sways the floods and lands
From Ind to Ind, but in fair daylight woke,
When from her wooden walls,—lit by sure hands,—
With thunders and with lightnings and with smoke,—
Peal after peal, the British battle broke,
Lulling the brine against the Coptic sands.
We taught him lowlier moods, when Elsinore
Heard the war moan along the distant sea,
Rocking with shattered spars, with sudden fires
Flamed over: at Trafalgar yet once more
We taught him: late he learned humility
Perforce, like those whom Gideon schooled with briars.

"If I were loved, as I desire to be"

If I were loved, as I desire to be,
What is there in the great sphere of the earth,
And range of evil between death and birth,
That I should fear,—if I were loved by thee?
All the inner, all the outer world of pain
Clear love would pierce and cleave, if thou wert mine.
As I have heard that, somewhere in the main,
Fresh-water springs come up through bitter brine.
'Twere joy, not fear, clasped hand in hand with thee,
To wait for death—mute—careless of all ills,
Apart upon a mountain, though the surge
Of some new deluge from a thousand hills
Flung leagues of roaring foam into the gorge
Below us, as far on as eye could see.

FRANCES ANNE KEMBLE
(1809–1893)

Born in London, the daughter of a theatrical family, Fanny Kemble, as she was known, entered upon her own stage career in 1829 when she played Juliet at Covent Garden. In 1832 she toured America with her father, and in 1834 she married a Georgia plantation owner. They were divorced in 1849, after which she gave a number of highly successful Shakespearean readings. A collection of her poems was published in 1844; her works include plays, poems, a novel, and a number of autobiographical books.

To Shakespeare

If from the height of that celestial sphere
Where now thou dwell'st, spirit powerful and sweet!
Thou yet canst love the race that sojourn here,
How must thou joy, with pleasure not unmeet
For thy exalted state, to know how dear
Thy memory is held throughout the earth,
Beyond the favored land that gave thee birth.

E'en in thy seat in heaven, thou mayst receive
Thanks, praise, and love, and wonder ever new,
From human hearts, who in thy verse perceive
All that humanity calls good and true;
Nor dost thou for each mortal blemish grieve.
They from thy glorious works have fallen away,
As from thy soul its outward form of clay.

EDGAR ALLAN POE
(1809–1849)

Poe was born in Boston; his actor father deserted his mother, an English-born actress who died in 1811, and Poe was raised by John Allan and his family in Richmond, Virginia. His first work, *Tamerlane and Other Poems* (1827), was published in Boston after his expulsion from the University of Virginia. He served briefly in the army and attended West Point for less than a year. Poe worked on a variety of newspapers in Richmond, Philadelphia, and New York. His major collection of poetry, *The Raven and Other Poems,* appeared in 1845.

To Science

Science, true daughter of Old Time thou art!
   Who alterest all things with thy peering eyes.
Why preyest thou thus upon the poet's heart,
   Vulture, whose wings are dull realities?
How should he love thee, or how deem thee wise,
   Who wouldst not leave him in his wandering
To seek for treasure in the jeweled skies,
   Albeit he soared with an undaunted wing?
Hast thou not dragged Diana from her car,
   And driven the Hamadryad from the wood
To seek a shelter in some happier star?
   Hast thou not torn the Naiad from her flood,
The Elfin from the green grass, and from me
The summer dream beneath the tamarind tree?

An Enigma

"Seldom we find," says Solomon Don Dunce,
  "Half an idea in the profoundest sonnet.
Through all the flimsy things we see at once
  As easily as through a Naples bonnet—
  Trash of all trash!—how *can* a lady don it?
Yet heavier far than your Petrarchan stuff—
Owl-downy nonsense that the faintest puff
  Twirls into trunk-paper while you con it."
And, veritably, Sol is right enough.
The general tuckermanities[1] are arrant
Bubbles—ephemeral and *so* transparent—
But *this* is, now,—you may depend upon it—
Stable, opaque, immortal—all by dint
Of the dear names that lie concealed within't.[2]

[1]tuckermanities/A reference to Henry Theodore Tuckerman (1813–
1871), critic, essayist, and poet, brother of Frederick
[2]names . . . concealed within't/The name of Sarah Anna Lewis,
poet and friend of Poe in his later years, is concealed in the poem.
It can be found by tracing out the first letter of the first line, the
second letter of the second line, etc., to the end of the sonnet.

Robert Browning
(1812–1889)

Browning, the son of a prosperous official of the Bank of England, was raised in Camberwell, outside of London, and was privately educated. He married Elizabeth Barrett in 1846 and lived with her for the most part in Italy. After her death in 1861, he returned to London. Browning wrote very few sonnets, his real genius being for the dramatic monologue and for longer narratives such as are to be found in volumes like *Bells and Pomegranates* (1841–1846), *Men and Women* (1855), *Dramatis Personae* (1864), and *The Ring and the Book* (1868–1869).

"Eyes, calm beside thee (Lady, could'st thou know!)"

Eyes, calm beside thee (Lady, could'st thou know!)
   May turn away thick with fast-gathering tears:
I glance not where all gaze: thrilling and low
   Their passionate praises reach thee—my cheek wears
Alone no wonder when thou passest by;
Thy tremulous lids bent and suffused reply
To the irrepressible homage which doth glow
   On every lip but mine: if in thine ears
Their accents linger—and thou dost recall
   Me as I stood, still, guarded, very pale,
Beside each votarist whose lighted brow
Wore worship like an aureole, "O'er them all
   My beauty," thou wilt murmur, "did prevail
Save that one only."—Lady, could'st thou know!

Why I Am a Liberal

"Why?" Because all I haply can and do,
   And that I am now, all I hope to be,—
   Whence comes it save from fortune setting free
Body and soul the purpose to pursue,
God traced for both? If fetters not a few,
   Of prejudice, convention, fall from me,
   These shall I bid men—each in his degree
Also God-guided—bear, and gaily, too?

But little do or can the best of us:
  That little is achieved through Liberty.
Who, then, dares hold, emancipated thus,
  His fellow shall continue bound? Not I,
Who live, love, labor freely, nor discuss
  A brother's right to freedom. That is "Why."

JONES VERY
(1813–1880)

The son of a ship captain, Very was born in Salem, Massachusetts. He graduated from Harvard in 1836 and was appointed a tutor in Greek. In 1837 he experienced a mystical revelation and began writing sonnets which he declared were "communicated" to him by the Lord. In 1838 he was asked to resign from Harvard and entered an insane asylum. His *Essays and Poems* (1839) was praised by Emerson, Channing, and Bryant. The latter part of his life was spent in quiet and disappointed retirement.

The Robin

Thou need'st not flutter from thy half-built nest,
Whene'er thou hear'st man's hurrying feet go by,
Fearing his eye for harm may on thee rest,
Or he thy young unfinished cottage spy;
All will not heed thee on that swinging bough,
Nor care that round thy shelter springs the leaves,
Nor watch thee on the pool's wet margin now,
For clay to plaster straws thy cunning weaves;
All will not hear thy sweet outpouring joy,
That with morn's stillness blends the voice of song;
For over-anxious cares their souls employ,
That else upon thy music borne along,
And the light wings or heart-ascending prayer,
Had learned that Heaven is pleased thy simple joys to share.

Yourself

'Tis to yourself I speak; you cannot know
Him whom I call in speaking such a one,
For you beneath the earth lie buried low,
Which he alone as living walks upon:
You may at times have heard him speak to you,
And often wished perchance that you were he;
And I must ever wish that it were true,
For then you could hold fellowship with me:
But now you hear us talk as strangers met
Above the room wherein you lie abed;
A word perhaps loud spoken you may get,
Or hear our feet when heavily they tread;
But he who speaks, or him who's spoken to,
Must both remain as strangers still to you.

Aubrey Thomas de Vere
(1814–1902)

De Vere was born in Ireland and educated at Trinity College,
Dublin. His father was also a poet. The younger de Vere formed
friendships with such English literary figures as Tennyson and
Browning. The *Waldenses* appeared in 1842, *The Search After
Proserpine* in 1843. After his conversion to Roman Catholicism
in 1851, de Vere devoted most of his poetry to religion and to
Irish history. His *Poetical Works* was published in 1884.

A Poet to a Painter

That which my fault has made me, O paint not:
Paint me as that which I desire to be.
The unaccomplished good that died in thought,
Deep buried in my heart, seek out, set free;
And all I might have been concede to me:
The veil my error and the world have wrought,
Remove: the cloud disperse: erase the blot:
Bid from my brow the temporal darkness flee.

In that celestial and pure font, whereof
Some drops affused by childhood, bathe me wholly;
And shield me from my own deserts: lest they
Who now but see me by the light of love,
A sterner insight learn from thee one day;
And love pass from them, like some outworn folly.

Correggio's Cupolas at Parma

Creatures all eyes and brows, and tresses streaming
By speed divine blown back; within, all fire
Of wondering zeal, and storm of bright desire;—
Round the broad dome the immortal throngs are beaming:
With elemental powers the vault is teeming.
We gaze, and, gazing, join the fervid choir,
In spirit launched on wings that ne'er can tire,
Like those that buoy the breasts of children dreaming.
The exquisitest hand that e'er in light
Revealed the subtlest smile of new-born pleasure
The depth here fathoms, and attains the height;
Is strong the strength of heavenly hosts to measure;
Draws back the azure curtain of the skies,
And antedates our promised Paradise.

George Eliot
(1819–1880)

Mary Ann (or Marian) Evans was born in Warwickshire near
Nuneaton. Two years after the death of her father she became an
assistant editor of *The Westminster Review.* Though not married,
she and George Henry Lewes, a writer and editor, lived together
as husband and wife from 1854 until his death in 1878. With the
publication of her first works of fiction in *Blackwood's,* gathered
together in the same year (1857) as *Scenes from Clerical Life,*
she assumed the pseudonym George Eliot. A major novelist of
the nineteenth century, Eliot also wrote a number of poems.
Brother and Sister, written in 1869, is a sequence of eleven
sonnets dealing with her childhood relationship with her brother,
Isaac Evans.

FROM BROTHER AND SISTER

I: *"I cannot choose but think upon the time"*

I cannot choose but think upon the time
When our two lives grew like two buds that kiss
At lightest thrill from the bee's swinging chime,
Because the one so near the other is.

He was the elder and a little man
Of forty inches, bound to show no dread,
And I the girl that puppy-like now ran,
Now lagged behind my brother's larger tread.

I held him wise, and when he talked to me
Of snakes and birds, and which God loved the best,
I thought his knowledge marked the boundary
Where men grew blind, though angels knew the rest.

   If he said "Hush!" I tried to hold my breath;
   Wherever he said "Come!" I stepped in faith.

XI: "School parted us . . ."

School parted us; we never found again
That childish world where our two spirits mingled
Like scents from varying roses that remain
One sweetness, nor can evermore be singled.

Yet the twin habit of that early time
Lingered for long about the heart and tongue:
We had been natives of one happy clime,
And its dear accent to our utterance clung,

Till the dire years whose awful name is Change
Had grasped our souls still yearning in divorce,
And pitiless shaped them in two forms that range
Two elements which sever their life's course.

But were another childhood-world my share,
I would be born a little sister there.

JAMES RUSSELL LOWELL
(1819–1891)

Lowell was born in Cambridge, Massachusetts, of a distinguished New England family. He graduated from Harvard, to which he returned as a professor in 1855. Although *A Year's Life and Other Poems* appeared in 1841, his literary reputation was thoroughly established in 1848 with the publication of *A Fable for Critics, The Vision of Sir Launfal,* and the first series of the *Bigelow Papers.* In addition to editing the *Atlantic Monthly* and the *North American Review,* Lowell served as American Minister to Spain and to England.

To the Spirit of Keats

Great soul, thou sittest with me in my room,
Uplifting me with thy vast, quiet eyes,
On whose full orbs, with kindly luster, lies
The twilight warmth of ruddy ember-gloom:

Thy clear, strong tones will oft bring sudden bloom
Of hope secure, to him who lonely cries,
Wrestling with the young poet's agonies,
Neglect and scorn, which seem a certain doom:
Yes! the few words which, like great thunder-drops,
Thy large heart down to earth shook doubtfully,
Thrilled by the inward lightning of its might,
Serene and pure, like gushing joy of light,
Shall track the eternal chords of Destiny,
After the moon-led pulse of ocean stops.

The Street

They pass me by like shadows, crowds on crowds,
Dim ghosts of men, that hover to and fro,
Hugging their bodies round them like thin shrouds
Wherein their souls were buried long ago:
They trampled on their youth, and faith, and love,
They cast their hope of human-kind away,
With Heaven's clear messages they madly strove,
And conquered,—and their spirits turned to clay:
Lo! how they wander round the world, their grave,
Whose ever-gaping maw by such is fed,
Gibbering at living men, and idly rave,
"We only truly live, but ye are dead."
Alas! poor fools, the anointed eye may trace
A dead soul's epitaph in every face!

FREDERICK GODDARD TUCKERMAN
(1821–1873)

A member of a distinguished family of academicians, church-men, and writers, Tuckerman was born in Boston. He was graduated from Harvard Law School in 1842 and admitted to the Bar in 1844, but soon after retired to Greenfield, Massachusetts, where he led a life of seclusion, devoting himself to literature, botany, and astronomy. His sonnets, far superior to those of his brother, Henry Theodore, were praised by his contemporaries.

"By this low fire . . ."

By this low fire I often sit to woo
Memory to bring the days forever done
And call the mountains, where our love begun
And the dear happy woodlands dipped in dew
And pore upon the landscape, like a book,
But cannot find her. Or there rise to me
Gardens and groves in light and shadow outspread.
Or on a headland far away, I see
Men marching slow in orderly review
And bayonets flash as, wheeling from the sun,
Rank after rank give fire. Or sad, I look
On miles of moonlit brine, with many a bed
Of wave-weed heaving. There the wet sands shine
And just awash, the low reef lifts its line.

"How oft in schoolboy days . . ."

How oft in schoolboy days, from the school's sway
Have I run forth to Nature as to a friend!—
With some pretext of o'erwrought sight, to spend
My school-time in green meadows far away!
Careless of summoning bell or clocks that strike,
I marked with flowers the minutes of my day.
For still the eye that shrank from hated hours,
Dazzled with decimal and dividend,
Knew each bleached alder-root that plashed across
The bubbling brook and every mass of moss;

Could tell the month, too, by the vervain-spike,—
How far the ring of purple tiny flowers
Had climbed—just starting, maybe, with the May,
Half-high, or tapering off at summer's end.

MATTHEW ARNOLD
(1822–1888)

Son of a famous headmaster of Rugby, Matthew Arnold was educated, in the family tradition, at Rugby and Oxford. In 1851 he was appointed an inspector of schools, in which capacity he made a considerable contribution to English education. From 1857 to 1867 he was professor of poetry at Oxford. *The Strayed Reveler, and Other Poems* appeared in 1849; *Empedocles on Etna, and Other Poems* in 1852; after 1860 the bulk of Arnold's work was in prose. He viewed poetry as "a criticism of life" and asserted the critical values of "high seriousness."

To a Friend

Who prop, thou ask'st, in these bad days, my mind?—
He much, the old man,[1] who, clearest-souled of men,
Saw The Wide Prospect, and the Asian Fen,
And Tmolus' Hill, and Smyrna Bay, though blind.
Much he, whose friendship I not long since won,
That halting slave;[2] who in Nicopolis
Taught Arrian, when Vespasian's brutal son
Cleared Rome of what most shamed him. But be his[3]
My special thanks, whose even-balanced soul,
From first youth tested up to extreme old age,
Business could not make dull, nor passion wild;
Who saw life steadily, and saw it whole;
The mellow glory of the Attic stage,
Singer of sweet Colonus, and its child.

[1] man/Homer
[2] slave/the Stoic philosopher Epictetus (c. A.D. 60–120)
[3] his/the Athenian playwright Sophocles (497–406 B.C.)

Shakespeare

Others abide our question. Thou art free.
We ask and ask—thou smilest and art still,
Out-topping knowledge. For the loftiest hill,
Who to the stars uncrowns his majesty,
Planting his steadfast footsteps in the sea,
Making the heaven of heavens his dwelling-place,
Spares but the cloudy border of his base
To the foiled searching of mortality;
And thou, who didst the stars and sunbeams know,
Self-schooled, self-scanned, self-honored, self-secure,
Didst tread on earth unguessed at.—Better so!
All pains the immortal spirit must endure,
All weakness which impairs, all griefs which bow,
Find their sole speech in that victorious brow.

To a Republican Friend, 1848

God knows it, I am with you. If to prize
Those virtues, prized and practiced by too few.
But prized, but loved, but eminent in you,
Man's fundamental life; if to despise

The barren optimistic sophistries
Of comfortable moles, whom what they do
Teaches the limit of the just and true
(And for such doing they require not eyes);

If sadness at the long heart-wasting show
Wherein earth's great ones are disquieted;
If thoughts, not idle, while before me flow

The armies of the homeless and unfed—
If these are yours, if this is what you are,
Then am I yours, and what you feel, I share.

Continued

Yet, when I muse on what life is, I seem
Rather to patience prompted, than that proud
Prospect of hope which France proclaims so loud—
France, famed in all great arts, in none supreme;

Seeing this vale, this earth, whereon we dream,
Is on all sides o'ershadowed by the high
Uno'erleaped Mountains of Necessity,
Sparing us narrower margin than we deem.

Nor will that day dawn at a human nod,
When, bursting through the network superposed
By selfish occupation—plot and plan,

Lust, avarice, envy—liberated man,
All difference with his fellow-mortal closed,
Shall be left standing face to face with God.

West London

Crouched on the pavement, close by Belgrave Square,
A tramp I saw, ill, moody, and tongue-tied.
A babe was in her arms, and at her side
A girl; their clothes were rags, their feet were bare.

Some laboring men, whose work lay somewhere there,
Passed opposite; she touched her girl, who hied
Across, and begged, and came back satisfied.
The rich she had let pass with frozen stare.

Thought I: "Above her state this spirit towers;
She will not ask of aliens, but of friends,
Of sharers in a common human fate.

"She turns from that cold succor, which attends
The unknown little from the unknowing great,
And points us to a better time than ours."

GEORGE HENRY BOKER
(1823–1890)

Boker was born in Philadelphia and graduated from Princeton (then the College of New Jersey) in 1842. His tragedy *Calaynos* was produced in London in 1849; his most successful play, *Francesca da Rimini*, in New York in 1855. *Plays and Poems* appeared in 1856 and his *Poems of War* in 1864. Boker served as American Minister to Turkey and Russia between 1871 and 1878. He wrote over 314 sonnets, many of which were praised by Leigh Hunt for their "true Shakespearean quality."

The Awaking of the Poetic Faculty

All day I heard a humming in my ears,
　A buzz of many voices, and a throng
　Of swarming numbers, passing with a song
Measured and stately as the rolling spheres.
I saw the sudden light of lifted spears,
　Slanted at once against some monster wrong;
　And then a fluttering scarf which might belong
To some sweet maiden in her morn of years.
I felt the chilling damp of sunless glades,
　Horrid with gloom; anon, the breath of May
　Was blown around me, and the lulling play
Of dripping fountains. Yet the lights and shades,
　The waving scarfs, the battle's grand parades
Seemed but vague shadows of that wondrous lay.

"Love is that orbit . . ."

Love is that orbit of the restless soul
　Whose circle grazes the confines of space,
　Bounding within the limits of its race
Utmost extremes; whose high and topmost pole
Within the very blaze of heaven doth roll;
　Whose nether course is through the darkest place
　Eclipsed by hell. What daring hand shall trace
The blended joys and sorrows that control

A heart whose journeys the fixed hand of Fate
    Points through this pathway? Who may soar so high,—
    Behold such glories with unwinking eye?
Who drop so low beneath his mortal state,
    And thence return with careful chart and date,
    To mark which way another's course must lie?

JAMES BAYARD TAYLOR
(1825–1878)

Born in Kennet Square, Pennsylvania, Taylor followed a phre-
nologist's prediction that he would become a traveler and a poet.
His career as a traveler began with an appointment as European
correspondent for several newspapers in 1844. In 1849 he went
to California and was with Perry in Japan in 1853. Taylor served
as secretary of the legation in St. Petersburg for a year and was
appointed Minister to Germany in the year of his death. His
literary works include *Poems of the Orient* (1854), *The Picture of
St. John* (1866), a translation of Goethe's *Faust* (1870–1871), and
Home Pastorals (1875).

FROM CHRISTMAS SONNETS

To G. H. B.[1]

If that my hand, like yours, dear George, were skilled
To win from Wordsworth's scanty plot of ground
A shining harvest, such as you have found,
Where strength and grace, fraternally fulfilled,
As in those sheaves whose rustling glories gild
The hills of August, folded are and bound:
So would I draw my loving tillage round
Its borders, let the gentlest rains be spilled,
The goldenest suns its happy growth compel,
And bind for you the ripe, redundant grain:
But ah! you stand amid your songful sheaves
So rich, this weed-born flower you might disdain,

Save that of me its growth and color tell,
And of my love some perfume haunt its leaves.

[1]G. H. B./George Henry Boker

FRANCES E. W. HARPER
(1825–1911)

Frances Ellen Watkins was born in Baltimore to free Negro parents. Orphaned at an early age, she was raised by her uncle William Watkins, a minister and educator. Active as an abolitionist, she lectured throughout the northeast and as far west as Ohio. Her marriage to Fenton Harper lasted only four years, until his death. From 1871 until her death she lived in Philadelphia. Her *Poems on Miscellaneous Subjects* (1845) was enormously popular. *Iola Leroy; or, Shadows Uplifted* (1892), a novel, is the first novel by a black to deal with the Reconstruction.

She's Free!

How say that by law we may torture and chase
A woman whose crime is the hue of her face?—
With her step on the ice, and her arm on her child,
The danger was fearful, the pathway was wild. . . .
But she's free! yes, free from the land where the slave,
From the hand of oppression, must rest in the grave;
Where bondage and blood, where scourges and chains,
Have placed on our banner indelible stains. . . .
The bloodhounds have miss'd the scent of her way,
The hunter is rifled and foiled of his prey,
The cursing of men and clanking of chains
Make sounds of strange discord on Liberty's plains. . . .
Oh! poverty, danger and death she can brave,
For the child of her love is no longer a slave.

HENRY TIMROD
(1828–1867)

Timrod's poetic output was small, but his war poems earned him a lasting reputation as the "Laureate of the Confederacy." He was born in Charleston, South Carolina, the son of a bookseller, studied at the University of Georgia for a year, read law, acted as a tutor, and finally became a journalist. Illness made Timrod's service in the Confederate Army brief. The only volume of his poems published in his lifetime appeared in 1860; a collection of *The Poems of Henry Timrod* was issued in 1873.

"Most men know love . . ."

Most men know love but as a part of life;
They hide it in some corner of the breast,
Even from themselves; and only when they rest
In the brief pauses of that daily strife,
Wherewith the world might else be not so rife,
They draw it forth (as one draws forth a toy
To soothe some ardent, kiss-exacting boy)
And hold it up to sister, child, or wife.
Ah me! why may not love and life be one?
Why walk we thus alone, when by our side,
Love, like a visible God, might be our guide?
How would the marts grow noble! and the street,
Worn like a dungeon floor by weary feet,
Seem then a golden courtway of the Sun!

DANTE GABRIEL ROSSETTI
(1828–1882)

The son of an Italian patriot who came to England in 1824, Rossetti studied at King's College, London, and at the Royal Academy, where he soon became disillusioned with contemporary fashions in painting. Along with Holman Hunt, John Everett Millais, and others, he formed the Pre-Raphaelite Brotherhood (1848) in reaction to the neoclassical imitativeness of the art of the time. Rossetti married Elizabeth Siddal in 1860 and buried his poems with her when she died in 1862. His reputation as a poet was established by the publication of these disinterred poems in 1870.

FROM THE HOUSE OF LIFE

The Sonnet

A sonnet is a moment's monument—
Memorial from the Soul's eternity
To one dead deathless hour. Look that it be,
Whether for lustral rite or dire portent,
Of its own arduous fullness reverent.
Carve it in ivory or in ebony,
As Day or Night may rule; and let Time see
Its flowering crest impearled and orient.
A sonnet is a coin; its face reveals
The Soul—its converse, to what Power 'tis due:—
Whether for tribute to the august appeals
Of life, or dower in Love's high retinue,
It serve; or 'mid the dark wharf's cavernous breath,
In Charon's palm it pay the toll to Death.

2. Bridal Birth

As when desire, long darkling, dawns, and first
The mother looks upon the newborn child,
Even so my Lady stood at gaze and smiled
When her soul knew at length the Love it nursed.

Born with her life, creature of poignant thirst
And exquisite hunger, at her heart Love lay
Quickening in darkness, till a voice that day
Cried on him, and the bonds of birth were burst.
Now, shadowed by his wings, our faces yearn
Together, as his fullgrown feet now range
The grove, and his warm hands our couch prepare;
Till to his song our bodiless souls in turn
Be born his children, when Death's nuptial change
Leaves us for light the halo of his hair.

6. *The Kiss*

What smoldering senses in death's sick delay
Or seizure of malign vicissitude
Can rob this body of honor, or denude
This soul of wedding raiment worn today?
For lo! even now my lady's lips did play
With these my lips such consonant interlude
As laureled Orpheus longed for when he wooed
The half-drawn hungering face with that last lay.
I was a child beneath her touch,—a man
When breast to breast we clung, even I and she,—
A spirit when her spirit looked through me,—
A god when all our life-breath met to fan
Our life-blood, till love's emulous ardors ran,
Fire within fire, desire in deity.

15. *The Birth-Bond*

Have you not noted, in some family
Where two were born of a first marriage-bed,
How still they own their gracious bond, though fed
And nursed on the forgotten breast and knee?—
How to their father's children they shall be
In act and thought of one goodwill; but each
Shall for the other have, in silence speech,
And in a word complete community?
Even so, when first I saw you, seemed it, love,
That among souls allied to mine was yet
One nearer kindred than life hinted of.

O born with me somewhere that men forget,
And though in years of sight and sound unmet,
Known for my soul's birth-partner well enough!

22. *Heart's Haven*

Sometimes she is a child within mine arms,
Cowering beneath dark wings that love must chase,—
With still tears showering and averted face,
Inexplicably filled with faint alarms:
And oft from mine own spirit's hurtling harms
I crave the refuge of her deep embrace,—
Against all ills the fortified strong place
And sweet reserve of sovereign counter-charms.
And Love, our light at night and shade at noon,
Lulls us to rest with songs, and turns away
All shafts of shelterless tumultuous day.
Like the moon's growth, his face gleams through his tune;
And as soft waters warble to the moon,
Our answering spirits chime one roundelay.

53. *Without Her*

What of her glass without her? The blank gray
There where the pool is blind of the moon's face.
Her dress without her? The tossed empty space
Of cloud-rack whence the moon has passed away.
Her paths without her? Day's appointed sway
Usurped by desolate night. Her pillowed place
Without her? Tears, ah me! for love's good grace,
And cold forgetfulness of night or day.
What of the heart without her? Nay, poor heart,
Of thee what word remains ere speech be still?
A wayfarer by barren ways and chill,
Steep ways and weary, without her thou art,
Where the long cloud, the long wood's counterpart,
Sheds doubled darkness up the laboring hill.

78. Body's Beauty (Lilith)

Of Adam's first wife, Lilith, it is told
(The witch he loved before the gift of Eve),
That, ere the snake's, her sweet tongue could deceive,
And her enchanted hair was the first gold.
And still she sits, young while the earth is old,
And, subtly of herself contemplative,
Draws men to watch the bright web she can weave,
Till heart and body and life are in its hold.
The rose and poppy are her flowers; for where
Is he not found, O Lilith, whom shed scent
And soft-shed kisses and soft sleep shall snare?
Lo! as that youth's eyes burned at thine, so went
Thy spell through him, and left his straight neck bent
And round his heart one strangling golden hair.

GEORGE MEREDITH
(1828–1909)

Meredith was apprenticed to a lawyer, but early turned to journalism and literature. His unhappy marriage to Mary Ellen Nichols, a daughter of Thomas Love Peacock, provided the background for the study of the dissolution of a marriage in *Modern Love* (1862). The sixteen-line poems of this sequence are sufficiently sonnetlike to be considered within the sonnet tradition. Meredith's critical acumen was demonstrated in the essay *On the Idea of Comedy and the Uses of the Comic Spirit* (1877), while his popular fame was assured by such novels as *The Egoist* (1879) and *Diana of the Crossways* (1885).

FROM MODERN LOVE

1. "By this he knew she wept . . ."

By this he knew she wept with waking eyes:
That, at his hand's light quiver by her head,

The strange low sobs that shook their common bed
Were called into her with a sharp surprise,
And strangled mute, like little gaping snakes,
Dreadfully venomous to him. She lay
Stone-still, and the long darkness flowed away
With muffled pulses. Then, as midnight makes
Her giant heart of Memory and Tears
Drink the pale drug of silence, and so beat
Sleep's heavy measure, they from head to feet
Were moveless, looking through their dead black years
By vain regret scrawled over the blank wall.
Like sculptured effigies they might be seen
Upon their marriage tomb, the sword between;
Each wishing for the sword that severs all.

3. "This was the woman . . ."

This was the woman; what now of the man?
But pass him. If he comes beneath a heel,
He shall be crushed until he cannot feel,
Or, being callous, haply till he can.
But he is nothing:—nothing? Only mark
The rich light striking out from her on him!
Ha! what a sense it is when her eyes swim
Across the man she singles, leaving dark
All else! Lord God, who mad'st the thing so fair,
See that I am drawn to her even now!
It cannot be such harm on her cool brow
To put a kiss? Yet if I meet him there!
But she is mine! Ah, no! I know too well
I claim a star whose light is overcast:
I claim a phantom-woman in the past.
The hour has struck, though I heard not the bell!

17. "At dinner, she is hostess . . ."

At dinner, she is hostess, I am host.
Went the feast ever cheerfuller? She keeps
The topic over intellectual deeps
In buoyancy afloat. They see no ghost.

With sparkling surface-eyes we ply the ball:
It is in truth a most contagious game:
Hiding the Skeleton, shall be its name.
Such play as this the devils might appal!
But here's the greater wonder: in that we,
Enamored of an acting naught can tire,
Each other, like true hypocrites, admire;
Warm-lighted looks, Love's ephemeridæ,
Shoot gaily o'er the dishes and the wine.
We waken envy of our happy lot.
Fast, sweet, and golden, shows the marriage knot.
Dear guests, you now have seen Love's corpse light shine.

50. "Thus piteously Love closed . . ."

Thus piteously Love closed what he begat:
The union of this ever-diverse pair!
These two were rapid falcons in a snare,
Condemned to do the flitting of the bat.
Lovers beneath the singing sky of May,
They wandered once; clear as the dew on flowers:
But they fed not on the advancing hours:
Their hearts held cravings for the buried day.
Then each applied to each that fatal knife,
Deep questioning, which probes to endless dole.
Ah, what a dusty answer gets the soul
When hot for certainties in this our life!—
In tragic hints here see what evermore
Moves dark as yonder midnight ocean's force,
Thundering like ramping hosts of warrior horse,
To throw that faint thin line upon the shore!

Lucifer in Starlight

On a starred night Prince Lucifer uprose.
Tired of his dark dominion, swung the fiend
Above the rolling ball, in cloud part screened,
Where sinners hugged their specter of repose.
Poor prey to his hot fit of pride were those.
And now upon his western wing he leaned,
Now his huge bulk o'er Afric's sands careened,
Now the black planet shadowed Arctic snows.

Soaring through wider zones that pricked his scars
With memory of the old revolt from Awe,
He reached a middle height, and at the stars,
Which are the brain of heaven, he looked, and sank.
Around the ancient track marched, rank on rank,
The army of unalterable law.

CHRISTINA ROSSETTI
(1830–1894)

Christina Rossetti, Dante Gabriel Rossetti's sister, contributed to the Pre-Raphaelite periodical *The Germ* and published her first book of poetry, *The Goblin Market and Other Poems,* in 1862. Most of her poetry was religious in nature; the relative seclusion of her life was reinforced by illness after 1871.

FROM MONNA INNOMINATA,[1] A SONNET OF SONNETS

2. *"I wish I could remember . . ."*

I wish I could remember that first day,
    First hour, first moment of your meeting me,
    If bright or dim the season, it might be
Summer or winter for aught I can say;
So unrecorded did it slip away,
    So blind was I to see and to foresee,
    So dull to mark the budding of my tree
That would not blossom yet for many a May.
If only I could recollect it, such
    A day of days! I let it come and go
    As traceless as a thaw of bygone snow;
It seemed to mean so little, meant so much;
If only now I could recall that touch,
    First touch of hand in hand—Did one but know!

[1] *Monna Innominata*/My Nameless Lady

7. " 'Love me, for I love you' . . ."

"Love me, for I love you"—and answer me,
    "Love me, for I love you": so shall we stand
    As happy equals in the flowering land
Of love, that knows not a dividing sea.
Love builds the house on rock and not on sand,
    Love laughs what while the winds rave desperately;
And who hath found love's citadel unmanned?
    And who hath held in bonds love's liberty?—
My heart's a coward though my words are brave—
    We meet so seldom, yet we surely part
    So often; there's a problem for your art!
    Still I find comfort in his Book who saith,
Though jealousy be cruel as the grave,
    And death be strong, yet love is strong as death.

14. "Youth gone, and beauty gone . . ."

Youth gone, and beauty gone if ever there
    Dwelt beauty in so poor a face as this;
    Youth gone and beauty, what remains of bliss?
I will not bind fresh roses in my hair,
To shame a cheek at best but little fair,—
    Leave youth his roses, who can bear a thorn,—
I will not seek for blossoms anywhere,
    Except such common flowers as blow with corn.
Youth gone and beauty gone, what doth remain?
The longing of a heart pent up forlorn,
        A silent heart whose silence loves and longs;
        The silence of a heart which sang its songs
While youth and beauty made a summer morn,
Silence of love that cannot sing again.

FROM LATER LIFE: A DOUBLE SONNET OF SONNETS

1. *"Before the mountains were brought forth . . ."*

Before the mountains were brought forth, before
    Earth and the world were made, then God was God:
And God will still be God when flames shall roar
    Round earth and heaven dissolving at His nod:
    And this God is our God, even while His rod
Of righteous wrath falls on us smiting sore:
And this God is our God for evermore,
    Through life, through death, while clod returns to clod.
For though He slay us we will trust in Him;
    We will flock home to Him by divers ways:
    Yea, though He slay us we will vaunt His praise,
Serving and loving with the Cherubim,
Watching and loving with the Seraphim,
    Our very selves His praise through endless days.

7. *"To love and to remember . . ."*

To love and to remember; that is good:
    To love and to forget; that is not well:
    To lapse from love to hatred; that is hell
And death and torment, rightly understood.
Soul dazed by love and sorrow, cheer thy mood;
    More blessed art thou than mortal tongue can tell:
    Ring not thy funeral but thy marriage bell,
And salt with hope thy life's insipid food.
Love is the goal, love is the way we wend,
    Love is our parallel unending line
        Whose only perfect Parallel is Christ,
Beginning not begun, End without end:
        For he Who hath the Heart of God sufficed
    Can satisfy all hearts,—yea, thine and mine.

26. *"This Life is full of numbness . . ."*

This Life is full of numbness and of balk,
  Of haltingness and baffled shortcoming,
  Of promise unfulfilled, of everything
That is puffed vanity and empty talk:
Its very bud hangs cankered on the stalk,
  Its very songbird trails a broken wing,
  Its very Spring is not indeed like Spring,
But sighs like Autumn round an aimless walk.
This Life we live is dead for all its breath;
  Death's self it is, set off on pilgrimage,
    Traveling with tottering steps the first short stage;
      The second stage is one mere desert dust
      Where Death sits veiled amid creation's rust:
Unveil thy face, O Death who art not Death.

THEODORE WATTS-DUNTON
(1832–1914)

A critic, novelist, and poet, Watts-Dunton practiced law in London, where he became friendly with many of the Pre-Raphaelite group. He wrote for the *Examiner* and the *Athenaeum*. Although *The Coming of Love, and Other Poems* (1897) and his novel *Aylwin* (1898) attracted considerable attention, Watts-Dunton is best known today for his association with Dante Gabriel Rossetti and above all with Swinburne, whom he cared for in his home from 1879 until Swinburne's death in 1909.

Coleridge

I see thee pine like her in golden story
  Who, in her prison, woke and saw, one day,
  The gates thrown open—saw the sunbeams play,
With only a web 'tween her and summer's glory;
Who, when that web—so frail, so transitory,
  It broke before her breath—had fallen away,
  Saw other webs and others rise for aye
Which kept her prisoned till her hair was hoary.

Those songs half-sung that yet were all-divine—
    That woke Romance, the queen, to reign afresh—
Had been but preludes from that lyre of thine,
    Could thy rare spirit's wings have pierced the mesh
    Spun by the wizard who compels the flesh,
But lets the poet see how heaven can shine.

THOMAS BAILEY ALDRICH
(1836–1907)

Born in Portsmouth, New Hampshire, of an old New England family, Aldrich began his literary career in New York City, where he held a series of editorial jobs. At the beginning of the Civil War, he served as a war correspondent. In 1865 he married, moved to Boston, and became editor of *Every Saturday*. In 1881 he became editor of the *Atlantic Monthly,* a post he held until his retirement in 1890. His poetry is little read today, and *The Story of a Bad Boy* (1870) is probably his best remembered work.

By the Potomac

The soft new grass is creeping o'er the graves
    By the Potomac; and the crisp ground-flower
    Lifts its blue cup to catch the passing shower;
The pinecone ripens, and the long moss waves
Its tangled gonfalons above our braves.
    Hark, what a burst of music from yon bower!—
    The Southern nightingale that, hour by hour,
In its melodious summer madness raves.
Ah, with what delicate touches of her hand,
    With what sweet voices, Nature seeks to screen
The awful Crime of this distracted land,—
    Sets her birds singing, while she spreads her green
Mantle of velvet where the Murdered lie,
As if to hide the horror from God's eye.

ALGERNON CHARLES SWINBURNE
(1837–1909)

Swinburne was educated at Eton and at Balliol College, Oxford. Leaving Oxford without a degree in 1861, he became friendly with Rossetti and others of the Pre-Raphaelite circle. The publication of *Atalanta in Calydon* (1865) made him famous; his popular reputation for dissipation and *Poems and Ballads* (1866) made him infamous. *Songs Before Sunrise* (1871) reasserted Swinburne's love of liberty, his hate for priests and kings. His interest in Elizabethan and Jacobean literature is seen in his critical writings as well as in his poetry.

On the Russian Persecution of the Jews

O son of man, by lying tongues adored,
  By slaughterous hands of slaves with feet red-shod
  In carnage deep as ever Christian trod
Profaned with prayer and sacrifice abhorred
And incense from the trembling tyrant's horde,
  Brute worshipers or wielders of the rod,
  Most murderous even of all that call thee God,
Most treacherous even that ever called thee Lord;
Face loved of little children long ago,
  Head hated of the priests and rulers then,
    If thou see this, or hear these hounds of thine
    Run ravening as the Gadarean swine,
Say, was not this thy Passion, to foreknow
  In death's worst hour the works of Christian men?

FROM SONNETS OF ENGLISH DRAMATIC POETS

Christopher Marlowe

Crowned, girdled, garbed and shod with light and fire,
  Son first-born of the morning, sovereign star!
  Soul nearest ours of all, that wert most far,
Most far off in the abysm of time, thy lyre
Hung highest above the dawn-enkindled quire
  Where all ye sang together, all that are,

And all the starry songs behind thy car
Rang sequence, all our souls acclaim thee sire.
"If all the pens that ever poets held
   Had fed the feeling of their masters' thoughts,"
   And as with rush of hurtling chariots
The flight of all their spirits were impelled
   Toward one great end, thy glory—nay, not then,
   Not yet might'st thou be praised enough of men.

Ben Jonson

Broad-based, broad-fronted, bounteous, multiform,
   With many a valley impleached with ivy and vine,
   Wherein the springs of all the streams run wine,
And many a crag full-faced against the storm,
The mountain where thy Muse's feet made warm
   Those lawns that reveled with her dance divine
   Shines yet with fire as it was wont to shine
From tossing torches round the dance aswarm.
Nor less, high-stationed on the gray grave heights,
High-thoughted seers with heaven's heart-kindling lights
   Hold converse; and the herd of meaner things
Knows or by fiery scourge or fiery shaft
When wrath on thy broad brows has risen, and laughed,
   Darkening thy soul with shadow of thunderous wings.

John Webster

Thunder: the flesh quails, and the soul bows down.
   Night: east, west, south, and northward, very night.
   Star upon struggling star strives into sight,
Star after shuddering star the deep storms drown.
The very throne of night, her very crown,
   A man lays hand on, and usurps her right.
   Song from the highest of heaven's imperious height
Shoots, as a fire to smite some towering town.
Rage, anguish, harrowing fear, heart-crazing crime,
Make monstrous all the murderous face of Time
   Shown in the spheral orbit of a glass
Revolving. Earth cries out from all her graves.
Frail, on frail rafts, across wide-wallowing waves,
   Shapes here and there of child and mother pass.

John Addington Symonds
(1840–1893)

Critic, poet, essayist, and translator, Symonds studied at Harrow and at Balliol College, Oxford. Much of his life was spent in Italy, and his most significant work was the seven volume *History of the Renaissance in Italy* (1875–1886). His collections of verse included *Many Moods* (1878), *New and Old* (1880), and *Animi Figura* (1882).

"Rebuke me not . . ."

Rebuke me not! I have nor wish nor skill
  To alter one hair's breath in all this house
  Of love, rising with domes so luminous
And air-built galleries on life's topmost hill!
Only I know that fate, chance, years that kill,
  Change that transmutes, have aimed their darts at us;
  Envying each lovely shrine and amorous
Reared on earth's soil by man's too passionate will.
Dread thou the moment when these glittering towers,
  These adamantine walls and gates of gems,
  Shall fade like forms of sun-forsaken cloud;
When dulled by imperceptible chill hours,
  The golden spires of our Jerusalems
  Shall melt to mist and vanish in night's shroud!

To Night, the Mother of Sleep and Death

Oh Mother, holiest Mother, Mother Night!
  Thou on thy marble throne of ebon hue
  Hast still the everlasting stars in view,
  The slumbering earth and dusk heavens infinite!
Turn thou those veiled eyes where never light
  Shone rudely yet, but dim purpureal blue
  Broods in the dawn of moonbeams, on these two
  Dread angels folded on thy bosom white:—
Sleep and his twin-born Death, entwined, embraced;
  Mingling soft breath, deep dreams, dark poppied hair;
  Lips pressed to lips, and hands in hands enlaced;

Thy children and our comforters, the pair
  From whom poor men, by earth enslaved, debased,
  Find freedom and surmount their life's despair!

WILFRID SCAWEN BLUNT
(1840–1922)

After study at Stonyhurst and at Oscott, Blunt entered the
diplomatic service, in which he remained until his marriage in
1869. He and his wife traveled widely; and in 1881 he bought a
house outside Cairo, where he lived in the manner of an Arab
patriarch. In addition to his poems, he wrote books of travel,
contemporary history, and politics. *Sonnets and Songs of Pro-
teus* was published in 1875, the sonnet sequence *Esther* in 1892.

FROM THE LOVE SONNETS OF PROTEUS

8. *As to His Choice of Her*

If I had chosen thee, thou shouldst have been
A virgin proud, untamed, immaculate,
Chaste as the morning star, a saint, a queen,
Scarred by no wars, no violence of hate.
Thou shouldst have been of soul commensurate
With thy fair body, brave and virtuous
And kind and just; and, if of poor estate,
At least an honest woman for my house.
I would have had thee come of honored blood
And honorable nature. Thou shouldst bear
Sons to my pride and daughters to my heart,
And men should hold thee happy, wise, and good.
Lo, thou art none of this, but only fair.
Yet must I love thee, dear, and as thou art.

49. "A 'woman with a past'..."

A "woman with a past." What happier omen
Could heart desire for mistress or for friend?
Phœnix of friends, and most divine of women,
Skilled in all fence to venture or defend
And with love's science at your fingers' end,
No tears to vex, no ignorance to bore,
A fancy ripe, the zest which sorrows lend!—
I would to God we had not met before!
—I would to God! and yet to God I would
That we had never met. To see you thus
Is grief and wounds and poison to my blood.
Oh, this is sacrilege and foul abuse.
You were a thing for honor not vile use,
Not for the mad world's wicked sinks and stews.

FROM ESTHER, A YOUNG MAN'S TRAGEDY

49. "I will not tell the secrets..."

I will not tell the secrets of that place.
    When Madame Blanche returned to us again
I was kneeling there, while Esther kissed my face
    And dried and comforted my tears. O vain
And happy tears! O griefs thrice comforted!
    I trembled, but not with fear. If I was dumb,
'Twas not for lack of speech where all was said.
    My doubts were ended and my fears o'ercome,
And joy had triumphed. Life has given me much
    And pleasure much, and Heaven may yet have store
Of nobler hopes to kindle and to touch,
    But never for all time, ah, never more,
That delicate dawn of wonder when lips move
First to the love of life and love of love.

SIDNEY LANIER
(1842–1881)

Born in Macon, Georgia, Lanier attended Oglethorpe University and served in the Confederate Army. In addition to his *Poems* of 1877, Lanier published *The Boy's Froissart* (1879), *The Boy's King Arthur* (1880), and *The Science of English Verse* (1880), a collection of lectures on versification which he had delivered at Johns Hopkins University. Poems like the "Song of the Chattahoochee" and "The Marshes of Glynn" show Lanier's interest in the union of music and poetry.

Laus Mariæ

Across the brook of Time man leaping goes
  On steppingstones of epochs, that uprise
Fixed, memorable, 'midst broad shallow flows
  Of neutrals, kill-times, sleeps, indifferences.
So 'twixt each morn and night rise salient heaps:
  Some cross with but a zigzag, jaded pace
From meal to meal: some with convulsive leaps
  Shake the green treacherous tussocks of disgrace;
And some advance, by system and deep art,
  O'er vantages of wealth, place, learning, tact.
But thou within thyself, dear manifold Heart,
  Dost bind all epochs in one dainty Fact.
    Oh, Sweet, my pretty Sum of history,
    I leaped the breadth of Time in loving thee!

"Whate'er has been . . ."

Whate'er has been, is, shall be—rind, pulp, core,
  O' the big and pied Eve's-apple of our life—
Thou gav'st: I ate, learned good and evil lore,
  And then was as a God, O Eve, O wife.
For who knows good, knows how the gods do grow,
  And feeds on fruits that godlike tissues build:
And who knows ill, in truth but good doth know,
  Ill is but good, wounding a hand unskilled.

Thus known, my Good brings double good alway,
  As bringing roses intermixed with fruit;
And Ill—tame viper—round my neck doth play,
  His fair white fangs not venom-bagged at root.
    Yea, thou, O sweeter Eve! my soul hast fed,
    And tamed, yet bruised not, the serpent's head.

ROBERT SEYMOUR BRIDGES
(1844–1930)

Robert Bridges attended Eton and Oxford and studied medicine
at St. Bartholomew's Hospital. His sonnet sequence *The Growth
of Love* was published anonymously in 1876, and two more
volumes of poems appeared in 1879 and 1880. In 1881 he retired
from medical practice and devoted himself entirely to literature.
Eros and Psyche, a long narrative poem, was published in 1885.
In 1913 he was appointed poet laureate. His eighty-fifth birthday
was marked by the publication of *The Testament of Beauty.*

FROM THE GROWTH OF LOVE

3. *"The whole world now . . ."*

The whole world now is but the minister
Of thee to me: I see no other scheme
But universal love, from timeless dream
Waking to thee his joy's interpreter.
I walk around and in the fields confer
Of love at large with tree and flower and stream,
And list the lark descant upon my theme,
Heaven's musical accepted worshiper.

  Thy smile outfaceth ill: and that old feud
'Twixt things and me is quashed in our new truce;
And nature now dearly with thee endued
No more in shame ponders her old excuse,
But quite forgets her frowns and antics rude,
So kindly hath she grown to her new use.

30. "My lady pleases me . . ."

My lady pleases me and I please her;
This know we both, and I besides know well
Wherefore I love her, and I love to tell
My love, as all my loving songs aver.
But what on her part could the passion stir,
Though 'tis more difficult for love to spell,
Yet can I dare divine how this befell,
Nor will her lips deny it if I err.

She loves me first because I love her, then
Loves me for knowing why she should be loved,
And that I love to praise her, loves again.
So from her beauty both our loves are moved,
And by her beauty are sustained; nor when
The earth falls from the sun is this disproved.

GERARD MANLEY HOPKINS
(1844–1889)

Hopkins was educated at Balliol College, Oxford, where he
studied under Walter Pater and had Robert Bridges for a friend.
Converted to Roman Catholicism, he became a Jesuit in 1868
and burned all his early poetry. He served in the slums of
Liverpool, in a church at Oxford, and finally was appointed to
the chair of Greek at Dublin University. He resumed his poetic
activity in Ireland and corresponded with Bridges and Coventry
Patmore. His poems, none of which were published in his life-
time, were collected and edited by Robert Bridges in 1918.
Hopkins's sonnets are notable for their structural variety and
experimentation.

God's Grandeur

The world is charged with the grandeur of God.
  It will flame out, like shining from shook foil;
  It gathers to a greatness, like the ooze of oil
Crushed. Why do men then now not reck his rod?

Generations have trod, have trod, have trod;
   And all is seared with trade; bleared, smeared with toil,
   And wears man's smudge and shares man's smell—the soil
Is bare now, nor can foot feel, being shod.

And for all this, nature is never spent;
   There lives the dearest freshness deep down things;
And though the last lights off the black West went
   Oh, morning, at the brown brink eastward, springs—
Because the Holy Ghost over the bent
   World broods with warm breast and with ah! bright wings.

The Caged Skylark

As a dare-gale skylark scanted in a dull cage
Man's mounting spirit in his bone-house, mean house, dwells—
That bird beyond the remembering his free fells;
This in drudgery, day-laboring-out life's age.

Though aloft on turf or perch or poor low stage,
Both sing sometímes the sweetest, sweetest spells,
Yet both droop deadly sómetimes in their cells
Or wring their barriers in bursts of fear or rage.

Not that the sweet-fowl, song-fowl, needs no rest—
Why, hear him, hear him babble and drop down to his nest,
But his own nest, wild nest, no prison.

Man's spirit will be flesh-bound when found at best,
But uncumbered: meadow-down is not distressed
For a rainbow footing it nor he for his bónes rísen.

Felix Randal

Felix Randal the farrier, O he is dead then? my duty all ended,
Who have watched his mold of man, big-boned and hardy-
    handsome
Pining, pining, till time when reason rambled in it and some
Fatal four disorders, fleshed there, all contended?

Sickness broke him. Impatient he cursed at first, but mended
Being anointed and all; though a heavenlier heart began some

Months earlier, since I had our sweet reprieve and ransom
Tendered to him. Ah well, God rest him all road ever he
        offended!

This seeing the sick endears them to us, us too it endears.
My tongue had taught thee comfort, touch had quenched thy
        tears,
Thy tears that touched my heart, child, Felix, poor Felix
        Randal;

How far from then forethought of, all thy more boisterous
        years,
When thou at the random grim forge, powerful amidst peers,
Didst fettle for the great gray drayhorse his bright and battering
        sandal!

Carrion Comfort

Not, I'll not, carrion comfort, Despair, not feast on thee;
Not untwist—slack they may be—these last strands of man
In me ór, most weary, cry *I can no more*. I can;
Can something, hope, wish day come, not choose not to be.
But ah, but O thou terrible, why wouldst thou rude on me
Thy wring-world right foot rock? lay a lionlimb against me?
        scan
With darksome devouring eyes my bruisèd bones? and fan,
O in turns of tempest, me heaped there; me frantic to avoid
        thee and flee?

  Why? That my chaff might fly; my grain lie, sheer and clear.
Nay in all that toil, that coil, since (seems) I kissed the rod,
Hand rather, my heart lo! lapped strength, stole joy, would
        laugh, chéer.
Cheer whom though? the hero whose heaven-handling flung
        me, fóot tród
Me? or me that fought him? O which one? is it each one? That
        night, that year
Of now done darkness I wretch lay wrestling with (my God!)
        my God.

Tom's Garland: upon the Unemployed[1]

Tom—garlanded with squat and surely steel
Tom; then Tom's fallowbootfellow piles pick
By him and rips out rockfire homeforth—sturdy Dick;
Tom Heart-at-ease, Tom Navvy: he is all for his meal
Sure, 's bed now. Low be it: lustily he his low lot (feel
That ne'er need hunger, Tom; Tom seldom sick,
Seldomer heartsore; that treads through, prickproof, thick
Thousands of thorns, thoughts) swings though. Commonweal

Little I reck ho! lacklevel in, if all had bread:
What! Country is honor enough in all us—lordly head,
With heaven's lights high hung round, or, mother-ground
That mammocks, mighty foot. But nó way sped,
Nor mind nor mainstrength; gold go garlanded
With, perilous, O nó; nor yet plod safe shod sound;
                Undenizened, beyond bound
Of earth's glory, earth's ease, all; no one, nowhere
In wide the world's weal; rare gold, bold steel, bare
              In both; care, but share care—
This, by Despair, bred Hangdog dull; by Rage,
Manwolf, worse; and their packs infest the age.

[1] Tom's Garland/This sonnet has two "codas" and is modeled on
Milton's "caudated" "On the New Forcers of Conscience . . ."

"Patience, hard thing! . . ."

Patience, hard thing! the hard thing but to pray,
But bid for, Patience is! Patience who asks
Wants war, wants wounds; weary his times, his tasks;
To do without, take tosses, and obey.
   Rare patience roots in these, and, these away,
Nowhere. Natural heart's ivy, Patience masks
Our ruins of wrecked past purpose. There she basks
Purple eyes and seas of liquid leaves all day.

We hear our hearts grate on themselves: it kills
To bruise them dearer. Yet the rebellious wills
Of us we do bid God bend to him even so.

And where is he who more and more distills
Delicious kindness?—He is patient. Patience fills
His crisp combs, and that comes those ways we know.

EUGENE LEE-HAMILTON
(1845–1907)

Eugene Lee-Hamilton was born in London, but received his early education in France and Germany. After leaving Oxford, he entered the diplomatic service, from which he resigned in 1875 because of illness. Completely incapacitated and forced to remain on his back, he devoted himself to poetry. *Imaginary Sonnets* appeared in 1888 and the autobiographical *Sonnets of the Wingless Hours* in 1894. By 1896 he had regained his health, visited Canada and the United States, and in 1898 he married. His grief at the death of his infant daughter is reflected in *Mimma Bella* (1909).

FROM IMAGINARY SONNETS

Luther to a Bluebottle Fly (1540)

Ay, buzz and buzz away. Dost thou suppose
  I know not who thou art, who all today
  Hast vexed and plagued me, as I write and pray,
And dared to settle on my very nose?

Thou thinkest thou canst trip me while I doze?
  Each time I snatch at thee thou slipp'st away;
  But wait till my next sermon: I will lay
Thee in the dust, thou Father of all Foes.

Ay, buzz about my Bible. But I wot,
  Unless thou wish to shrivel, thou'lt not dare
To settle on the page, thou live blue blot!

Out, Beelzebub, or thou wilt make me swear.
  Buzz back to Hell: old Martin fears thee not,
Thou god of Flies, though thou shouldst fill the air!

What the Sonnet Is

Fourteen small broidered berries on the hem
  Of Circe's mantle, each of magic gold;
  Fourteen of lone Calypso's tears that rolled
Into the sea, for pearls to come of them;

Fourteen clear signs of omen in the gem
  With which Medea human fate foretold;
  Fourteen small drops, which Faustus, growing old,
Craved of the Fiend, to water Life's dry stem.

It is the pure white diamond Dante brought
  To Beatrice; the sapphire Laura wore
When Petrarch cut it sparkling out of thought;

The ruby Shakespeare hewed from his heart's core;
  The dark, deep emerald that Rossetti wrought
For his own soul, to wear for evermore.

ALICE CHRISTINA MEYNELL
(1847–1922)

Alice Meynell was educated by her father, Thomas James
Thompson, and became a Catholic when he was converted.
Aubrey De Vere encouraged the publication of her first volume,
Preludes (1875). In 1877 she married Wilfrid Meynell and as-
sisted him in his journalistic activities. *The Color of Life,* a
collection of essays published in 1896, was praised by George
Meredith and Coventry Patmore. Her poems reflect the depth of
her religious feeling.

To a Daisy

Slight as thou art, thou art enough to hide,
  Like all created things, secrets from me,
  And stand a barrier to eternity.
And I, how can I praise thee well and wide
From where I dwell—upon the hither side?

Thou little veil for so great mystery,
  When shall I penetrate all things and thee,
And then look back? For this I must abide,
Till thou shalt grow and fold and be unfurled
Literally between me and the world.
  Then I shall drink from in beneath a spring,
And from a poet's side shall read his book.
O daisy mine, what will it be to look
  From God's side even on such a simple thing?

Renouncement

I must not think of thee; and, tired yet strong,
  I shun the thought that lurks in all delight—
  The thought of thee—and in the blue Heaven's height,
And in the sweetest passage of a song.

O just beyond the fairest thoughts that throng
  This breast, the thought of thee waits hidden yet bright;
  But it must never, never come in sight;
I must stop short of thee the whole day long.

But when sleep comes to close each difficult day,
  When night gives pause to the long watch I keep,
    And all my bonds I needs must loose apart,

Must doff my will as raiment laid away,
  With the first dream that comes with the first sleep
    I run, I run, I am gathered to thy heart.

EMMA LAZARUS
(1849–1887)

Born in New York, Emma Lazarus was a poet and essayist. Her early poems appeared in the volume *Admetus and Other Poems* (1871). She lectured and wrote poems advocating Jewish causes, and in 1882 she published *Songs of a Semite*. Her famous poem is engraved on the pedestal of the Statue of Liberty.

The New Colossus

Not like the brazen giant of Greek fame,
With conquering limbs astride from land to land,
Here at our sea-washed, sunset-gates shall stand
A mighty woman with a torch, whose flame
Is the imprisoned lightning, and her name
Mother of Exiles. From her beacon-hand
Glows world-wide welcome, her mild eyes command
The air-bridged harbor that twin-cities frame.
"Keep, ancient lands, your storied pomp!" cries she,
With silent lips. "Give me your tired, your poor,
Your huddled masses yearning to breathe free,
The wretched refuse of your teeming shore,
Send these, the homeless, tempest-tost to me,
I lift my lamp beside the golden door!"

HENRIETTA CORDELIA RAY
(1850–1916)

Daughter of a distinguished minister and abolitionist, Henrietta Cordelia Ray was born in Falmouth, Massachusetts. She was raised in New York where she attended New York University and the Sauveveur School of Languages. Proficient in Greek, Latin, French, and German, she taught for many years in Grammar School Number 80. Her works include *Sonnets* (1893) and *Poems* (1910).

Robert G. Shaw[1]

When War's red banner trailed along the sky,
And many a manly heart grew all aflame
With patriotic love and purest aim,
There rose a noble soul who dared to die,
If only Right could win. He heard the cry
Of struggling bondmen and he quickly came,
Leaving the haunts where Learning tenders fame
Unto her honored sons; for it was ay
A loftier cause that lured him on to death.
Brave men who saw their brothers held in chains,
Beneath his standard battled ardently.
O friend! O hero! thou who yielded breath
That others might share Freedom's priceless gains,
In rev'rent love we guard thy memory.

[1] Robert Gould Shaw (1837–1863), born in Boston, a white abolitionist, as colonel led the 54th Massachusetts Regiment of Negro troops in the attack on Fort Wagner at Charleston, South Carolina, in which he was killed.

To My Father[1]

A leaf from Freedom's golden chaplet fair,
We bring to thee, dear father. Near her shrine
None came with holier purpose, nor was thine
Alone the soul's mute sanction; every prayer
Thy captive brother uttered found a share

In thy wide sympathy; to every sigh
That told the bondman's need thou didst incline.
No thought of guerdon hadst thou but to bear
A long part in Freedom's strife. To see
Sad lives illumined, fetters rent in twain,
Tears dried in eyes that wept for length of days—
Ah! was not that a recompense for thee?
And now where all life's mystery is plain,
Divine approval is thy sweetest praise.

[1] Rev. Charles B. Ray

OSCAR WILDE
(1856–1900)

Wilde studied at Trinity College, Dublin, and was graduated from Oxford in 1878. He quickly became a public figure, the colorful exponent of aestheticism; in 1882 he made a lecture tour of the United States. The larger portion of his dramatic, poetic, and prose work appeared between 1888 and 1895, when scandal and imprisonment ended his career. *The Picture of Dorian Gray,* a novel, was published in 1891; among his finest comedies were *Lady Windermere's Fan* (1892) and *The Importance of Being Earnest* (1895). After release from prison in 1897, he moved to France.

Hélas[1]

To drift with every passion till my soul
Is a stringed lute on which all winds can play
Is it for this that I have given away
Mine ancient wisdom, and austere control?
Methinks my life is a twice-written scroll
Scrawled over on some boyish holiday
With idle songs for pipe and virelay,
Which do but mar the secret of the whole.
Surely there was a time I might have trod
The sunlit heights, and from life's dissonance

Struck one clear chord to reach the ears of God:
Is that time dead? lo! with a little rod
I did but touch the honey of romance—
And must I lose a soul's inheritance?

[1] *Hélas*/Alas!

E Tenebris[1]

Come down, O Christ, and help me! reach thy hand,
    For I am drowning in a stormier sea
    Than Simon on thy lake of Galilee:
The wine of life is spilt upon the sand,
My heart is as some famine-murdered land
    Whence all good things have perished utterly,
    And well I know my soul in Hell must lie
If I this night before God's throne should stand.
"He sleeps perchance, or rideth to the chase,
    Like Baal, when his prophets howled that name
    From morn to noon on Carmel's smitten height."
Nay, peace, I shall behold, before the night,
    The feet of brass, the robe more white than flame,
The wounded hands, the weary human face.

[1] *E Tenebris*/"Out of darkness"

Francis Thompson
(1859–1907)

Thompson, a Roman Catholic, attended Ushaw College, where his religious faith was encouraged and strengthened. After a brief attempt at studying medicine, he went to London, where he failed to earn a living and through illness and opium was reduced to utter destitution, In 1888 he sent two poems to *Merry England*, a magazine edited by Wilfrid Meynell. With the aid of the Meynells he was rescued from opium addiction, and his first collection of verse was published in 1893. His best known poem is "The Hound of Heaven."

All's Vast

O nothing, in this corporal earth of man,
   That to the imminent heaven of his high soul
Responds with color and with shadow, can
   Lack correlated greatness. If the scroll
Where thoughts lie fast in spell of hieroglyph
   Be mighty through its mighty inhabitants;
If God be in His Name; grave potence if
   The sounds unbind of hieratic chants;
All's vast that vastness means. Nay, I affirm
   Nature is whole in her least things exprest,
Nor know we with what scope God builds the worm.
    Our towns are copied fragments from our breast;
     And all man's Babylons strive but to impart
     The grandeurs of his Babylonian heart.

Ad Amicam

Dear Dove, that bear'st to my sole-laboring ark
   The olive branch of so long wished rest,
When the white solace glimmers through my dark
   Of nearing wings, what comfort in my breast!
Oh, may that doubted day not come, not come,
   When you shall fail, my heavenly messenger,
And drift into the distance and the doom
   Of all my impermissible things that were!

Rather than so, now make the sad farewell,
  Which yet may be with not too-pained pain,
Lest I again the acquainted tale should tell
  Of sharpest loss that pays for shortest gain.
    Ah, if my heart should hear no white wings thrill
    Against its waiting window, open still!

ERNEST DOWSON
(1867–1900)

Dowson lived a brief, irregular life in London after leaving Oxford in 1887. The fine lyrics of his *Verses* (1896) epitomize the spirit of the *fin de siècle*. "*Non Sum Qualis Eram Sub Regno Cynarae*," with its refrain of "I have been faithful to thee, Cynara! in my fashion," is undoubtedly his best-known poem.

To One in Bedlam

With delicate, mad hands, behind his sordid bars,
Surely he hath his posies, which they tear and twine;
Those scentless wisps of straw, that miserably line
His strait, caged universe, whereat the dull world stares,
Pedant and pitiful. Oh, how his rapt gaze wars
With their stupidity! Know they what dreams divine
Lift his long, laughing reveries like enchanted wine,
And make his melancholy germane to the stars?
O lamentable brother! if those pity thee,
Am I not fain of all thy lone eyes promise me;
Half a fool's kingdom, far from men who sow and reap,
All their days, vanity? Better than mortal flowers,
Thy moon-kissed roses seem: better than love or sleep,
The star-crowned solitude of thine oblivious hours!

Gray Nights

A while we wandered (thus it is I dream!)
Through a long, sandy track of No Man's Land,
Where only poppies grew among the sand,

The which we, plucking, cast with scant esteem,
And ever sadlier, into the sad stream,
Which followed us, as we went, hand in hand,
Under the estranged stars, a road unplanned,
Seeing all things in the shadow of a dream.
And ever sadlier, as the stars expired,
We found the poppies rarer, till thine eyes
Grown all my light, to light me were too tired,
And at their darkening, that no surmise
Might haunt me of the lost days we desired,
After them all I flung those memories!

TRUMBULL STICKNEY
(1874–1904)

Born in Geneva, Switzerland, Stickney immigrated with his family to the United States when he was five years old. He was graduated from Harvard in 1895 and then went to France to study at the Sorbonne. After the publication of a book of poems, he was invited to come back to Harvard as an instructor. About to be married, with a promising career before him, he died at the age of thirty of a brain tumor. His work has been praised by a number of contemporary poets.

Mt. Lykaion

Alone on Lykaion since man hath been
Stand on the height two columns, where at rest
Two eagles hewn of gold sit looking east
Forever; and the sun goes up between.
Far down around the mountain's oval green
An order keeps the falling stones abreast.
Below within the chaos last and least
A river like a curl of light is seen.
Beyond the river lies the even sea,
Beyond the sea another ghost of sky,—
O God, support the sickness of my eye
Lest the far space and long antiquity

Suck out my heart, and on this awful ground
The great wind kill my little shell with sound.

On Some Shells Found Inland

These are my murmur-laden shells that keep
A fresh voice though the years lie very gray.
The wave that washed their lips and tuned their lay
Is gone, gone with the faded ocean sweep,
The royal tide, gray ebb and sunken neap
And purple midday,—gone! To this hot clay
Must sing my shells, where yet the primal day,
Its roar and rhythm and splendor will not sleep.
What hand shall join them to their proper sea
If all be gone? Shall they forever feel
Glories undone and worlds that cannot be?—
'T were mercy to stamp out this aged wrong,
Dash them to earth and crunch them with the heel
And make a dust of their seraphic song.

PART FOUR

The Twentieth Century

THOMAS HARDY
(1840–1928)

Hardy's father was a building contractor and at an early age Hardy was apprenticed to an ecclesiastical architect. He first began writing poetry, but turned to novels when no one published his poems. After *Jude the Obscure* (1895) was badly received, Hardy turned from novels back to poetry. He published *Wessex Poems* in 1898, *Poems of the Past and Present* in 1902. His Napoleonic epic drama, *The Dynasts*, was published from 1903 to 1904. Other volumes include *Satires of Circumstance* (1914) and *Late Lyrics and Earlier* (1922).

Hap

If but some vengeful god would call to me
From up the sky, and laugh: "Thou suffering thing,
Know that thy sorrow is my ecstasy,
That thy love's loss is my hate's profiting."
Then would I bear it, clench myself, and die,
Steeled by the sense of ire unmerited;
Half-eased in that a Powerfuller than I
Had willed and meted me the tears I shed.

But not so. How arrives it joy lies slain,
And why unblooms the best hope ever sown?
—Crass Casualty obstructs the sun and rain,
And dicing Time for gladness casts a moan. . . .
These purblind Doomsters had as readily strown
Blisses about my pilgrimage as pain.

Departure (Southampton Docks: October 1899)

While the far farewell music thins and fails,
And the broad bottoms rip the bearing brine—
All smalling slowly to the gray sea-line—
And each significant red smoke-shaft pales,
Keen sense of severance everywhere prevails,

Which shapes the late long tramp of mounting men
To seeming words that ask and ask again:
"How long, O striving Teutons, Slavs, and Gaels

Must your wroth reasonings trade on lives like these,
That are as puppets in a playing hand?—
When shall the saner softer polities
Whereof we dream, have sway in each proud land
And patriotism, grown Godlike, scorn to stand
Bondslave to realms, but circle earth and seas?"

Rome: Building a New Street in the Ancient Quarter

These umbered cliffs and gnarls of masonry
Outskeleton Time's central city, Rome;
Whereof each arch, entablature, and dome
Lies bare in all its gaunt anatomy.
And cracking frieze and rotten metope
Express, as though they were an open tome
Top-lined with caustic monitory gnome;
"Dunces, learn here to spell Humanity!"

And yet within these ruins' very shade
The singing workmen shape and set and join
Their frail new mansion's stuccoed cove and quoin
With no apparent sense that years abrade,
Though each rent wall their feeble works invade
Once shamed all such in power of pier and groin.

In the Cemetery

"You see those mothers squabbling there?"
Remarks the man of the cemetery.
"One says in tears, ''Tis mine lies here!'
Another, 'Nay, mine, you Pharisee!'
Another, 'How dare you move my flowers
And put your own on this grave of ours!'
But all their children were laid therein
At different times, like sprats in a tin.

"And then the main drain had to cross,
And we moved the lot some nights ago,
And packed them away in the general foss
With hundreds more. But their folks don't know,
And as well cry over a new-laid drain
As anything else, to ease your pain!"

WILLIAM BUTLER YEATS
(1865–1939)

Born near Dublin of Anglo-Irish parentage, Yeats was the son of a portrait painter. He was very influential in the Irish literary revival, moving from Celtic mysticism in *The Wanderings of Oisin* (1889) to more universal themes in such volumes as *Responsibilities* (1914), *The Wild Swans at Coole* (1919), *Michael Robartes and the Dancer* (1921), *The Tower* (1928), and *Last Poems* (1936–1939). Yeats was not a frequent user of the sonnet, but "Leda and the Swan" must stand in any list of remarkable sonnets.

At The Abbey Theatre
(Imitated from Ronsard)

Dear Craoibhin Aoibhin, look into our case.
When we are high and airy hundreds say
That if we hold that flight they'll leave the place,
While those same hundreds mock another day
Because we have made our art of common things,
So bitterly, you'd dream they longed to look
All their lives through into some drift of wings.
You've dandled them and fed them from the book
And know them to the bone; impart to us—
We'll keep the secret—a new trick to please.
Is there a bridle for this Proteus
That turns and changes like his draughty seas?
Or is there none, most popular of men,
But when they mock us, that we mock again?

Leda and the Swan

A sudden blow: the great wings beating still
Above the staggering girl, her thighs caressed
By the dark webs, her nape caught in his bill,
He holds her helpless breast upon his breast.

How can those terrified vague fingers push
The feathered glory from her loosening thighs?
And how can body, laid in that white rush,
But feel the strange heart beating where it lies?

A shudder in the loins engenders there
The broken wall, the burning roof and tower
And Agamemnon dead.
                              Being so caught up,
So mastered by the brute blood of the air,
Did she put on his knowledge with his power
Before the indifferent beak could let her drop?

A Crazed Girl

That crazed girl improvising her music,
Her poetry, dancing upon the shore,
Her soul in division from itself
Climbing, falling she knew not where,
Hiding amid the cargo of a steamship,
Her knee-cap broken, that girl I declare
A beautiful lofty thing, or a thing
Heroically lost, heroically found.

No matter what disaster occurred
She stood in desperate music wound,
Wound, wound, and she made in her triumph
Where the bales and the baskets lay
No common intelligible sound
But sang, "O sea-starved, hungry sea."

EDWIN ARLINGTON ROBINSON
(1869–1935)

Robinson was born at Head Tide, Maine, and spent his boyhood in Gardiner, the "Tilbury Town" of his poems. He attended Harvard for two years. His first two volumes, *The Torrent and the Night Before* (1896) and *The Children of the Night* (1897), were printed at his own expense. Theodore Roosevelt, however, admired his work, got him a Customs House appointment in New York, and helped to get *The Town down the River* (1910) published. *The Man Who Died Twice* (1924), *Collected Poems* (1921), and *Tristram* (1927) all won Pulitzer Prizes. Primarily interested in long narrative, Robinson nonetheless found the sonnet a congenial form for his bleak portraits.

Aaron Stark

Withal a meager man was Aaron Stark—
Cursed and unkempt, shrewd, shriveled, and morose.
A miser was he, with a miser's nose.
And eyes like little dollars in the dark.
His thin, pinched mouth was nothing but a mark;
And when he spoke there came like sullen blows
Through scattered fangs a few snarled words and close,
As if a cur were chary of its bark.

Glad for the murmur of his hard renown,
Year after year he shambled through the town—
A loveless exile moving with a staff;
And oftentimes there crept into his ears
A sound of alien pity, touched with tears—
And then (and only then) did Aaron laugh.

Cliff Klingenhagen

Cliff Klingenhagen had me in to dine
With him one day; and after soup and meat,
And all the other things there were to eat,
Cliff took two glasses and filled one with wine
And one with wormwood. Then, without a sign

For me to choose at all, he took the draught
Of bitterness himself, and lightly quaffed
It off, and said the other one was mine.

And when I asked him what the deuce he meant
By doing that, he only looked at me
And grinned, and said it was a way of his.
And though I know the fellow, I have spent
Long time awondering when I shall be
As happy as Cliff Klingenhagen is.

Reuben Bright

Because he was a butcher and thereby
Did earn an honest living (and did right),
I would not have you think that Reuben Bright
Was any more a brute than you or I;
For when they told him that his wife must die,
He stared at them, and shook with grief and fright,
And cried like a great baby half the night,
And made the women cry to see him cry.

And after she was dead, and he had paid
The singers and the sexton and the rest,
He packed a lot of things that she had made
Most mournfully away in an old chest
Of hers, and put some chopped-up cedar boughs
In with them, and tore down the slaughterhouse.

Calvary

Friendless and faint, with martyred steps and slow,
Faint for the flesh, but for the spirit free,
Stung by the mob that came to see the show,
The Master toiled along to Calvary;
We gibed him, as he went, with houndish glee,
Till his dimmed eyes for us did overflow;
We cursed his vengeless hands thrice wretchedly,—
And this was nineteen hundred years ago.

But after nineteen hundred years the shame
Still clings, and we have not made good the loss

That outraged faith has entered in his name.
Ah, when shall come love's courage to be strong!
Tell me, O Lord—tell me, O Lord, how long
Are we to keep Christ writhing on the cross!

JAMES WELDON JOHNSON
(1871–1938)

Born in Jacksonville, Florida, Johnson was educated at Atlanta University and Columbia. He was the first black admitted to the bar in Florida and served as American consul in Venezuela and Nicaragua. Johnson helped found and for many years (1916–1930) was secretary of the National Association for the Advancement of Colored People. *Autobiography of an Ex-Coloured Man,* a novel, was published anonymously in 1912 and caused considerable comment. Johnson acknowledged the work as his when it was reprinted in 1927. In his later years Johnson taught at Fisk and served as a visiting professor at New York University. The editor of a number of volumes, his works include *God's Trombones* (1927) and *Manhattan* (1930). His autobiography, *Along This Way,* was published in 1930.

Mother Night

Eternities before the first-born day,
   Or ere the first sun fledged his wings of flame,
   Calm Night, the everlasting and the same,
A brooding mother over chaos lay.
And whirling suns shall blaze and then decay,
   Shall run their fiery courses and then claim
   The haven of the darkness whence they came;
Back to Nirvanic peace shall grope their way.

So when my feeble sun of life burns out,
   And sounded is the hour for my long sleep,
   I shall, full weary of the feverish light,
Welcome the darkness without fear or doubt,
   And heavy-lidded, I shall softly creep
   Into the quiet bosom of the Night.

PAUL LAURENCE DUNBAR
(1872–1906)

Dunbar, a novelist and poet, the son of former slaves, was born in Dayton, Ohio. He gained considerable popularity for his use of folk materials and dialect. *Lyrics of Lowly Life* (1896) established his reputation as a poet. The stories in *Folks from Dixie* (1898) depict the lives of southern blacks; *The Sport of the Gods*, a novel, was published in 1902. Dunbar's collections of poetry include *Oak and Ivy* (1893) and *Majors and Minors* (1895); his *Complete Poems* (1913) was not published until after his death.

Robert Gould Shaw[1]

Why was it that the thunder voice of Fate
   Should call thee, studious, from the classic groves,
   Where calm-eyed Pallas with still footsteps roves,
And charge thee seek the turmoil of the State?
What bade thee hear the voice and rise elate,
   Leave home and kindred and thy spicy loaves,
   To lead th' unlettered and despised droves
To manhood's home and thunder at the gate?

Far better the slow blaze of Learning's light,
   The cool and quiet of her dearer fane,[2]
Than this hot terror of a hopeless fight,
   This cold endurance of the final pain,—
Since thou and those who with thee died for right
   Have died, the Present teaches, but in vain!

[1] Robert Gould Shaw (1837–1863), American abolitionist. See Henrietta Cordelia Ray's sonnet on the same subject, and note (p. 257).
[2] fane/temple.

Douglass[1]

Ah, Douglass, we have fall'n on evil days,
   Such days as thou, not even thou didst know,
   When thee, the eyes of that harsh long ago

Saw, salient, at the cross of devious ways,
And all the country heard thee with amaze.
  Not ended then, the passionate ebb and flow,
  The awful tide that battled to and fro;
We ride amid a tempest of dispraise.

Now, when the waves of swift dissension swarm,
  And Honor, the strong pilot, lieth stark,
Oh, for thy voice high-sounding o'er the storm,
  For thy strong arm to guide the shivering bark,
The blast-defying power of thy form,
  To give us comfort through the lonely dark.

[1]Frederick Douglass (c. 1817–1895), American abolitionist and journalist.

AMY LOWELL
(1874–1925)

Born in Brookline, Massachusetts, to a prominent New England family, Amy Lowell distinguished herself as a poet, critic, and biographer. Her interest as a child in the Romantic poets led to the precocious publication of *Dream Drops, or Stories from Fairy Land, by a Dreamer* in 1887. In 1902, after attending the opening night performance of Eleanora Duse, the internationally acclaimed Italian actress, in a play by Gabriel D'Annunzio, Duse's lover, Lowell found her poetic inspiration. The blank verse she reports having written that evening eventually became the six-sonnet sequence named for the actress. After the publication of her first collection of poetry, *A Dome of Many-Coloured Glass* (1912), she traveled to England where, among other poets and writers, she met Ezra Pound and became a major figure in the Imagist movement. *Can Grande's Castle* (1918) and *Pictures of the Floating World* (1919) contain important Imagist poems. Her critical works include *Six French Poets* (1915) and *Tendencies in Modern American Poetry* (1917). Her lifelong love of Keats led to her most ambitious project, the two-volume biography published in the year of her death. *What's O'Clock* (1925), printed posthumously, was awarded the Pulitzer Prize.

6. *"Seeing you stand once more before my eyes"*

Seeing you stand once more before my eyes
In your pale dignity and tenderness,
Wearing your frailty like a misty dress
Draped over the great glamour which denies
To years their domination, all disguise
Time can achieve is but to add a stress,
A finer fineness, as though some caress
Touched you a moment to a strange surprise.
Seeing you after these long lengths of years,
I only know the glory come again,
A majesty bewildered by my tears,
A golden sun spangling slant shafts of rain,
Moonlight delaying by a sick man's bed,
A rush of daffodils where wastes of dried leaves spread.

To John Keats

Great master! Boyish, sympathetic man!
  Whose orbed and ripened genius lightly hung
  From life's slim, twisted tendril and there swung
In crimson-sphered completeness; guardian
Of crystal portals through whose openings fan
  The spicéd winds which blew when earth was young,
  Scattering wreaths of stars, as Jove once flung
A golden shower from heights cerulean.
  Crumbled before thy majesty we bow.
  Forget thy empurpled state, thy panoply
Of greatness, and be merciful and near;
  A youth who trudged the highroad we tread now
  Singing the miles behind him; so may we
Faint throbbings of thy music overhear.

ROBERT FROST
(1875–1963)

Frost was born in California, but in 1885 he and his mother returned to Lawrence, Massachusetts, after his father's death. Frost studied at Harvard between 1897 and 1899, and in 1900 began farming and teaching at Derry, New Hampshire. In 1912 he moved his family to England, where *A Boy's Will* (1913) achieved immediate success. *North of Boston* (1914) came next, and *Mountain Interval* appeared in 1916 after Frost had returned to New Hampshire. Other works include *New Hampshire* (1923), *West-Running Brook* (1928), *A Further Range* (1936), *A Witness Tree* (1942), *Steeple Bush* (1947), and *In the Clearing* (1962). Frost held various appointments in poetry at Dartmouth, Wesleyan, Yale, Michigan, and Harvard. In 1961 he read "The Gift Outright" at the inauguration of President Kennedy.

The Oven Bird

There is a singer everyone has heard,
Loud, a midsummer and a mid-wood bird,
Who makes the solid tree trunks sound again.
He says that leaves are old and that for flowers
Midsummer is to spring as one to ten.
He says the early petal-fall is past
When pear and cherry bloom went down in showers
On sunny days a moment overcast;
And comes that other fall we name the fall.
He says the highway dust is over all.
The bird would cease and be as other birds
But that he knows in singing not to sing.
The question that he frames in all but words
Is what to make of a diminished thing.

Once by the Pacific

The shattered water made a misty din.
Great waves looked over others coming in,
And thought of doing something to the shore
That water never did to land before.

The clouds were low and hairy in the skies,
Like locks blown forward in the gleam of eyes.
You could not tell, and yet it looked as if
The shore was lucky in being backed by cliff,
The cliff in being backed by continent;
It looked as if a night of dark intent
Was coming, and not only a night, an age.
Someone had better be prepared for rage.
There would be more than ocean-water broken
Before God's last *Put out the Light* was spoken.

Acquainted with the Night

I have been one acquainted with the night.
I have walked out in rain—and back in rain.
I have outwalked the furthest city light.

I have looked down the saddest city lane.
I have passed by the watchman on his beat
And dropped my eyes, unwilling to explain.

I have stood still and stopped the sound of feet
When far away an interrupted cry
Came over houses from another street,

But not to call me back or say good-bye;
And further still at an unearthly height,
One luminary clock against the sky

Proclaimed the time was neither wrong nor right.
I have been one acquainted with the night.

Design

I found a dimpled spider, fat and white,
On a white heal-all, holding up a moth
Like a white piece of rigid satin cloth—
Assorted characters of death and blight
Mixed ready to begin the morning right,
Like the ingredients of a witches' broth—
A snow-drop spider, a flower like froth,
And dead wings carried like a paper kite.

What had that flower to do with being white,
The wayside blue and innocent heal-all?
What brought the kindred spider to that height,
Then steered the white moth thither in the night?
What but design of darkness to appall?—
If design govern in a thing so small.

The Silken Tent

She is as in a field a silken tent
At midday when a sunny summer breeze
Has dried the dew and all its ropes relent,
So that in guys it gently sways at ease,
And its supporting central cedar pole,
That is its pinnacle to heavenward
And signifies the sureness of the soul,
Seems to owe naught to any single cord,
But strictly held by none, is loosely bound
By countless silken ties of love and thought
To everything on earth the compass round,
And only by one's going slightly taut
In the capriciousness of summer air
Is of the slightest bondage made aware.

Never Again Would Birds' Song Be the Same

He would declare and could himself believe
That the birds there in all the garden round
From having heard the daylong voice of Eve
Had added to their own an oversound,
Her tone of meaning but without the words.
Admittedly an eloquence so soft
Could only have had an influence on birds
When call or laughter carried it aloft.
Be that as may be, she was in their song.
Moreover her voice upon their voices crossed
Had now persisted in the woods so long
That probably it never would be lost.
Never again would birds' song be the same.
And to do that to birds was why she came.

ALICE DUNBAR-NELSON
(1875–1935)

Alice Ruth Moore was born in New Orleans. Her first book, *Violets and Other Tales,* was privately printed in 1895. The poet Paul Laurence Dunbar, whom she later married, was an early admirer of her poetry. While married to Dunbar, she taught in New York City and was active in the National Association of Colored Women, which she served as recording secretary. In 1916, she married Robert John Nelson, the publisher of the *Wilmington Advocate,* a newspaper concerned with black rights. Throughout her life she was active as a poet, teacher, short story writer, and political activist. She edited a number of anthologies and in her later years wrote a column for the *Washington Eagle.*

Sonnet

I had no thought of violets of late,
The wild, shy kind that spring beneath your feet
In wistful April days, when lovers mate
And wander through the fields in raptures sweet.
The thought of violets meant florists' shops,
And bows and pins, and perfumed papers fine;
And garish lights, and mincing little fops
And cabarets and songs, and deadening wine.
So far from sweet real things my thoughts had strayed,
I had forgot wide fields, and clear brown streams;
The perfect loveliness that God has made,—
Wild violets shy and Heaven-mounting dreams.
And now—unwittingly, you've made me dream
Of violets, and my soul's forgotten gleam.

ANNA HEMPSTEAD BRANCH
(1875–1937)

Anna Hempstead Branch was born in New London, Connecticut, and received her education at Smith College. Her early volumes of poetry, *The Shoes that Danced* (1905) and *Rose of the World* (1910), established her reputation. She was a founding member of the Poets' Guild at the New York settlement house, Christadora House, along with other well-known writers, including Edwin Arlington Robinson. Her *Sonnets from a Lock Box* (1929), a sequence of thirty-eight sonnets, is especially interesting for the way in which Branch deals with religious belief.

FROM SONNETS FROM A LOCK BOX

1. *"How nonchalantly I spend with little thrift"*

How nonchalantly I spend with little thrift
His proud sparse earnings which were the frugal pay
Of a man's stout will and honorable day.
What insolent spending of that sturdy gift!
When I reflect on him he seems like one
Who on a bleak hill set a lonely pine.
He saw the North Star in its branches shine.
His honest valors are by me undone.
Why I should own his box I cannot see.
For his scant legacy I am unfit.
Yet since he's in the yard I have his key,
And somehow I am master over it.
I am like one who decks the Holy Tree
With tinsel shapes; then casts it in the pit.

William Ellery Leonard
(1876–1944)

A professor of English at the University of Wisconsin for many years, Leonard's sonnet sequence *Two Lives* (1922), a highly personal account of his courtship, marriage, and his wife's tragic suicide, received considerable acclaim. His first collection, *Sonnets and Poems*, appeared in 1906, and his selected poems, *A Son of Earth*, in 1928; another sonnet sequence, *A Man Against Time, An Heroic Dream*, was published in 1945. He also wrote scholarly works and translations of Lucretius and *Beowulf*.

———————————

FROM TWO LIVES

"*Love's primal want . . .*"

Love's primal want, foreshadowed by Love's quest
Of young seclusion, and, if Love's to thrive,
Proven in practice by all lovers alive,
And by all lovers gone to their long rest
(Beyond the Aegyptian river to the West
No more to love, to linger, and to strive),
Is through the ages not the noisy hive,
But the dear quiet of self-built nest.
She wakes one impulse even as she weans
From others; than herself more great is she,
The Aphrodite of reality,
For her own ends creative of her means:
Through her, mortality forgets to roam,
And plants a tree and stablishes a home.

"*True marriage is true love . . .*"

True marriage is true love; but love is free
In its blithe exultation, swift to take
Each own hour only for that hour's own sake
Or for its thrill of splendid prophecy.
Today Love walks by mountain, stream, and sea
In Love's own woodlands, wondrously awake,—
But yet Tomorrow may its finger shake:

"Lo, marriage was not meant for such as ye."
True marriage is true love—but more than love
In long, severe, but eloquent, routine;
And spring's brief instinct of the deer and dove
Alone founds little that outlasts the green—
True mates in love, under one law of life,
May, under another, mate not as man and wife.

JOHN MASEFIELD
(1878–1967)

At fifteen Masefield went to sea on a windjammer. After three
years in New York, he returned to London in 1897 and began
writing. His first book of poems, *Salt-Water Ballads* (1902),
contained his best-known poem, "Sea Fever." Masefield fol-
lowed Robert Bridges as poet laureate in 1930 and received the
Order of Merit in 1935.

Posted

Dream after dream I see the wrecks that lie
Unknown of man, unmarked upon the charts,
Known of the flat-fish with the withered eye,
And seen by women in their aching hearts.

World-wide the scattering is of those fair ships
That trod the billow tops till out of sight:
The cuttle mumbles them with horny lips,
The shells of the sea-insects crust them white.

In silence and in dimness and in greenness
Among the indistinct and leathery leaves
Of fruitless life they lie among the cleanness.
Fish glide and flit, slow under-movement heaves:

But no sound penetrates, not even the lunge
Of ships passing, nor the gannet's plunge.

D. H. LAWRENCE
(1885–1930)

The son of a miner and a schoolteacher, D. H. Lawrence was born in Eastwood, Nottinghamshire, a locale he later used for several of his novels. His first poems to appear in print were published in the *English Review* in 1909; his first novel, *The White Peacock,* was published in 1911. One of the major writers of the twentieth century, Lawrence was also one of the most controversial. In 1912 he eloped with Frieda von Richthofen Weekley, the wife of a professor of philology, and spent most of the rest of his life traveling. Lawrence was very prolific, writing novels, short stories, novellas, poems, plays, essays and accounts of his travels, and critical works. He did not find the sonnet form congenial, but could use it for the expression of his critical views.

When I Read Shakespeare—

When I read Shakespeare I am struck with wonder
that such trivial people should muse and thunder
in such lovely language.

Lear, the old buffer, you wonder his daughters
didn't treat him rougher,
the old chough, the old chuffer!

And Hamlet, how boring, how boring to live with,
so mean and self-conscious, blowing and snoring
his wonderful speeches, full of other folks' whoring!

And Macbeth and his Lady, who should have been choring,
such suburban ambition, so messily goring
old Duncan with daggers!

How boring, how small Shakespeare's people are!
Yet the language so lovely! like the dyes from gas-tar.

ELINOR WYLIE
(1885–1928)

Poet and novelist, Elinor Wylie was born in New Jersey and raised in Rosemont, outside of Philadelphia, and in Washington, D.C. She left her first husband to elope with Horace Wylie. Divorced in 1923, she married the poet William Rose Benét. *Nets to Catch the Wind* (1921), *Black Armour* (1923), and other volumes brought her great popularity in the 1920s. Her sonnets invite comparison with those of Edna St. Vincent Millay.

FROM ONE PERSON

5. *"The little beauty that I was allowed"*

The little beauty that I was allowed—
The lips new-cut and colored by my sire,
The polished hair, the eyes' perceptive fire—
Has never been enough to make me proud:
For I have moved companioned by a cloud,
And lived indifferent to the blood's desire
Of temporal loveliness in vain attire:
My flesh was but a fresh-embroidered shroud.

Now do I grow indignant at the fate
Which made me so imperfect to compare
With your degree of noble and of fair;
Our elements are the farthest skies apart;
And I enjoin you, ere it is too late,
To stamp your superscription on my heart.

16. *"I hereby swear that to uphold your house"*

I hereby swear that to uphold your house
I would lay my bones in quick destroying lime
Or turn my flesh to timber for all time;
Cut down my womanhood; lop off the boughs
Of that perpetual ecstasy that grows
From the heart's core; condemn it as a crime
If it be broader than a beam, or climb
Above the stature that your roof allows.

I am not the hearthstone nor the cornerstone
Within this noble fabric you have builded;
Not by my beauty was its cornice gilded;
Not on my courage were its arches thrown:
My lord, adjudge my strength, and set me where
I bear a little more than I can bear.

EZRA POUND
(1885–1972)

Born in Hailey, Idaho, Pound was graduated from Hamilton
College in 1905 and then studied romance languages at the
University of Pennsylvania. In 1908 he expatriated himself and
lived in London, Paris, and Rapallo, Italy. He was associated for
a time with Amy Lowell and the Imagists and acted as foreign
correspondent for Harriet Monroe's *Poetry: A Magazine of
Verse*. He encouraged T. S. Eliot and with him must be consid-
ered one of the chief motivators of the modern movement in
poetry. *Personae* first appeared in 1913; publication of *The Can-
tos* began in 1917, and *Hugh Selwyn Mauberley* was published in
1920. Pound's work also includes a considerable body of prose.

Silet

When I behold how black, immortal ink
Drips from my deathless pen—ah, well-away!
Why should we stop at all for what I think?
There is enough in what I chance to say.

It is enough that we once came together;
What is the use of setting it to rime?
When it is autumn do we get spring weather,
Or gather May of harsh northwindish time?

It is enough that we once came together;
What if the wind has turned against the rain?
It is enough that we once came together;
Time has seen this, and will not turn again.

And who are we, who know that last intent,
To plague tomorrow with a testament!

A Virginal

No, no! Go from me. I have left her lately.
I will not spoil my sheath with lesser brightness,
For my surrounding air hath a new lightness;
Slight are her arms, yet they have bound me straitly
And left me cloaked as with a gauze of ether;
As with sweet leaves; as with subtle clearness.
Oh, I have picked up magic in her nearness
To sheathe me half in half the things that sheathe her.
No, no! Go from me. I have still the flavor,
Soft as spring wind that's come from birchen bowers.
Green come the shoots, aye April in the branches,
As winter's wound with her sleight hand she staunches,
Hath of the trees a likeness of the savor:
As white their bark, so white this lady's hours.

SIEGFRIED SASSOON
(1886–1967)

Sassoon attended Clare College, Cambridge, which made him an
Honorary Fellow in 1953. He enlisted in the army at the begin-
ning of World War I and was awarded the Military Cross. His
detestation of war is reflected in *Counter-Attack* (1918). *Col-
lected Poems, 1908–1956* appeared in 1961.

Dreamers

Soldiers are citizens of death's gray land,
    Drawing no dividend from time's tomorrows.
In the great hour of destiny they stand,
    Each with his feuds, and jealousies, and sorrows.
Soldiers are sworn to action; they must win
    Some flaming, fatal climax with their lives.
Soldiers are dreamers; when the guns begin
    They think of firelit homes, clean beds, and wives.

I see them in foul dugouts, gnawed by rats,
    And in the ruined trenches, lashed with rain,
Dreaming of things they did with balls and bats,
    And mocked by hopeless longing to regain
Bank holidays, and picture shows, and spats,
    And going to the office in the train.

On Passing the New Menin Gate

Who will remember, passing through this Gate,
The unheroic Dead who fed the guns?
Who shall absolve the foulness of their fate,—
Those doomed, conscripted, unvictorious ones?
Crudely renewed, the Salient holds its own,
Paid are its dim defenders by this pomp;
Paid, with a pile of peace-complacent stone,
The armies who endured that sullen swamp.

Here was the world's worst wound. And here with pride
"Their name liveth for ever," the Gateway claims.
Was ever an immolation so belied
As these intolerably nameless names?
Well might the Dead who struggled in the slime
Rise and deride this sepulchre of crime.

RUPERT BROOKE
(1887–1915)

His father a housemaster at Rugby, Brooke was educated there and at King's College, Cambridge. *Poems* appeared in 1911. In 1914 he was commissioned in the Royal Naval Division, and he died on the island of Skyros on April 23, 1915. His *Collected Poems* was published in 1915. His personal attractiveness, early death, and in particular his war sonnets encouraged the romantic myth which has tended to obscure his real merits as a poet.

"Oh! Death will find me . . ."

Oh! Death will find me, long before I tire
  Of watching you; and swing me suddenly
Into the shade and loneliness and mire
  Of the last land! There, waiting patiently,

One day, I think, I'll feel a cool wind blowing,
  See a slow light across the Stygian tide,
And hear the Dead about me stir, unknowing,
  And tremble. And I shall know that you have died,

And watch you, a broad-browed and smiling dream,
  Pass, light as ever, through the lightless host,
Quietly ponder, start, and sway, and gleam—
  Most individual and bewildering ghost!—

And turn, and toss your brown delightful head
Amusedly, among the ancient Dead.

The Hill

Breathless, we flung us on the windy hill,
Laughed in the sun, and kissed the lovely grass.
You said, "Through glory and ecstasy we pass;
Wind, sun, and earth remain, the birds sing still,
When we are old, are old. . . ." "And when we die
All's over that is ours; and life burns on
Through other lovers, other lips," said I,
"Heart of my heart, our heaven is now, is won!"

"We are Earth's best, that learnt her lesson here.
Life is our cry. We have kept the faith!" we said;
"We shall go down with unreluctant tread
Rose-crowned into the darkness! . . ." Proud we were,
And laughed, that had such brave true things to say.
And then you suddenly cried, and turned away.

The Soldier

If I should die, think only this of me;
  That there's some corner of a foreign field
That is for ever England. There shall be
  In that rich earth a richer dust concealed;
A dust whom England bore, shaped, made aware,
  Gave, once, her flowers to love, her ways to roam,
A body of England's breathing English air,
  Washed by the rivers, blessed by suns of home.

And think, this heart, all evil shed away,
  A pulse in the eternal mind, no less
    Gives somewhere back the thoughts by England given;
Her sights and sounds; dreams happy as her day;
  And laughter, learned of friends; and gentleness,
    In hearts at peace, under an English heaven.

ROBINSON JEFFERS
(1887–1962)

Robinson Jeffers was born in Pittsburgh, Pennsylvania, and attended schools in Germany and Switzerland. He graduated from Occidental College at eighteen, took a Master of Arts degree at the University of Southern California, and began to study medicine. After 1912, however, he devoted himself to literature, settling at Carmel, California, in 1914. His *Selected Poetry* was published in 1938.

Love the Wild Swan

"I hate my verses, every line, every word,
Oh pale and brittle pencils ever to try
One grass-blade's curve, or the throat of one bird
That clings to twig, ruffled against white sky.
Oh cracked and twilight mirrors ever to catch
One color, one glinting flash, of the splendor of things.
Unlucky hunter, Oh bullets of wax,
The lion beauty, the wild-swan wings, the storm of the wings."
—This wild swan of a world is no hunter's game.
Better bullets than yours would miss the white breast,
Better mirrors than yours would crack in the flame.
Does it matter whether you hate your . . . self? At least
Love your eyes that can see, your mind that can
Hear the music, the thunder of the wings. Love the wild swan.

Shiva

There is a hawk that is picking the birds out of the sky.
She killed the pigeons of peace and security,
She has taken honesty and confidence from nations and men,
She is hunting the lovely heron of liberty.
She loads the arts with nonsense, she is very cunning,
Silence with dreams and the state with powers to catch them at
    last.
Nothing will escape her at last, flying or running.
This is the hawk that picks out the stars' eyes.
This is the only hunter that will ever catch the wild swan;

The prey she will take last is the wild white swan of the beauty
    of things.
Then she will be alone, pure destruction, achieved supreme,
Empty darkness under the death-tent wings.
She will build a nest of the swan's bones and hatch a new
    brood,
Hang new heavens with new birds, all be renewed.

JOHN CROWE RANSOM
(1888–1974)

Born in Pulaski, Tennessee, Ransom graduated from Vanderbilt
University in 1909 and then studied at Oxford as a Rhodes
scholar. He served in the field artillery in World War I, after
which he returned to Vanderbilt to teach, and was one of the
founders of *The Fugitive* in 1922. Ransom was one of the
"Twelve Southerners" who issued the agrarian essays of *I'll
Take My Stand* in 1930. Becoming Carnegie Professor of English
at Kenyon College in 1937, he founded and edited the influential
Kenyon Review there. Ransom's *Selected Poems* appeared in
1945; his critical works include *The World's Body* (1938), *The
New Criticism* (1941), and *Poems and Essays* (1955).

The Tall Girl

The Queens of Hell had lissome necks to crane
At the tall girl approaching with long tread
And, when she was caught up even with them, nodded:
"If the young miss with gold hair might not disdain,
We would esteem her company over the plain,
To profit us where the dogs will be out barking;
And we'll walk by the windows where the young men are
    working
And tomorrow we will all come home again."

But the Queen of Heaven on the other side of the road
In the likeness, I hear, of a fine motherly woman
Made a wry face, despite it was so common

To be worsted by the smooth ladies of hell,
And crisped her sweet tongue: "This will never come to good!
Just an old woman, my pet, that wishes you well."

Piazza Piece

—I am a gentleman in a dust coat trying
To make you hear. Your ears are soft and small
And listen to an old man not at all,
They want the young men's whispering and sighing.
But see the roses on your trellis dying
And hear the spectral singing of the moon;
For I must have my lovely lady soon,
I am a gentleman in a dust coat trying.

—I am a lady young in beauty waiting
Until my truelove comes, and then we kiss.
But what gray man among the vines is this
Whose words are dry and faint as in a dream?
Back from my trellis, sir, before I scream!
I am a lady young in beauty waiting.

Conrad Aiken
(1889–1973)

Conrad Aiken was born in Savannah, Georgia. He was a member of the Harvard class of 1911, which included among other notables T. S. Eliot, Van Wyck Brooks, John Reed, and Walter Lippmann. Aiken lived in South Yarmouth and Brewster, Massachusetts; Sussex, England; and in New York City. As well as poetry he wrote short stories, novels, plays, and criticism. His *Selected Poems* won the Pulitzer Prize for 1929. Aiken held the Chair of Poetry in the Library of Congress for 1950–1951, and in 1953, he received the National Book Award for his *Collected Poems*. His sonnet sequence *And in the Human Heart* (1940) was praised for its music and attacked for its rhetoric.

FROM AND IN THE HUMAN HEART

1. *"Bend as the bow bends . . ."*

Bend as the bow bends, and let fly the shaft,
the strong cord loose its word as light as flame;
speak without cunning, love, as without craft,
careless of answer, as of shame or blame:
this is to be known, that love is love, despite
knowledge of ignorance, truth, untruth, despair;
careless of all things, if that love be bright,
careless of hate and fate, careless of care.
Spring the word as it must, the leaf or flower
broken or bruised, yet let it, broken, speak
of time transcending this too transient hour,
and space that finds the beating heart too weak:
thus, and thus only, will our tempest come
by continents of snow to find a home.

28. *"Green, green, and green again . . ."*

Green, green, and green again, and greener still,
spring towards summer bends the immortal bow,
and northward breaks the wave of daffodil,

and northward breaks the wave of summer's snow:
green, green, and green again, and greener yet,
wide as this forest is, which counts its leaves,
wide as this kingdom, in a green sea set,
which round its shores perpetual blossom weaves—
green, green, and green again, and green once more,
the season finds its term—then greenest, even,
when frost at twilight on the leaf lies hoar,
and one cold star shines bright in greenest heaven:
but love, like music, keeps no seasons ever;
like music, too, once known is known forever.

CLAUDE MCKAY
(1890–1948)

Born in Jamaica, McKay studied at the Tuskegee Institute and at
Kansas State College. In 1914 he moved to Harlem and became
one of the most important writers in the Harlem Renaissance.
He traveled widely and was active in radical causes. For a time
he worked as an editor for *The Liberator* and *The Masses*.
Harlem Shadows, his most important book of poetry, was pub-
lished in 1922. McKay also wrote a number of novels, including
the best seller *Home to Harlem* (1927), as well as *Banjo* (1929)
and *Banana Bottom* (1933). "If We Must Die" was written in
response to the race riots in Harlem in 1919 and received inter-
national acclaim.

If We Must Die

If we must die, let it not be like hogs
Hunted and penned in an inglorious spot,
While round us bark the mad and hungry dogs,
Making their mock at our accursed lot.
If we must die, O let us nobly die,
So that our precious blood may not be shed
In vain; then even the monsters we defy
Shall be constrained to honor us though dead!
O kinsmen! we must meet the common foe!

Though far outnumbered let us show us brave,
And for their thousand blows deal one deathblow!
What though before us lies the open grave?
Like men we'll face the murderous, cowardly pack,
Pressed to the wall, dying, but fighting back!

Africa

The sun sought thy dim bed and brought forth light,
The sciences were sucklings at thy breast;
When all the world was young in pregnant night
Thy slaves toiled at thy monumental best.
Thou ancient treasure-land, thou modern prize,
New peoples marvel at thy pyramids!
The years roll on, thy sphinx of riddle eyes
Watches the mad world with immobile lids.
The Hebrews humbled them at Pharaoh's name.
Cradle of Power! Yet all things were in vain!
Honor and Glory, Arrogance and Fame!
They went. The darkness swallowed thee again.
Thou art the harlot, now thy time is done,
Of all the mighty nations of the sun.

The Harlem Dancer

Applauding youths laughed with young prostitutes
And watched her perfect, half-clothed body sway;
Her voice was like the sound of blended flutes
Blown by black players upon a picnic day.
She sang and danced on gracefully and calm,
The light gauze hanging loose about her form;
To me she seemed a proudly-swaying palm
Grown lovelier for passing through a storm.
Upon her swarthy neck black shiny curls
Luxuriant fell; and tossing coins in praise,
The wine-flushed, bold-eyed boys, and even the girls,
Devoured her shape with eager, passionate gaze;
But looking at her falsely-smiling face,
I knew her self was not in that strange place.

JOHN PEALE BISHOP
(1892–1944)

Bishop attended Princeton, where he was friendly with Edmund Wilson and F. Scott Fitzgerald. He served as a lieutenant in World War I. After living in France for ten years (1923–1933), he returned to the United States and was appointed a Fellow of the Library of Congress in 1942. His *Collected Poems* was published posthumously in 1948.

A Recollection

Famously she descended, her red hair
Unbound and bronzed by sea-reflections, caught
Crinkled with sea-pearls. The fine slender taut
Knees that let down her feet upon air,

Young breasts, slim flanks and golden quarries were
Odder than when the young distraught
Unknown Venetian, painting her portrait, thought
He'd not imagined what he painted there.

And I too commerced with that golden cloud:
Lipped her delicious hands and had my ease
Faring fantastically, perversely proud.

All loveliness demands our courtesies.
Since she was dead I praised her as I could
Silently, among the Barberini bees.

"Sleep brought me vision . . ."

Sleep brought me vision of my lady dead,
    Robed as of old time in a silken gown,
With violets clustered round her perfect head,
    And violets gathered where her robe fell down
    Even to where her silken shoes were sewn
With dust of silver and stained purple thread;
    Her vesture's dyes were something fainter grown;
And the dusk buds held memory of scents shed.

But in her face there seemed a heavier change,
    As when a rose is ruined by long rain
And the rich hues show rust; a sorrow strange
    Brooded within her eyes, and the wet stain
Tarnished her cheeks, as to mine own thought's range
    She sighed: "There is no love where I have lain!"

Edna St. Vincent Millay
(1892–1950)

Born in Rockland, Maine, Edna St. Vincent Millay became one of the most successful and popular poets of her time. Her first volume of poetry, *Renascence,* was published in 1917, the same year she was graduated from Vassar. She received the Pulitzer Prize for *The Ballad of the Harp Weaver* (1922). A member of the Provincetown Players, she wrote a number of verse dramas, including *Aria da Capo* (1920) and *Two Slatterns and a King* (1921). In 1927 she wrote the libretto for Deems Taylor's opera *The King's Henchmen.* Millay is one of the best and most prolific sonneteers of the twentieth century; *Fatal Interview* (1931), an extended sequence, reveals her mastery of the form.

"I do but ask that you be always fair"

I do but ask that you be always fair,
That I for ever may continue kind;
Knowing me what I am, you should not dare
To lapse from beauty ever, nor seek to bind
My alterable mood with lesser cords:
Weeping and such soft matters but invite
To further vagrancy, and bitter words
Chafe soon to irremediable flight.
Wherefore I pray you if you love me dearly
Less dear to hold me than your own bright charms,
Whence it may fall that until death or nearly
I shall not move to struggle from your arms;
Fade if you must; I would but bid you be
Like the sweet year, doing all things graciously.

"What lips my lips have kissed . . ."

What lips my lips have kissed, and where, and why,
I have forgotten, and what arms have lain
Under my head till morning; but the rain
Is full of ghosts tonight, that tap and sigh
Upon the glass and listen for reply,
And in my heart there stirs a quiet pain
For unremembered lads that not again
Will turn to me at midnight with a cry.
Thus in the winter stands the lonely tree,
Nor knows what birds have vanished one by one,
Yet knows its boughs more silent than before:
I cannot say what loves have come and gone,
I only know that summer sang in me
A little while, that in me sings no more.

"Euclid alone has looked on Beauty bare"

Euclid alone has looked on Beauty bare.
Let all who prate of Beauty hold their peace,
And lay them prone upon the earth and cease
To ponder on themselves, the while they stare
At nothing, intricately drawn nowhere
In shapes of shifting lineage; let geese
Gabble and hiss, but heroes seek release
From dusty bondage into luminous air.
O blinding hour, O holy, terrible day,
When first the shaft into his vision shone
Of light anatomized! Euclid alone
Has looked on Beauty bare. Fortunate they
Who, though once only and then but far away,
Have heard her massive sandal set on stone.

"Love is not all . . ."

Love is not all: it is not meat nor drink
Nor slumber nor a roof against the rain;
Nor yet a floating spar to men that sink
And rise and sink and rise and sink again;
Love cannot fill the thickened lung with breath,
Nor clean the blood, nor set the fractured bone;
Yet many a man is making friends with death
Even as I speak, for lack of love alone.
It may well be that in a difficult hour,
Pinned down by pain and moaning for release,
Or nagged by want past resolution's power,
I might be driven to sell your love for peace,
Or trade the memory of this night for food.
It well may be. I do not think I would.

"I will put Chaos into fourteen lines"

I will put Chaos into fourteen lines
And keep him there; and let him thence escape
If he be lucky; let him twist, and ape
Flood, fire, and demon—his adroit designs
Will strain to nothing in the strict confines
Of this sweet Order, where, in pious rape,
I hold his essence and amorphous shape,
Till he with Order mingles and combines.
Past are the hours, the years, of our duress,
His arrogance, our awful servitude:
I have him. He is nothing more than less
Than something simple not yet understood;
I shall not even force him to confess;
Or answer. I will only make him good.

ARCHIBALD MACLEISH
(1892–1983)

Born in Glencoe, Illinois, MacLeish graduated from Yale in 1915. He enlisted in the army in 1917 and served in France. From 1923 to 1928 he lived in Paris, his return being marked by *The Hamlet of A. MacLeish* (1928). *Conquistador* appeared in 1932; his growing social consciousness was evident in *New Found Land* (1930) and the satirical *Frescoes for Mr. Rockefeller's City* (1933). In 1939 MacLeish was appointed Librarian of Congress; from 1944 to 1945 he served as Assistant Secretary of State. *Actfive and Other Poems* was published in 1948, *J. B.: A Play in Verse* in 1958. In 1949 MacLeish was appointed Boylston Professor at Harvard.

The End of the World

Quite unexpectedly as Vasserot
The armless ambidextrian was lighting
A match between his great and second toe
And Ralph the lion was engaged in biting
The neck of Madame Sossman while the drum
Pointed, and Teeny was about to cough
In waltz time swinging Jocko by the thumb—
Quite unexpectedly the top blew off:

And there, there overhead, there, there, hung over
Those thousands of white faces, those dazed eyes,
There in the starless dark the poise, the hover,
There with vast wings across the canceled skies,
There in the sudden blackness the black pall
Of nothing, nothing, nothing—nothing at all.

Aeterna Poetae Memoria

The concierge at the front gate where relatives
Half after two till four Mondays and Fridays
Do not turn always to look at the hospital,
Brown now and rusty with sunlight and bare
As the day you died in it, stump of the knee gangrenous,

"Le ciel dans les yeux" and the flea-bitten priest with the wafer
Forgiving you everything—You!—the concierge hadn't
Heard of you: *"Rimbaud? Comment s'écrit ça, Rimbaud?"*

But Sidis the, well, American dealer in manuscripts—
Sidis has sold the original ink decree:
Verlaine versus Verlaine (Divorce) with your name as
How do we say between gentlemen—anyway all
OK, the facts, the actual story . . .

Men remember you, dead boy—the lover of verses!

WILFRED OWEN
(1893–1918)

Educated at Birkenhead Institute and London University, Owen
enlisted in the army in 1916. In June 1917 he was invalided home.
Siegfried Sassoon, a patient in the same hospital, encouraged
Owen to continue writing poetry. Owen returned to combat in
August, 1918, was awarded the Military Cross for gallantry in
October, and was killed in November. Sassoon collected his
poems and published them in 1920. Owen was recognized as an
outstanding poet of the war. "Anthem for Doomed Youth" must
be ranked among the finest of sonnets.

To a Child

Sweet in your antique body, not yet young.
Beauty withheld from youth that looks for youth.
Fair only for your father. Dear among
Masters in art. To all men else uncouth
Save me, who know your smile comes very old,
Learnt of the happy dead that laughed with gods;
For earlier suns than ours have lent you gold,
Sly fauns and trees have given you jigs and nods.

But soon your heart, hot-beating like a bird's,
Shall slow down. Youth shall lop your hair,

And you must learn wry meanings in our words.
Your smile shall dull, because too keen aware;
And when for hopes your hand shall be uncurled,
Your eyes shall close, being opened to the world.

Anthem for Doomed Youth

What passing-bells for these who die as cattle?
  Only the monstrous anger of the guns.
  Only the stuttering rifles' rapid rattle
Can pattern out their hasty orisons.
No mockeries for them; no prayers nor bells,
Nor any voice of mourning save the choirs,—
The shrill, demented choirs of wailing shells;
And bugles calling for them from sad shires.

What candles may be held to speed them all?
  Not in the hands of boys, but in their eyes
Shall shine the holy glimmers of good-byes.
  The pallor of girls' brows shall be their pall;
Their flowers the tenderness of patient minds,
And each slow dusk a drawing-down of blinds.

The Next War

>   *War's a joke for me and you,*
>   *While we know such dreams are true.*—SASSOON

Out there, we've talked quite friendly up to Death;
  Sat down and eaten with him, cool and bland,—
  Pardoned his spilling mess-tins in our hand.
We've sniffed the green thick odor of his breath,—
Our eyes wept, but our courage didn't writhe.
  He's spat at us with bullets and he's coughed
  Shrapnel. We chorused when he sang aloft;
We whistled while he shaved us with his scythe.

Oh, Death was never an enemy of ours!
  We laughed at him, we leagued with him, old chum.
No soldier's paid to kick against his powers.

We laughed, knowing that better men would come,
And greater wars; when each proud fighter brags
He wars on Death—for Life; not men—for flags.

E. E. CUMMINGS
(1894–1962)

E[dward] E[stlin] Cummings was born in Cambridge, Massachusetts, and was educated at Harvard. *The Enormous Room* (1922) recounts the experiences of his imprisonment for criticizing the military while he was serving in an ambulance corps in France in 1916. A painter as well as a poet, he studied art in Paris for several years. He won the *Dial* poetry prize in 1925. The sonnet especially suited Cummings's lyrical bent; his typographical innovations do not really alter the form in any fundamental way.

_____

"the Cambridge ladies . . ."

the Cambridge ladies who live in furnished souls
are unbeautiful and have comfortable minds
(also, with the church's protestant blessings
daughters, unscented shapeless spirited)
they believe in Christ and Longfellow, both dead,
are invariably interested in so many things—
at the present writing one still finds
delighted fingers knitting for the is it Poles?
perhaps. While permanent faces coyly bandy
scandal of Mrs. N and Professor D
. . . . the Cambridge ladies do not care, above
Cambridge if sometimes in its box of
sky lavender and cornerless, the
moon rattles like a fragment of angry candy

"i like my body . . ."

i like my body when it is with your
body. It is so quite new a thing.

Muscles better and nerves more.
i like your body. i like what it does,
i like its hows. i like to feel the spine
of your body and its bones, and the trembling
-firm-smooth ness and which i will
again and again and again
kiss, i like kissing this and that of you,
i like, slowly stroking the, shocking fuzz
of your electric fur, and what-is-it comes
over parting flesh. . . . And eyes big love-crumbs,

and possibly i like the thrill

of under me you so quite new

"*when my sensational moments are no more*"

when my sensational moments are no more
unjoyously bullied of vilest mind

and sweet uncaring earth by thoughtful war
heaped wholly with high wilt of human rind—
when over hate has triumphed darkly love

and the small spiritual cry of spring
utters a striving flower,
                                  just where strove
the droll god-beasts
                                  do thou distinctly bring
thy footstep, and the rushing of thy deep
hair and smiting smile didst love to use
in other ways (drawing my Mesd from sleep
whose stranger dreams thy strangeness must abuse. . . .)

Time being not for us, purple roses were
sweeter to thee
                                  perchance to me deeper.

Robert Graves
(1895–1985)

In the course of a career spanning half a century Graves wrote more than 130 volumes of poetry, fiction, essays, and criticism. He was educated at Charterhouse and St. John's College, Oxford. He recounted his experiences in World War I in France in the Royal Welsh Fusiliers in his classic autobiography, *Goodbye to All That* (1929). From 1961 to 1968 he was Professor of Poetry at Oxford. His novel *I, Claudius* (1934) was the basis for an immensely successful BBC television series. He lived on the island of Majorca, which made him an honorary citizen in 1968.

The Troll's Nosegay

A simple nosegay! was that much to ask?
(Winter still nagged, with scarce a bud yet showing.)
He loved her ill, if he resigned the task.
"Somewhere," she cried, "there must be blossom blowing."

It seems my lady wept and the troll swore
By heaven he hated tears: he'd cure her spleen—
Where she had begged one flower he'd shower fourscore,
A bunch fit to amaze a China Queen.

Cold fog-drawn Lily, pale mist-magic Rose
He conjured, and in a glassy cauldron set
With elvish unsubstantial Mignonette
And such vague bloom as wandering dreams enclose.
But she?
      Awed,
          Charmed to tears,
               Distracted,
                    Yet—
Even yet, perhaps, a trifle piqued—who knows?

Spoils

When all is over and you march for home,
The spoils of war are easily disposed of:

Standards, weapons of combat, helmets, drums
May decorate a staircase or a study,
While lesser gleanings of the battlefield—
Coins, watches, wedding rings, gold teeth and such—
Are sold anonymously for solid cash.

The spoils of love present a different case,
When all is over and you march for home:
That lock of hair, these letters and the portrait
May not be publicly displayed; nor sold;
Nor burned; nor returned (the heart being obstinate)—
Yet never dare entrust them to a safe
For fear they burn a hole through two-foot steel.

LOUISE BOGAN
(1897–1970)

Influential poetry critic at *The New Yorker* from 1931 to 1969,
Louise Bogan was born in Livermore Falls, Maine. Bogan began
writing poetry as a student at Girls' Latin School in Boston
where her family had moved in 1909. Her early volumes of
poetry, *Body of This Death* (1923) and *Dark Summer* (1929),
established her reputation. In 1945 and 1946 she was Consultant
in Poetry at the Library of Congress. In 1954 she was awarded
the Bollingen Prize for her *Collected Poems*. Her last book of
poems, *The Blue Estuaries: Poems 1923–1968*, was published
just a year before her death.

Simple Autumnal

The measured blood beats out the year's delay.
The tearless eyes and heart forbidden grief,
Watch the burned, restless, but abiding leaf,
The brighter branches arming the bright day.

The cone, the curving fruit should fall away,
The vine-stem crumble, ripe grain know its sheaf.
Bonded to time, fires should have done, be brief,
But, serfs to sleep, they glitter and they stay.

Because not last nor first, grief in its prime
Wakes in the day, and knows of life's intent.
Anguish would break the seal set over time
And bring the baskets where the bough is bent.

Full seasons come, yet filled trees keep the sky,
And never scent the ground where they will lie.

Single Sonnet

Now, you great stanza, you heroic mold,
Bend to my will, for I must give you love:
The weight in the heart that breathes, but cannot move,
Which to endure flesh only makes so bold.

Take up, take up, as it were lead or gold
The burden; test the dreadful mass thereof.
No stone, slate, metal under or above
Earth, is so ponderous, so dull, so cold.

Too long as ocean bed bears up the ocean,
As earth's core bears the earth, have I borne this;
Too long have lovers, bending for their kiss,
Felt bitter force cohering without motion.

Staunch meter, great song, it is yours, at length,
To prove how stronger you are than my strength.

HART CRANE
(1899–1932)

Born in Garrettsville, Ohio, Hart Crane, according to his own account, had a very unhappy youth. Never finishing high school, he supported himself with a variety of jobs. He went to Mexico in 1931 and 1932 on a Guggenheim fellowship, and committed suicide by jumping overboard on his return voyage to New York. His largest and probably greatest work, *The Bridge,* appeared in 1930.

To Emily Dickinson

You who desired so much—in vain to ask—
Yet fed your hunger like an endless task,
Dared dignify the labor, bless the quest—
Achieved that stillness ultimately best,

Being, of all, least sought for: Emily, hear!
O sweet, dead Silencer, most suddenly clear
When singing that Eternity possessed
And plundered momently in every breast;

—Truly no flower yet withers in your hand,
The harvest you descried and understand
Needs more than wit to gather, love to bind.
Some reconcilement of remotest mind—

Leaves Ormus rubyless, and Ophir chill.
Else tears heap all within one clay-cold hill.

To Shakespeare

Through torrid entrances, past icy poles
A hand moves on the page! Who shall again
Engrave such hazards as thy might controls—
    Conflicting, purposeful yet outcry vain
Of all our days, being pilot,—tempest, too!
    Sheets that mock lust and thorns that scribble hate

Are lifted from torn flesh with human rue,
    And laughter, burnished brighter than our fate,
Thou wieldest with such tears that every faction
    Swears high in Hamlet's throat, and devils throng
Where angels beg for doom in ghast distraction
    And fall, both! Yet thine Ariel holds his song:
And that serenity that Prospero gains
Is justice that has canceled earthly chains.

ALLEN TATE
(1899–1979)

Born in Kentucky, Tate was educated at Vanderbilt University, where, along with Robert Penn Warren and John Crowe Ransom, he was associated with *The Fugitive*. Tate edited the *Sewanee Review* from 1944 to 1946 and held the Chair of Poetry in the Library of Congress for 1943–1944. He received the Bollingen Prize for Poetry in 1956. He was a Professor of English at the University of Minnesota from 1951 until 1968. His *Collected Poems* appeared in 1977.

FROM SONNETS AT CHRISTMAS

1. "This is the day . . ."

This is the day His hour of life draws near,
Let me get ready from head to foot for it
Most handily with eyes to pick the year
For small feed to reward a feathered wit.
Some men would see it an epiphany
At ease, at food and drink, others at chase
Yet I, stung lassitude, with ecstasy
Unspent argue the season's difficult case
So: Man, dull critter of enormous head,
What would he look at in the coiling sky?
But I must kneel again unto the Dead
While Christmas bells of paper white and red,
Figured with boys and girls spilt from a sled,
Ring out the silence I am nourished by.

2. "Ah, Christ . . ."

Ah, Christ, I love you rings to the wild sky
And I must think a little of the past:
When I was ten I told a stinking lie
That got a black boy whipped; but now at last
The going years, caught in an accurate glow,
Reverse like balls englished upon green baize—
Let them return, let the round trumpets blow
The ancient crackle of the Christ's deep gaze.
Deafened and blind, with senses yet unfound,
Am I, untutored to the after-wit
Of knowledge, knowing a nightmare has no sound;
Therefore with idle hands and head I sit
In late December before the fire's daze
Punished by crimes of which I would be quit.

YVOR WINTERS
(1900–1968)

Born in Chicago, Yvor Winters studied at the University of
Chicago, the University of Colorado, and Stanford University,
where he taught for many years. With the publication of *Primitivism and Decadence: A Study of American Experimental Poetry* in 1937 he established a major reputation as a critic. Though
he published his first book of verse, *The Immobile Wind* (1921),
quite early, recognition as a poet came later. He was awarded the
Bollingen Prize in 1961 for his *Collected Poems*.

To Emily Dickinson

Dear Emily, my tears would burn your page,
But for the fire-dry line that makes them burn—
Burning my eyes, my fingers, while I turn
Singly the words that crease my heart with age.
If I could make some tortured pilgrimage
Through words or Time or the blank pain of Doom
And kneel before you as you found your tomb,
Then I might rise to face my heritage.

Yours was an empty upland solitude
Bleached to the powder of a dying name;
The mind, lost in a word's lost certitude
That faded as the fading footsteps came
To trace an epilogue to words grown odd
In that hard argument which led to God.

Apollo and Daphne

Deep in the leafy fierceness of the wood,
Sunlight, the cellular and creeping pyre,
Increased more slowly than aethereal fire:
But it increased and touched her where she stood.
The god had seized her, but the powers of good
Struck deep into her veins; with rending flesh
She fled all ways into the grasses' mesh
And burned more quickly than the sunlight could.

And all her heart broke still in leafy flame
That neither rose nor fell, but stood aghast;
And she, rooted in Time's slow agony,
Stirred dully, hard-edged laurel, in the past;
And, like a cloud of silence or a name,
The god withdrew into Eternity.

OSCAR WILLIAMS
(1900–1964)

Oscar Williams began writing poetry when he was still quite young. His first book of poems, *The Golden Darkness*, was published in the Yale Series of Younger Poets. In 1944 *Poetry* awarded him the Fellowship Prize. Among his many volumes of poetry, the last was *Selected Poems* (1964). Oscar Williams lived most of his life in New York City.

The Spritely Dead

There was a man within our tenement
who died upon a worn down step of day:
the wreath they hung upon the doorway meant
that there was nothing else for him to do.
But he was obstinate, he would not rest:
he dragged the flesh of silence everywhere
on crippled wings, and we would hear him whir
while on our memory's sill his eyes would roost.
We saw him wring his thoughts in deep despair
and stamp the color from our backyard scene:
careless, without his body, he would peer
to find out if we noticed his new sin.
He was afraid, afraid: he climbed our vines
and hid, on hands and knees, along our veins.

Picture Postcard of a Zoo

The zoo is full of cages and it lies
deep in the park but all around mankind:
the deadly bitterness of nature's lees
here gathers from foul pockets of the mind:
a temple to morbidity, it sprawls
through trees and down the vistas of the fictions:
giraffes live high in air, the bison drools;
the birds are screaming in a hundred factions.
The sky races above the tragedy:
the deer is nibbling at a crippled bird,
its fawn now stomps its hoof down on it hard;

next to the cage in which the yak will die
the boys are watching in a great to-do
the zebra's yardlong idling in the zoo.

COUNTEE CULLEN
(1903–1946)

The son of a Methodist Episcopal minister, Cullen was born in New York City. He received his undergraduate degree from New York University and an M.A. in English from Harvard in 1926. A major writer in the Harlem Renaissance, in his early years Cullen was recognized for his style, modeled on Keats, and the mild quality of his protest. In the 1930s his mood and the tone of his work darkened considerably. His volumes of poetry include *Color* (1925), *Copper Sun* (1927), *The Ballad of the Brown Girl* (1927), and *On These I Stand* (1947). His *Caroling Dusk* (1927) is an important anthology of black writers.

Yet Do I Marvel

I doubt not God is good, well-meaning, kind,
And did He stoop to quibble could tell why
The little buried mole continues blind,
Why flesh that mirrors Him must some day die,
Make plain the reason tortured Tantalus
Is baited by the fickle fruit, declare
If merely brute caprice dooms Sisyphus
To struggle up a never-ending stair.
Inscrutable His ways are, and immune
To catechism by a mind too strewn
With petty cares to slightly understand
What awful brain compels His awful hand.
Yet do I marvel at this curious thing:
To make a poet black, and bid him sing!

From the Dark Tower

We shall not always plant while others reap
The golden increment of bursting fruit,

Not always countenance, abject and mute,
That lesser men should hold their brothers cheap;
Not everlastingly while others sleep
Shall we beguile their limbs with mellow flute,
Not always bend to some more subtle brute;
We were not made eternally to weep.

The night whose sable breast relieves the stark,
White stars is no less lovely being dark,
And there are buds that cannot bloom at all
In light, but crumple, piteous, and fall;
So in the dark we hide the heart that bleeds,
And wait, and tend our agonizing seeds.

MERRILL MOORE
(1903–1957)

Merrill Moore was a psychiatrist who developed a "compulsive addiction" to the sonnet. He was born in Columbia, Tennessee, and received both B.A. and M.D. degrees from Vanderbilt University, where he was a member of the group connected with *The Fugitive*. He served in the Army Medical Corps in the Pacific during World War II. The prolific Dr. Moore wrote two to five sonnets a day; among his books are *M: One Thousand Autobiographical Sonnets* (1938), *Illegitimate Sonnets* (1950), and *A Case Record from a Sonnetorium* (1952).

In Magic Words

Wordsworth to the contrary notwithstanding,
Milton's and Shakespeare's statements also doubted:
A sonnet's force is not so easily routed
That flying one should not seek the safest landing.

As much as anything, a magic word
Is what a sonnet is, that quickly falls
If touched indelicately or shaken hard,
Or if it be reared too heavy or too tall.

Sonnets possess impertinence; they have bliss,
They require excitement in at least one line,
They need specific gravity and this
Especially is important—to be in focus;

Rarely a sonnet deserves to be exhibited;
Most of them should be (and they are) inhibited.

E. S. MILLER
(b.1904)

E. S. Miller was born in Ohio and educated at Bethany College,
Ohio State, and the University of North Carolina. He taught on
various faculties here and abroad, longest at Stephens College.
He has published scholarly articles, and many poems in a vari-
ety of magazines. His *Selected Poems* was published in 1972;
Amaryllis in the Shade in 1987. He went around the world before
World War II.

_____

To My Lady

For dateless consummation dateless days
rig-ripped by wind and bashed abeam by sea
or fixed upon a vast vacuity
becalmed and trembling hot, uncharted ways
wandering, I wearied you-ward. Each phase
around your still-eyed you-ness blew at me
a typhoon in limbo and left debris
rusty and parched, the blank of your blue gaze
from everywhere, until together, Love,
we navigate such seas as, scudding deep
through us, pitching and rolling us above
all helm and whirling compass, wreck us, sweep
us off. The crests dwindle. The relics of
the sanctified float motionless asleep.

CECIL DAY-LEWIS
(1904–1972)

C. Day-Lewis's name is linked with those of Auden, Spender, and MacNeice for his poetic activity in the 1930s. He was educated at Oxford and between 1927 and 1935 taught school. He served in the Ministry of Information during World II. From 1951 to 1956 he was Professor of Poetry at Oxford, and in 1967 he was appointed Poet Laureate, a post he held until his death. *Collected Poems* appeared in 1954, followed by *Pegasus and Other Poems* (1957) and *The Whispering Roots and Other Poems* (1970). His autobiography, *The Buried Day*, was published in 1960. C. Day-Lewis wrote a number of detective novels under the pseudonym of Nicholas Blake.

"This man was strong . . ."

This man was strong, and like a seacape parted
The tides. There were not continents enough
For all his fledged ambitions. The hard-hearted
Mountains were moved by his explosive love.
Was young: yet between island and island
Laid living cable and whispered across seas:
When he sang, our feathery woods fell silent:
His smile put the fidgeting hours at ease.
See him now, a cliff chalk-faced and crumbling,
Eyes like craters of volcanoes dead;
A miser with the tarnished minutes fumbling,
A queasy traveler from board to bed:
The voice that charmed spirits grown insane
As the barking of dogs at the end of a dark lane.

Maple and Sumach

Maple and sumach down this autumn ride—
Look, in what scarlet character they speak!
For this their russet and rejoicing week
Trees spend a year of sunsets on their pride.
You leaves drenched with the lifeblood of the year
What flamingo dawns have wavered from the east,

What eves have crimsoned to their toppling crest
To give the fame and transience that you wear!
Leaf-low he shall lie soon: but no such blaze
Briefly can cheer man's ashen, harsh decline;
His fall is short of pride, he bleeds within
And paler creeps to the dead end of his days.
O light's abandon and the fire-crest sky
Speak in me now for all who are to die!

FROM OH DREAMS, OH DESTINATIONS

"Symbols of gross experience . . ."

Symbols of gross experience!—our grief
Flowed, like a sacred river, underground:
Desire bred fierce abstractions on the mind,
Then like an eagle soared beyond belief.
Often we tried our breast against the thorn,
Our paces on the turf: whither we flew,
Why we should agonize, we hardly knew—
Nor what ached in us, asking to be born.
Ennui of youth!—thin air above the clouds,
Vain divination of the sunless stream
Mirror that impotence, till we redeem
Our birthright, and the shadowplay concludes.
Ah, not in dreams, but when our souls engage
With the common mesh and moil, we come of age.

PHYLLIS MCGINLEY
(1905–1978)

Born in Ontario, Oregon, Phyllis McGinley was educated at the Convent of the Sacred Heart and the University of Utah and began writing while still in college. A frequent contributor to *The New Yorker*, she published a great many volumes of poetry. Her *Times Three* (1960) received the Pulitzer Prize in 1961.

Evening Musicale

Candles. Red tulips, ninety cents the bunch.
　　Two lions, Grade B. A newly tuned piano.
No cocktails, but a dubious kind of punch,
　　Lukewarm and weak. A harp and a soprano.
The "Lullaby" of Brahms. Somebody's cousin
　　From Forest Hills, addicted to the pun.
Two dozen gentlemen; ladies, three dozen,
　　Earringed and powdered. Sandwiches at one.

The ash trays few, the ventilation meager.
　　Shushes to greet the late-arriving guest
Or quell the punch-bowl group. A young man eager
　　To render "Danny Deever" by request.
And sixty people trying to relax
On little rented chairs with gilded backs.

Occupation: Housewife

Her health is good. She owns to forty-one,
　　Keeps her hair bright by vegetable rinses,
Has two well-nourished children—daughter and son—
　　Just now away at school. Her house, with chintzes
Expensively curtained, animates the caller.
　　And she is fond of Early American glass
Stacked in an English breakfront somewhat taller
　　Than her best friend's. Last year she took a class

In modern drama at the County Center.
　　Twice, on Good Friday, she's heard *Parsifal* sung.

She often says she might have been a painter,
 Or maybe writer; but she married young.
She diets. And with Contract she delays
The encroaching desolation of her days.

W. H. AUDEN
(1907–1973)

Auden was born in York and educated at Christ Church, Oxford.
He traveled and wrote documentary films; in 1938 he came to the
United States, later becoming a citizen. His first *Poems* ap-
peared in 1930. Auden collaborated with Christopher Isherwood
on the verse plays *The Dog Beneath the Skin* (1935), *The Ascent
of F 6* (1936), and *On the Frontier* (1938). *Letters from Iceland*
(1937) was written with Louis MacNeice. Other volumes include
Another Time (1940), *For the Time Being* (1944), and *The Dyer's
Hand* (1963). Professor of Poetry at Oxford from 1956 to 1961,
Auden received the National Medal for Literature in 1967. A
very prolific poet, Auden distinguished himself as a critic and
librettist as well.

Who's Who

A shilling life will give you all the facts:
How Father beat him, how he ran away,
What were the struggles of his youth, what acts
Made him the greatest figure of his day:
Of how he fought, fished, hunted, worked all night,
Though giddy, climbed new mountains; named a sea:
Some of the last researchers even write
Love made him weep his pints like you and me.

With all his honors on, he sighed for one
Who, say astonished critics, lived at home;
Did little jobs about the house with skill
And nothing else; could whistle; would sit still
Or potter round the garden; answered some
Of his long marvelous letters but kept none.

Petition

Sir, no man's enemy, forgiving all
But will its negative inversion, be prodigal:
Send to us power and light, a sovereign touch
Curing the intolerable neutral itch,
The exhaustion of weaning, the liar's quinsy,
And the distortions of ingrown virginity.
Prohibit sharply the rehearsed response
And gradually correct the coward's stance;
Cover in time with beams those in retreat
That, spotted, they turn though the reverse were great;
Publish each healer that in city lives
Or country houses at the end of drives;
Harrow the house of the dead; look shining at
New styles of architecture, a change of heart.

FROM THE QUEST

The Door

Out of it steps the future of the poor,
Enigmas, executioners and rules,
Her Majesty in a bad temper or
The red-nosed Fool who makes a fool of fools.

Great persons eye it in the twilight for
A past it might so carelessly let in,
A widow with a missionary grin,
The foaming inundation at a roar.

We pile our all against it when afraid,
And beat upon its panels when we die:
By happening to be open once, it made

Enormous Alice see a wonderland
That waited for her in the sunshine, and,
Simply by being tiny, made her cry.

The City

In villages from which their childhoods came
Seeking Necessity, they had been taught
Necessity by nature is the same,
No matter how or by whom it be sought.

The city, though, assumed no such belief,
But welcomed each as if he came alone,
The nature of Necessity like grief
Exactly corresponding to his own.

And offered them so many, every one
Found some temptation fit to govern him;
And settled down to master the whole craft

Of being nobody; sat in the sun
During the lunch-hour round the fountain rim;
And watched the country kids arrive, and laughed.

FROM IN TIME OF WAR

2. "They wondered why . . ."

They wondered why the fruit had been forbidden;
It taught them nothing new. They hid their pride,
But did not listen much when they were children;
They knew exactly what to do outside.

They left; immediately the memory faded
Of all they'd learned; they could not understand
The dogs now who, before, had always aided;
The stream was dumb with whom they'd always planned.

They wept and quarreled: freedom was so wild.
In front, maturity, as he ascended,
Retired like a horizon from the child;

The dangers and the punishments grew greater;
And the way back by angels was defended
Against the poet and the legislator.

12. "And the age ended . . ."

And the age ended, and the last deliverer died.
In bed, grown idle and unhappy; they were safe:
The sudden shadow of the giant's enormous calf
Would fall no more at dusk across the lawn outside.

They slept in peace: in marshes here and there no doubt
A sterile dragon lingered to a natural death,
But in a year the spoor had vanished from the heath;
The kobold's knocking in the mountain petered out.

Only the sculptors and the poets were half sad,
And the pert retinue from the magician's house
Grumbled and went elsewhere. The vanquished powers were
    glad

To be invisible and free: without remorse
Struck down the sons who strayed their course
And ravished the daughters, and drove the fathers mad.

Louis MacNeice
(1907–1963)

Louis MacNeice was born in Ireland and educated at Marlborough and Merton College, Oxford. He was a lecturer in classics at the University of Birmingham from 1930 to 1936 and at Bedford College for Women from 1936 to 1940. From 1941 to 1949 he worked for the British Broadcasting Company as a writer and a producer. His first volume, *Blind Fireworks*, was published in 1929, *Poems* in 1935. *Solstices* appeared in 1961.

Spring Voices

The small householder now comes out warily
Afraid of the barrage of sun that shouts cheerily,
Spring is massing forces, birds wink in air,
The battlemented chestnuts volley green fire,

The pigeons banking on the wind, the hoots of cars,
Stir him to run wild, gamble on horses, buy cigars;
Joy lies before him to be ladled and lapped from his hand—
Only that behind him, in the shade of his villa, memories stand
Breathing on his neck and muttering that all this has happened
    before,
Keep the wind out, cast no clout, try no unwarranted jaunts
    untried before,
But let the spring slide by nor think to board its car
For it rides west to where the tangles of scrap iron are;
Do not walk, these voices say, between the bucking clouds
    alone
Or you may loiter into a suddenly howling crater, or fall, jerked
    back, garroted by the sun.

Sunday Morning

Down the road someone is practicing scales,
The notes like little fishes vanish with a wink of tails,
Man's heart expands to tinker with his car
For this is Sunday morning, Fate's great bazaar,
Regard these means as ends, concentrate on this Now,
And you may grow to music or drive beyond Hindhead anyhow,
Take corners on two wheels until you go so fast
That you can clutch a fringe or two of the windy past,
That you can abstract this day and make it to the week of time
A small eternity, a sonnet self-contained in rhyme.

But listen, up the road, something gulps, the church spire
Opens its eight bells out, skulls' mouths which will not tire
To tell how there is no music or movement which secures
Escape from the weekday time. Which deadens and endures.

STEPHEN SPENDER
(b.1909)

Spender met W. H. Auden, Louis MacNeice, and C. Day-Lewis at Oxford, and his name is linked with theirs in any mention of the poetry of the 1930s. His *Collected Poems: 1928–1953* appeared in 1955. Spender was co-editor of *Horizon,* and co-editor of *Encounter* from its establishment in 1953 until 1967. His literary criticism includes *The Destructive Element* (1935) and *The Making of the Poem* (1955). An early autobiography, *World within World,* appeared in 1951; *The Thirties and After,* a volume of memoirs, was published in 1978; his *Chinese Journal* in 1982.

"Without that once clear aim . . ."

Without that once clear aim, the path of flight
To follow for a lifetime through white air,
This century chokes me under roots of night
I suffer like history in Dark Ages, where
Truth lies in dungeons, from which drifts no whisper:
We hear of towers long broken off from sight
And tortures and war, in dark and smoky rumor,
But on men's buried lives there falls no light.
Watch me who walk through coiling streets where rain
And fog drown every cry: at corners of day
Road drills explore new areas of pain,
Nor summer nor light may reach down here to play.
The city builds its horror in my brain,
This writing is my only wings away.

"You were born; must die; were loved; must love"

You were born; must die; were loved; must love;
Born naked; were clothed; still naked walk
Under your clothes. Under your skin you move
Naked; naked under acts and talk.
    The miles and hours upon you feed.
They eat your eyes out with their distance
They eat your heart out with devouring need
They eat your death out with lost significance.

There is one fate beneath those ignorances
Those flesh and bone parcels in which you're split
O thing of skin and words hanging on breath:
Harlequin skeleton, it
Strums on your gut such songs and merry dances
Of love, of loneliness, of life being death.

PEYTON HOUSTON
(b.1910)

Peyton Houston's published work includes *Sonnet Variations* (1962), *Occasions in a World* (1969), *The Changes* (1977), and *Arguments of Idea* (1980). In the *Sonnet Variations* the sonnet is used through many transformations ranging from simple forms to a sonnet fugue and canzone, as a basic unifying principle to permit a wide diversity of approach and topic and the final resolution of this diversity. He sees the sonnet "not as a containing formula but as an architectural idea which is essentially invariant under change," so that *Sonnet Variations*, which contains 106 poems, stands as one of the most innovative explorations of the form. Houston was born in Cincinnati, Ohio, but has lived most of his life in Connecticut.

FROM SONNET VARIATIONS

17: *The Doll*

Or this doll of death, hideous, we treasure
In such cellar memories, whose cold
And livid cheek combs our touch seizure
Of an eternal sawdust. Your sister gave jewels here
For it: for it a strong lord died. It too is old,
Misgiven in all its misgivings. The embryonic fire,
The amniotic waters, could not quicken it.
No birth: birth is where you accept thought

Caught given, giving, a living to loving. Again, what
Amethyst eyes regarding out of a high sky

Welded again the idea into such grave clay? Day
Shatters its moment against this mechanic plight

Before the voice says momma, so exercised in rote,
And pretty curls fall out and eyes click shut.

77. Time's Mirror

I have been bent no less
In that arrogant nothingness,
In the lengthening shadows saw
Ghostly visitants of the new,
Sons of my sons and their sons' sons,
Private dreams and public bones,
All formulated in the flash
Of that fiery thought and wish.

They had their being in a wink
Out of my being, in that air,
Turbulent and wild as I,
A grimmer burden back to bear
All that living is to think
All that living is to die.

Act to act and love to love
I breathed that breath, I walked that ground.
My flesh risen there begot
Mannikin man-child of that mind,
Everything that love could prove
Before the turning wind forgot.

Private bones, the public dreams,
Each has its action, either tames
The beast that runs, the beast that turns.
Love rises fiercer as flesh burns.
The bow must arch, the shaft must pierce
Deeper distance, sharper force.
They are now and I am then
When all this dream is gone again.

105: "The/Quick gold, slant blue, sharp scarlet"

The
Quick gold, slant blue, sharp scarlet
Deaths we arrive at—
A fire's usage: we
Alter into strange silences, under a crown of sky
Mingle moment a thousand wonders, so come into what
White kingdom, the tall window, the straight
Door, solace of possibility—

O
I have prayed that my death might be in a green place
In a new season under blossoming boughs,
And that love might attend me as I put on the garment of a new
     use,
And that I might make my celebration just in a clear peace
So.

106: Canzone

II

Love, which is least sure and most dared, the pure, keen
                   unsparing
                         and immediate
Requirement we perceive and
           would avoid, comes now to us day, a
                  sun through the
Fogs of our dead findings, losings, a clean
           new, baring
               all we have hidden. We
Cannot compel it, demand
       it, deceive it. Its strict ray
              burns truth, the yet

Unarrived possible which
          experience organizes us
               towards, met
On the threshold of a new eye. To withstand
         begins, to
           go further, to see,

Is risk. The thorn bush burns. But to enrich
        soul to thus
               hazarded joy, to free
Thought to its use
        is an assent so large, so strange, you
               may direct it, abet

It only obliquely, in the twitch
        of an eye seized, in
               the corner of so
Slant a heart-beat. And God gets loose,
        panther or lion, lays waste
               country of all
Your secure denials. Not here
        can you walk mountain
               of any safety, pretend

The voice mute, reduce
        meaning a rote hope. You must taste
               death, digest it, and no
Rampart of iron angels can guard you. Death is near
        always,
               and strength is small.
In weakness each learns how to dare.
        Daring, can praise.
               Praising, use act to his end.

Roy Fuller
(b.1912)

Born at Failsworth near Manchester, Roy Fuller served in the Royal Navy from 1941 to 1946. Until his retirement in 1969 he practiced law. His first collection of poems was published in 1939; *The Middle of the War* (1942), which concentrated on war, was well received. His *Collected Poems* appeared in 1962, *New Poems,* for which he received the Duff Cooper Memorial Prize, in 1967. Fuller was Professor of Poetry at Oxford University from 1968 to 1973.

FROM MYTHOLOGICAL SONNETS

2. *"There actually stood . . ."*

There actually stood the fabled riders,
Their faces, to be truthful, far from white;
Their tongue incomprehensible, their height
Negligible: in a word, complete outsiders.

Why had they come? To wonder at the tarts,
Trade smelly hides, gawk at the statuary,
Copy our straddling posture and our arts?
How right that we had not thought fit to flee!

"Join us at cocktails, bathing?" No reply.
"Let's see your wild dances, hear your simple airs."
No move save the shifting of a shifty eye.

Trailing great pizzles, their dun stallions
Huddled against the hedges while our mares
Cavorted on the grass, black, yellow, bronze.

7. *"Well now, the virgin . . ."*

Well now, the virgin and the unicorn—
Although its point and details are obscure
The theme speeds up the pulses, to be sure.

No doubt it is the thought of that long horn
Inclined towards a lady young, well-born,
Unfearful, naïve, soft, ecstatic, pure.
How often, dreaming, have we found the cure
For our malaise, to tear or to be torn!

In fact, the beast and virgin merely sat,
I seem to think, in some enameled field;
He milky, muscular, and she complete
In kirtle, bodice, wimple. Even that
Tame conjugation makes our eyeballs yield
Those gems we long to cast at someone's feet.

16. "How startling to find . . ."

How startling to find the portraits of the gods
Resemble men! Even those parts where we
Might have expected to receive the odds
Are very modest, perhaps suspiciously.

For we cannot forget that these aloof and splendid
Figures with negligible yards and curls
Arranged in formal rising suns descended,
With raging lust, on our astonished girls—

No doubt because they were intimidated
By their own kind (those perfect forms that man,
Ironically, has always adulated)
And craved the extravagance of nature's plan.

So that humanity's irregular charms
In time fused with divine breasts, buttocks, arms.

George Barker
(b.1913)

Born in Essex, George Barker attended the Marlborough Road School in Chelsea, but dropped out at fourteen and worked at a series of odd jobs. His first novel and first book of verse were published in 1933. Barker spent a year in Japan as Professor of English Literature at the Imperial Tohoku University and then came to the United States where he stayed until 1943. Although he has written many long poems, especially *The True Confessions of George Barker* (1950, 1957), notable for its candor, his lyrics are especially fine. His *Collected Poems, 1930–1965* was issued in 1965.

Sonnet of Fishes

Bright drops the morning from its trophied nets
Looped along a sky flickering fish and wing,
Cobbles like salmon crowd up waterfalling
Streets where life dies thrashing as the sea forgets,
True widow, what she has lost; and, ravished, lets
The knuckledustered sun shake bullying
A fist of glory over her. Every thing,
Even the sly night, gives up its lunar secrets.

And I with pilchards cold in my pocket make
Red-eyed a way to the bed. But in my blood
Crying I hear, still, the leap of the silver diver
Caught in four cords after his fatal strike:
And then, the immense imminence not understood,
Death, in a dark, in a deep, in a dream, for ever.

To My Mother

Most near, most dear, most loved and most far,
Under the window where I often found her
Sitting as huge as Asia, seismic with laughter,
Gin and chicken helpless in her Irish hand,
Irresistible as Rabelais, but most tender for
The lame dogs and hurt birds that surround her,—

She is a procession no one can follow after
But be like a little dog following a brass band.

She will not glance up at the bomber, or condescend
To drop her gin and scuttle to a cellar,
But leans on the mahogany table like a mountain
Whom only faith can move, and so I send
O all my faith, and all my love to tell her
That she will move from mourning into morning.

To Any Member of My Generation

What was it you remember—the summer mornings
Down by the river at Richmond with a girl,
And as you kissed, clumsy in bathing costumes,
History guffawed in a rosebush. O what a warning—
If only we had known, if only we had known!
And when you looked in mirrors was this meaning
Plain as the pain in the center of a pearl?
Horrible tomorrow in Teutonic postures
Making absurd the past we cannot disown?

Whenever we kissed we cocked the future's rifles
And from our wild-oat words, like dragon's teeth,
Death underfoot now arises; when we were gay
Dancing together in what we hoped was life,
Who was it in our arms but the whores of death
Whom we have found in our beds today, today?

MURIEL RUKEYSER
(1913–1980)

Born in New York, where she lived most of her life, Muriel
Rukeyser was educated at Vassar and Columbia University. At
an early age she trained as an aviator, and this experience
informs her first book, *Theory of Flight* (1935), published in the
Yale Series of Younger Poets. Concerned with social injustice
and the atrocities of World War II, Rukeyser produced a great
many books, including *Mediterranean* (1938), *The Turning Wind*
(1939), *The Soul and Body of John Brown* (1940), *Wake Island*
(1942), *Beast in View* (1944), and *The Green Wave* (1948). After
the war, she taught at the California School of Labor and,
returning to New York, at Sarah Lawrence. Her later poems
continue her earlier political interests, but are also concerned
with feminist themes. In her later years Rukeyser provided great
inspiration for a great many women poets. Her *Collected Poems*
were published in 1978.

FROM NINE POEMS FOR THE UNBORN CHILD

2. *"They came to me and said, 'There is a child.'"*

They came to me and said, "There is a child."
Fountains of images broke through my land.
My swords, my fountains spouted past my eyes
And in my flesh at last I saw.   Returned
To when we drove in the high forest, and earth
Turned to glass in the sunset where the wild
Trees struck their roots as deep and visible
As their high branches, the double planted world.

"There is no father," they came and said to me.
—I have known fatherless children, the searching, walk
The world, look at all faces for their father's life.
Their choice is death or the world.   And they do choose.
Earn their brave set of bone, the seeking marvelous look
Of those who lose and use and know their lives.

Believing in Those Inexorable Laws

Believing in those inexorable laws
After long rebellion and long discipline
I am cut down to the moment in all my flaws
Creeping to the feet of my master the sun
On the sea-beach, tides beaten by the moon woman,
And will not think of you, but lie at my full length
Among the great breakers. I find the clear outwater
Shine crash speaking of truth behind the law.

The many-following waves turn into you.
I see in vision that northern bay : pines, villages,
And the flat water suddenly rears up
The high wave races against all edicts, taller,
Finally powerful. Water becomes your mouth,
And all laws all polarities your truth.

ROBERT HAYDEN
(1913–1980)

Hayden was born in Detroit and educated at Wayne State University and the University of Michigan, where he received two Hopwood Awards for his writing. He taught for many years at Fisk and later at Michigan. His books of poetry include *Heartshape in the Dust* (1940), *A Ballad for Remembrance* (1962), for which he received the Grand Prize in 1966 at the World Festival of Negro Arts in Dakar, Senegal, *Selected Poems* (1966), *Words in the Mourning Time* (1970), and *The Night-Blooming Cereus* (1972). *Angle of Ascent, New and Selected Poems* was published in 1975.

Frederick Douglass[1]

When it is finally ours, this freedom, this liberty, this beautiful
and terrible thing, needful to man as air,
usable as earth; when it belongs at last to all,
when it is truly instinct, brain matter, diastole, systole,

reflex action; when it is finally won; when it is more
than the gaudy mumbo jumbo of politicians:
this man, this Douglass, this former slave, this Negro
beaten to his knees, exiled, visioning a world
where none is lonely, none hunted, alien,
this man, superb in love and logic, this man
shall be remembered. Oh, not with statues' rhetoric,
not with legends and poems and wreaths of bronze alone,
but with the lives grown out of his life, the lives
fleshing his dream of the beautiful, needful thing.

[1]Frederick Douglass (c.1817–1885), American abolitionist and
journalist. For another sonnet on the same subject see Paul
Laurence Dunbar, p. 274.

DELMORE SCHWARTZ
(1913–1966)

Schwartz was born in Brooklyn and educated at New York
University. From 1943 to 1955 he was an editor of *Partisan
Review*. He received the Bollingen Prize for *Summer Knowledge*
(1959). In addition to poetry and criticism Schwartz was the
author of two collections of short fiction. *Last and Lost Poems*
was published in 1979. Saul Bellow modeled his character Von
Humboldt Fleisher in *Humboldt's Gift* on Schwartz.

Sonnet on Famous and Familiar Sonnets and Experiences
(With much help from Robert Good, William Shakespeare, John Milton, and little Catherine Schwartz)

Shall I compare her to a summer play?
She is too clever, too devious, too subtle, too dark:
Her lies are rare, but then she paves the way
Beyond the summer's sway, within the jejune park
Where all souls' aspiration to true nobility
Obliges Statues in the Frieze of Death
And when this pantomime and Panama of Panorama Fails,
"I'll never speak to you agayne"—or waste her panting breath.

When I but think of how her years are spent
Deadening that one talent which—for woman is—
Death or paralysis, denied: nature's intent
That each girl be a mother—whether or not she is
Or has become a lawful wife or bride
—O Alma Magna Mater, deathless the living death of pride.

JOHN FREDERICK NIMS
(b.1913)

A translator of poems from several languages, Nims has published numerous books of his own poetry: *The Iron Pastoral* (1947), *A Fountain in Kentucky* (1950), *Knowledge of the Evening* (1960), *Of Flesh and Bone* (1967), and *The Kiss* (1982). Nims has taught at Notre Dame, the University of Illinois, and The University of Chicago, and has served as a visiting editor for *Poetry* magazine.

Agamemnon Before Troy

> *Er will bloss zeigen, wie es eigentlich gewesenist*[1]—RANKE

A-traipsin' from a shindig, I unsaddles—
Three floozies an' a blatherin' buckaroo
Wangled the whole caboodle, and skedaddles.
You in cahoots with thet shebang, skidoo!—
Seein' if yer the critters I suspicion,
You varmints ain't a-goin' to hotfoot far.
Sartin galoots is sp'ilin' fer conniptions—
Wal, they's a posse hustlin' here an' thar

Fixin' to put the kibosh on shenanigans
By landin' scalawags in the calaboose.
Hornswoggled! sich palaver with bamboozlin'
Coyotes gits my dander up! Vamoose
Totin' spondulicks an' the cutie too!
They're itchin' fer a whangdang howdy-do!

[1] He merely wants to point out how it actually happened.

John Berryman
(1914–1972)

Berryman's works include the biographical ode *Homage to Mistress Bradstreet* (1956), *77 Dream Songs* (1964), with its complex ironic persona of Henry, for which he was awarded the Pulitzer Prize, and which was completed by *Dream Songs* in 1969, *Love and Fame* (1970), and the posthumous *Henry's Fate* (1977). *Berryman's Sonnets* (1967), a sequence of 115 Petrarchan sonnets, established his place in the sonnet tradition. *Recovery,* published in 1973 after his death by suicide, is an incomplete autobiographical novel about his struggle with alcoholism. He was born in Oklahoma, educated in the United States and England, and taught at the University of Minnesota.

The Poet's Final Instructions

Dog-tired, suisired, will now my body down
near Cedar Avenue in Minneap,
when my crime comes. I am blazing with hope.
Do me glory, come the whole way across town.

I couldn't rest from hell just anywhere,
in commonplaces. Choiring & strange my pall!
I might not lie still in the waste of St Paul
or buy DAD's root beer; good signs I forgive.

Drop here, with honour due, my trunk & brain
among the passioning of my countrymen
unable to read, rich, proud of their tags
and proud of me. Assemble all my bags!
Bury me in a hole, and give a cheer,
near Cedar on Lake Street, where the used cars live.

FROM BERRYMAN'S SONNETS

9: *"Great citadels whereon the gold sun falls"*

Great citadels whereon the gold sun falls
Miss you O Lise sequestered to the West
Which wears you Mayday lily at its breast,
Part and not part, proper to balls and brawls,
Plains, cities, or the yellow shore, not false
Anywhere, free, native and Danishest
Profane and elegant flower,—whom suggest
Frail and not frail, blond rocks and madrigals.

Once in the car (cave of our radical love)
Your darker hair I saw than golden hair
Above your thighs whither than white-gold hair,
And where the dashboard lit faintly your least
Enlarged scene, O the midnight bloomed . . . the East
Less gorgeous, wearing you like a long white glove!

15: *"What was Ashore, then? . . ."*
(After Petrarch & Wyatt)[1]

What was Ashore, then? . . . Cargoed with Forget,
My ship runs down a midnight winter storm
Between whirlpool and rock, and my white love's form
Gleams at the wheel, her hair streams. When we met
Seaward, Thought frank & guilty to each oar set
Hands careless of port as of the waters' harm.
Endless a wet wind wears my sail, dark swarm
Endless of sighs and veering hopes, love's fret.

Rain of tears, real, mist of imagined scorn,
No rest accords the fraying shrouds, all thwart
Already with mistakes, foresight so short.
Muffled in capes of waves my clear sighs, torn,
Hitherto most clear,—Loyalty and Art.
And I begin now to despair of port.

[1] See Wyatt, p. 4.

40: "Marble nor monuments whereof then we spoke"

Marble nor monuments whereof then we spoke
We speak of more; spasmodic as the wasp
About my windowpane, our short songs rasp—
Not those alone before their singers choke—
Our sweetest; none hopes now with one smart stroke
Or whittling years to crack away the hasp
Across the ticking future; all our grasp
Cannot beyond the butt secure its smoke.

A Renaissance fashion, not to be recalled.
We dinch 'eternal numbers' and go out.
We understand exactly what we are.
. . . Do we? Argent I craft you as the star
Of flower-shut evening: who stays on to doubt
I sang true? ganger with trobador and scald!

DYLAN THOMAS
(1914–1953)

Dylan Thomas was born in Swansea, Wales, and was educated at
Swansea Grammar School. His first book appeared in 1934, and
he soon won the praise of many older poets. Thomas was an
outstanding reader of poetry, and the rich language of his poems
reflects the musical tradition of Wales. He also wrote radio plays
for the British Broadcasting Company; *Under Milk Wood* is his
most popular play "for voices." His *Collected Poems* was pub-
lished a year before he died in New York City. "Altarwise by
Owl-Light" is a sonnet sequence which shows his full powers as
a lyric poet.

FROM ALTARWISE BY OWL-LIGHT

1. "Altarwise by owl-light . . ."

Altarwise by owl-light in the half-way house
The gentleman lay graveward with his furies;

Abaddon in the hangnail cracked from Adam,
And, from his fork, a dog among the fairies,
The atlas-eater with a jaw for news,
Bit out the mandrake with tomorrow's scream.
Then, penny-eyed, that gentleman of wounds,
Old cock from nowheres and the heaven's egg,
With bones unbuttoned to the half-way winds,
Hatched from the windy salvage on one leg,
Scraped at my cradle in a walking word
That night of time under the Christward shelter:
I am the long world's gentleman, he said,
And share my bed with Capricorn and Cancer.

2. "Death is all metaphors . . ."

Death is all metaphors, shape in one history;
The child that sucketh long is shooting up,
The planet-ducted pelican of circles
Weans on an artery the gender's strip;
Child of the short spark in a shapeless country
Soon sets alight a long stick from the cradle;
The horizontal cross-bones of Abaddon,
You by the cavern over the black stairs,
Rung bone and blade, the verticals of Adam,
And, manned by midnight, Jacob to the stars.
Hairs of your head, then said the hollow agent,
Are but the roots of nettles and of feathers
Over these groundworks thrusting through a pavement
And hemlock-headed in the wood of weathers.

When All My Five and Country Senses See

When all my five and country senses see,
The fingers will forget green thumbs and mark
How, through the halfmoon's vegetable eye,
Husk of young stars and handfull zodiac,
Love in the frost is pared and wintered by,
The whispering ears will watch love drummed away
Down breeze and shell to a discordant beach,
And, lashed to syllables, the lynx tongue cry
That her fond wounds are mended bitterly.
My nostrils see her breath burn like a bush.

My one and noble heart has witnesses
In all love's countries, that will grope awake;
And when blind sleep drops on the spying senses,
The heart is sensual, though five eyes break.

Among Those Killed in the Dawn Raid Was a Man Aged a Hundred

When the morning was waking over the war
He put on his clothes and stepped out and he died,
The locks yawned loose and a blast blew them wide,
He dropped where he loved on the burst pavement stone
And the funeral grains of the slaughtered floor.
Tell his street on its back he stopped a sun
And the craters of his eyes grew springshoots and fire
When all the keys shot from the locks, and rang.
Dig no more for the chains of his gray-haired heart.
The heavenly ambulance drawn by a wound
Assembling waits for the spade's ring on the cage.
O keep his bones away from that common cart,
The morning is flying on the wings of his age
And a hundred storks perch on the sun's right hand.

WILLIAM STAFFORD
(b.1914)

Stafford was born in Kansas and educated at the University of Kansas and the University of Iowa. The prose *Down in My Heart* (1947) recounts his experiences as a conscientious objector during World War II. He began his long teaching career at Lewis and Clark College in Portland, Oregon in 1948. *Traveling Through the Dark* (1962) won the National Book Award. Among his other collections of poetry are *The Rescued Year* (1966), *Allegiances* (1970), *Someday, Maybe* (1973), *Stories That Could Be True* (1977), and *A Glass Face in the Rain* (1982).

A Stared Story

Over the hill came horsemen, horsemen whistling.
They were all hard-driven, stamp, stamp, stamp.
Legs withdrawn and delivered again like pistons,
down they rode into the winter camp,
and while earth whirled on its forgotten center
those travelers feasted till dark in the lodge of their chief.
Into the night at last on earth their mother
they drummed away; the farthest hoofbeat ceased.

Often at cutbanks where roots hold dirt together
survivors pause in the sunlight, quiet, pretending
that stared story—and gazing at earth their mother:
all journey far, hearts beating, to some such ending.
And all, slung here in our cynical constellation,
whistle the wild world, live by imagination.

Time

The years to come (empty boxcars
waiting on a siding while someone forgets
and the tall grass tickles their bellies)
will sometime stay, rusted still;
and a little boy who clambers up,
saved by his bare feet, will run
along the top, jump to the last car,

and gaze down at the end into that river
near every town.
     Once when I was a boy
I took that kind of walk,
beyond the last houses, out where the grass
lived, then the tired siding where trains whistled.
The river was choked with old Chevies and Fords.
And that was the day the world ended.

JOHN MANIFOLD
(b.1915)

Manifold was born in Melbourne, Australia, and educated at
Jesus College, Cambridge University. He served in the Intel-
ligence Corps in World War II. His first collection, *The Death of
Ned Kelly and Other Ballads,* was published in 1941. His inter-
est in the sonnet is seen in *Selected Verse* (1946) and in *Op. 8:
Poems 1961–1969* (1970) as well as in *Six Sonnets on Human
Ecology* (1974). His *Collected Poems* were published in 1978. In
addition to poetry he has written extensively on music.

The Sirens

Odysseus heard the sirens; they were singing
Music by Wolf and Weinberger and Morley
About a region where the swans go winging,
Vines are in color, girls growing surely
Into nubility, and pylons bringing
Leisure and power to farms that live securely
Without a landlord. Still, his eyes were stinging
With salt and seablink, and the ropes hurt sorely.
Odysseus saw the sirens; they were charming,
Blonde, with snub breasts and little neat posteriors,
But could not take his mind off the alarming
Weather report, his mutineers in irons,
The radio failing; it was bloody serious.
In twenty minutes he forgot the sirens.

MARGARET WALKER
(b.1915)

Margaret Walker was born in Birmingham, Alabama, the daughter of a Methodist minister. She was educated at Northwestern University and the University of Iowa, from which she received her Ph.D. in 1965. Her first book of poetry, *For My People* (1942), was published in the Yale Series of Younger Poets. She has for many years been a Professor of English at Jackson State College in Mississippi. As the title of her first book indicates, Walker has long been concerned with black culture and human rights issues. Other collections include *Prophets for a New Day* (1970) and *October Journey* (1973). Her historical novel, *Jubilee* (1966), earned her the Houghton Mifflin Literary Fellowship. In 1970 she published *How I Wrote Jubilee*. Other works include *A Poetic Equation: Conversations with Nikki Giovanni* (1974) and *The Daemonic Genius of Richard Wright* (1984).

Childhood

When I was a child I knew red miners
dressed raggedly and wearing carbide lamps.
I saw them come down red hills to their camps
dyed with red dust from old Ishkooda mines.
Night after night I met them on the roads,
or on the streets in town I caught their glance;
the swing of dinner buckets in their hands,
and grumbling undermining all their words.

I also lived in low cotton country
where moonlight hovered over ripe haystacks,
or stumps of trees, and croppers' rotting shacks
with famine, terror, flood, and plague near by;
where sentiment and hatred still held sway
and only bitter land was washed away.

For Malcolm X[1]

All you violated ones with gentle hearts;
You violent dreamers whose cries shout heartbreak;
Whose voices echo clamors of our cool capers,
And whose black faces have hollowed pits for eyes.
All you gambling sons and hooked children and bowery bums
Hating white devils and black bourgeoisie,
Thumbing your noses at your burning red suns,
Gather round this coffin and mourn your dying swan.

Snow-white moslem head-dress around a dead black face!
Beautiful were your sand-papering words against our skins!
Our blood and water pour from your flowing wounds.
You have cut open our breasts and dug scalpels in our brains.
When and where will another come to take your holy place?
Old man mumbling in his dotage, or crying child, unborn?

[1] Malcolm X, born 1925, black nationalist leader, was assassinated in 1965.

GAVIN EWART
(b. 1916)

Ewart's *Poems and Songs* was published in 1939. After World War II he worked in advertising and then as a free-lance writer. His first collection, *Poems and Songs,* was published in 1939, his second, *Londoners,* in 1964. *The Collected Ewart* appeared in 1980 and *The new ewart: 1980–1982* in 1982. A master of the limerick, the clerihew, and of occasional verse, Ewart edited *The Penguin Book of Light Verse* (1980) and *Other People's Clerihews* (1983).

Sonnet: Supernatural Beings

You can't ever imagine the Virgin Mary having vulvitis or
      thrush—
she's not a real woman, she's a supernatural being,
not like the real women who are snoring and farting.

Aldous Huxley in an essay said that the angels
painted so often in Italian pictures
would need huge pectoral muscles if they were ever to fly . . .
But angels, like the Virgin, are supernatural beings.
It's all done by magic. If you can, you believe it.

And not so much *if you can,* more *if you want to*—
if you want to imagine something a bit kinder than people,
full of love and bursting with benevolence
you go for these smiling supernatural do-gooders
that look a little patronizing to an ordinary man
and still can't prevent you getting cancer or a cold.

Sonnet: Equality of the Sexes

I'm sure if I were a woman I should hate
being regarded as someone designed by Nature
to answer the telephone, make sandwiches, make tea;
or be fucked, look after a family, wash, cook, sew.
I would want to be an engineer, I would want to be regarded
as a person whose sex, though inescapable, was accidental
and not of the first importance. Though we don't deny
there *are* maternal feelings—and traces of masochism . . .

still, though men are in the rat race, and the American Satan
with not much help from others could burn us all up,
even so—if men are devils—we mustn't think all women
are perfect, downtrodden angels. There are nasty people about
of both sexes—surely you know some? Equally nasty
(or equally nice?)—that's one 'equality of the sexes'.

ROBERT LOWELL
(1917–1977)

Born in Boston, Robert Lowell was educated at St. Mark's, Harvard, and Kenyon College. He became a Roman Catholic in 1940 and was imprisoned as a conscientious objector during 1943 and 1944. His works include *Lord Weary's Castle* (1946), which received the Pulitzer Prize for Poetry, *The Mills of the Kavanaughs* (1951), *Life Studies* (1959), *Imitations* (1961), *For the Union Dead* (1964), *Notebooks, 1967–68* (1969), *The Dolphins* (1973), a cycle of sonnets for which he received a second Pulitzer Prize, and *Selected Poems* (1976). His final book of poems, *Day by Day*, appeared in the year of his death.

Salem

In Salem seasick spindrift drifts or skips
To the canvas flapping on the seaward panes
Until the knitting sailor stabs at ships
Nosing like sheep of Morpheus through his brain's
Asylum. Seamen, seamen, how the draft
Lashes the oily slick about your head,
Beating up whitecaps! Seamen, Charon's raft
Dumps its damned goods into the harbor-bed,—
There sewage sickens the rebellious seas.
Remember, seamen, Salem fishermen
Once hung their nimble fleets on the Great Banks.
Where was it that New England bred men
Who quartered the Leviathan's fat flanks
And fought the British Lion to his knees?

The Shako
(After Rilke)

Night, and its muffled creakings, as the wheels
Of Blücher's caissons circle with the clock;
He lifts his eyes and drums until he feels
The clavier shudder and allows the rock
And Scylla of her eyes to fix his face:

It is as though he looks into a glass
Reflecting on this guilty breathing-space
His terror and the salvos of the brass
From Brandenburg. She moves away. Instead,
Wearily by the broken altar, Abel
Remembers how the brothers fell apart
And hears the friendless hacking of his heart,
And strangely foreign on the mirror-table
Leans the black shako with its white death's-head.

In the Cage

The lifers file into the hall,
According to their houses—twos
Of laundered denim. On the wall
A colored fairy tinkles blues
And titters by the balustrade;
Canaries beat their bars and scream.
We come from tunnels where the spade
Pickax and hod for plaster steam
In mud and insulation. Here
The Bible-twisting Israelite
Fasts for his Harlem. It is night,
And it is vanity, and age
Blackens the heart of Adam. Fear,
The yellow chirper, beaks its cage.

FROM WRITERS

7: "Robert Frost"

Robert Frost at midnight, the audience gone
to vapor, the great act laid on the shelf in mothballs,
his voice musical, raw and raw—he writes in the flyleaf:
"Robert Lowell from Robert Frost, his friend in the art."
"Sometimes I feel too full of myself," I say.
And he, misunderstanding, "When I am low,
I stray away. My son wasn't your kind. The night
we told him Merrill Moore[1] would come to treat him,
he said, 'I'll kill him first.' One of my daughters thought things,
knew every male she met was out to make her;

the way she dresses, she couldn't make a whorehouse."
And I, "Sometimes I'm so happy I can't stand myself."
And he, "When I am too full of joy, I think
how little good my health did anyone near me."

[1] Merrill Moore, poet and psychiatrist, see p. 315. Frost's son later committed suicide.

GWENDOLYN BROOKS
(b. 1917)

Gwendolyn Brooks was born in Topeka, Kansas, but grew up and has spent a large part of her life in Chicago. Her acclaim as a poet was established with *A Street in Bronzeville* (1945). She received a Pulitzer Prize for *Annie Allen* (1950). During her distinguished career she has received many awards, including two Guggenheim fellowships and the American Academy of Letters Award in 1946. Her numerous volumes include *Bronzeville Boys and Girls* (1956), *The Bean Eaters* (1960), *Selected Poems* (1963), *In the Mecca* (1968), *Riot* (1969), *The World of Gwendolyn Brooks* (1971), *Aloneness* (1972), *Beckonings* (1975), and *To Disembark* (1981). Her novel, *Maud Martha*, was published in 1953; her autobiography, *Report from Part One*, in 1972.

What Shall I Give My Children?

What shall I give my children? who are poor,
Who are adjudged the leastwise of the land,
Who are my sweetest lepers, who demand
No velvet and no velvety velour;
But who have begged me for a brisk contour,
Crying that they are quasi, contraband
Because unfinished, graven by a hand
Less than angelic, admirable or sure.
My hand is stuffed with mode, design, device.
But I lack access to my proper stone.
And plentitude of plan shall not suffice

Nor grief nor love shall be enough alone
To ratify my little halves who bear
Across an autumn freezing everywhere.

the rites for Cousin Vit

Carried her unprotesting out the door.
Kicked back the casket-stand. But it can't hold her,
That stuff and satin aiming to enfold her,
The lid's contrition nor the bolts before.
Oh oh. Too much. Too much. Even now, surmise,
She rises in the sunshine. There she goes,
Back to the bars she knew and the repose
In love-rooms and the things in people's eyes.
Too vital and too squeaking. Must emerge.
Even now she does the snake-hips with a hiss,
Slops the bad wine across her shantung, talks
Of pregnancy, guitars and bridgework, walks
In parks or alleys, comes haply on the verge
Of happiness, haply hysterics. Is.

CHARLES CAUSLEY
(b.1917)

Charles Causley was born in Launceston, Cornwall, where, except for the six years during World War II that he served in the Royal Navy, he has spent most of his life. His first collection of poetry, *Farewell, Aggie Weston,* was published in 1951. Much of his early poetry was concerned with the war, but later he became increasingly interested in folk material and has written a number of works for children. His books include: *Survivor's Leave* (1953), *Union Street* (1957), *Johnny Alleluia* (1961), *Underneath the Water* (1968), and *Figgie Hobbin* (1970), a collection for children. His *Collected Poems: 1951–75* was published in 1975.

Autobiography

Now that my seagoing self-possession wavers
I sit and write the letter you will not answer.
The razor at my wrist patiently severs
Passion from thought, of which the flesh is censor.
I walk by the deep canal where moody lovers
Find their Nirvana on each other's tongues,
And in my naked bed the usual fevers
Invade the tropic sense, brambling the lungs.
I am drowned to the sound of seven flooding rivers
The distant Bombay drum and the ghazel[1] dancer,
But the English Sunday, monstrous as India, shivers,
And the voice of the muezzin is the voice of the station
      announcer.
The wet fields blot the bitterness of the cry,
And I turn from the tactful friend to the candid sky.

[1] ghazel/Ghazel or ghezal is a form of Oriental lyric poetry often accompanied by dancing.

JOHN HEATH-STUBBS
(b.1918)

Troubled in his early years by failing eyesight, Heath-Stubbs spent a year at the Worcester College for the Blind before going on to Oxford. He has taught at a number of universities, among them the University of Leeds, the University of Cairo, and the University of Michigan. Heath-Stubbs has written many volumes of poetry and *The Darkling Plain,* a critical work.

Watching Tennis

Light, in light breezes and a favoring sun,
You moved, like a dancer, to the glancing ball,
And the dance and the game seemed one
To me, unmarked spectator by the wall—

Always spectator, nor apt at any sport—
And you free burgess of the summer air;
Embraced with the iron maiden, Thought,
I of my body's poverty am aware.

How could I guess that all-consoling night,
Confider and concealer of secrets, should conduct
You to lie easy in my fumbling arms?

Yet, by the chances of the game betrayed,
Your mouth on mine found out its silent need,
And my discordant nerves peace in your limbs.

Howard Nemerov
(b.1920)

The author of stories and novels as well as essays and critical works, Howard Nemerov was born in New York City. Educated at Harvard, he served with the Royal Canadian Air Force and the United States Army Air Force during World War II. His first book of poems, *The Image and the Law,* was published in 1947. Nemerov was Consultant in Poetry at the Library of Congress in 1963–64, and co-winner of the Bollingen Prize in 1979. He taught at Bennington for many years and now teaches at Washington University in St. Louis. His *Collected Poems* was published in 1977.

The Remorse for Time

When I was a boy, I used to go to bed
By daylight, in the summer, and lie awake
Between the cool, white, reconciling sheets,
Hearing the talk of birds, watching the light
Diminish through the shimmering planes of leaf
Outside the window, until sleep came down
When darkness did, eyes closing as the light
Faded out of them, silencing the birds.

Sometimes still, in the sleepless dark hours
Tormented most by the remorse for time,
Only for time, the mind speaks of that boy
(he did no wrong, then why had he to die?)
Falling asleep on the current of the stars
Which even then washed him away past pardon.

Ozymandias II[1]

I met a guy I used to know, who said:
"You take your '57 Karnak, now,
The model that they called their Coop de Veal
That had the pointy rubber boobs for bumpers—
You take that car, owned by a nigger now
Likelier'n not, with half its chromium teeth

Knocked down its throat and aerial ripped off,
Side stitched with like bullets where the stripping's gone
And rust like a fungus spreading on the fenders,

Well, what I mean, that fucking car still runs,
Even the moths in the upholstery are old
But it gets around, you see one on the street
Beat-up and proud, well, Jeezus what a country,
Where even the monuments keep on the move."

[1] See Shelley's "Ozymandias," p. 182.

RICHARD WILBUR
(b.1921)

Wilbur was educated at Amherst and Harvard and after service in the U.S. Army in the Second World War taught at Harvard, Wellesley, and Wesleyan University. He has gained distinction for his translations, especially of Molière, as well as for his own poetry. In 1957 he received the Pulitzer Prize for *Things of This World* (1956). *Poems 1943–1956* was published in 1957; other collections include *The Poems* (1963), *Complaint* (1968), *Walking to Sleep: New Poems and Translations* (1969), *Seed Leaves: Homage to R.F.* (1974), and *The Mind Reader* (1976). He has also written poems for children and the lyrics for a comic opera version of *Candide* for which Lillian Hellman wrote the libretto and Leonard Bernstein the music.

"The winter deepening . . ."

The winter deepening, the hay all in,
The barn fat with cattle, the apple crop
Conveyed to market or fragrant bin,
He thinks the time has come to make a stop.

And sinks half-grudging in his firelit seat,
Though with his heavy body's full consent,
In what would be the posture of defeat,
But for that look of rigorous content.

Outside, the night drives down like one great crow
Against his cast-off clothing where it stands
Up to the knees in miles of hustled snow,

Flapping and jumping like a kind of fire,
And floating skyward its abandoned hands
In gestures of invincible desire.

HAYDEN CARRUTH
(b.1921)

Hayden Carruth was born in Connecticut and received degrees
from the University of North Carolina and the University of
Chicago. His awards for poetry include the Vachel Lindsay Prize
and the Harriet Monroe Poetry Award. *The Crow and the Heart*
appeared in 1959. Other collections are *Nothing for Tigers:
Poems, 1959–1964* (1965), *For You* (1970), *From Snow and Rock,
from Chaos* (1973), *The Bloomingdale Papers* (1975), *Brothers, I
Loved You All: Poems, 1969–1977* (1978), and *Asphalt Georgics*
(1985).

Sonnet

Cry, crow,
caw and caw, clawing
on black wings over hot black pines. What's
one more voice?

This morning the spring gave out,
no water in pipe. Hustled to spring, peered
in and saw three salamanders, very pallid;
saw water-level below pipe-end.

No more syphon. What's that? What? *And*
the brook is polluted.
               Weather going to pot,
each year drier than last, and hotter.

What's the trouble? Long time, 25 years, was I
mad.
      Won through, does anyone know?
      Hey, crow, does anyone know?
I see a chance for peace! What about water?

Late Sonnet

For that the sonnet no doubt was my own true
singing and suchlike other song, for that
I gave it up half-coldheartedly to set
my lines in a fashion that proclaimed its virtue
original in young arrogant artificers who
had not my geniality nor voice, and yet
their fashionableness was persuasive to me,—what
shame and sorrow I pay!
            And that I knew
that beautiful hot old man Sidney Bechet
and heard his music often but not what he
was saying, that tone, phrasing, and free play
of feeling mean more than originality,
these being the actual qualities of song.
Nor is it essential to be young.

Philip Larkin
(1922–1985)

Born in Coventry, England and educated at St. John's College, Oxford, Larkin, author of two novels as well as poetry, was librarian at Hull University. The poems in *The Northship* (1945), *The Less Deceived* (1955), *The Whitsun Weddings* (1964), and *High Windows* (1974) brought him consideration as a possible poet laureate, about which he remarked, "I dream about that sometimes—and wake up screaming. With any luck they'll pass me over."

Whatever Happened?

At once whatever happened starts receding.
Panting, and back on board, we line the rail
With trousers ripped, light wallets, and lips bleeding.

Yes, gone, thank God! Remembering each detail
We toss for half the night, but find next day
All's kodak-distant. Easily, then (though pale),

"Perspective brings significance," we say,
Unhooding our photometers, and, snap!
What can't be printed can be thrown away.

Later, it's just a latitude: the map
Points out how unavoidable it was:
"Such coastal bedding always means mishap."

Curses? The dark? Struggling? Where's the source
Of these yarns now (except in nightmares, of course)?

ANTHONY HECHT
(b.1923)

Born in New York City and educated at Bard and Columbia, Hecht served in the U.S. Army in World War II. His first collection, *A Summoning of Stones*, was published in 1954. *The Hard Hours* (1967) was awarded the Pulitzer Prize. Other collections include *The Seven Deadly Sins* (1958), *Millions of Strange Shadows* (1977), and *The Venetian Vespers* (1979). Hecht writes in traditional verse forms. A comic offshoot of that interest is *Jiggerry-pokery: A Compendium of Double Dactyls* (1967) edited with John Hollander.

Double Sonnet

I recall everything, but more than all,
Words being nothing now, an ease that ever
Remembers her to my unfailing fever,
How she came forward to me, letting fall
Lamplight upon her dress till every small
Motion made visible seemed no mere endeavor
Of body to articulate its offer,
But more a grace won by the way from all
Striving in what is difficult, from all
Losses, so that she moved but to discover
A practice of the blood, as the gulls hover,
Winged with their life, above the harbor wall,
Tracing inflected silence in the tall
Air with a tilt of mastery and quiver
Against the light, as the light fell to favor
Her coming forth; this chiefly I recall.

It is a part of pride, guiding the hand
At the piano in the splash and passage
Of sacred dolphins, making numbers human
By sheer extravagance that can command
Pythagorean heavens to spell their message
Of some unlooked-for peace, out of the common;
Taking no thought at all that man and woman,
Lost in the trance of lamplight, felt the presage

Of the unbidden terror and bone hand
Of gracelessness, and the unspoken omen
That yet shall render all, by its first usage,
Speechless, inept, and totally unmanned.

ALAN DUGAN
(b.1923)

Dugan was born in Brooklyn and educated at Queens College, Olivet College, and Mexico City College. He served in the U.S. Army Air Force in World War II and later worked in advertising and publishing. He taught for a number of years at Sarah Lawrence College. His *Poems* (1961) received both the Pulitzer Prize and the National Book Award. His *Collected Poems* appeared in 1969 and *New and Collected Poems, 1961–1983* in 1983.

To a Red-Headed Do-Good Waitress

Every morning I went to her charity and learned
to face the music of her white smile so well
that it infected my black teeth as I escaped,
and those who saw me smiled too and went in
the White Castle, where she is the inviolable lady.

There cripples must be bright, and starvers noble:
no tears, no stomach-cries, but pain made art
to move her powerful red pity toward philanthropy.
So I must wear my objectively stinking poverty
like a millionaire clown's rags and sing, "Oh I

got plenty o'nuttin'," as if I made
a hundred grand a year like Gershwin, while
I get a breakfast every day from her for two
weeks and nothing else but truth: she has
a policeman and a wrong sonnet in fifteen lines.

JAMES CAMP
(b.1923)

Born in Louisiana, James Camp was educated at Louisiana State University, Columbia, and the University of Michigan, where he won a Hopwood Award for his poetry and received his Ph.D. *An Edict from the Emperor* was published in 1968, *Carnal Refreshment* in 1975. He has collaborated with X. J. Kennedy and Keith Waldrop on many projects, including *Pegasus Descending* (1971), "a treasury of the best bad verse," and *Three Tenors, One Vehicle: A Book of Songs* (1975). He has lived in New York City for the last twenty-five years.

Female Dancer

Consider for a moment how the body of a dancer
Attaches to itself the attributes of love.
More graceful than the masculine fencer,
How forcefully, how subtly the muscles move
The plunging foot, the arched androgynous leg.
Love is here beyond deserts of Araby,
Fornication sublimed to a liveable ecstasy,
The white, the yolk, the fertilized egg
Of a freed-inshelled desire.
                She'll never beg
Bones in the local market, or ever endure
The turning away of wintry and expensive eyes.

Yet harsh and whirling is the dance.
                      Pure
Love comes hard. She prays for strength
To move her soul until her body dies.

W. D. SNODGRASS
(b.1926)

Snodgrass's first volume of poems, *Heart's Needle*, was awarded
the Pulitzer Prize in 1960. *The Führer Bunker* (1977) is written in
the voices of Nazi leaders at the end of World War II. Other
works include *Gallows Songs of Christian Morgenstern* (1967),
After Experience (1968), and *Remains*. He was educated at the
University of Iowa and has taught at Wayne State University and
Syracuse University.

──────────────

Μητιζ . . . Ομτιζ[1]
For R. M. Powell

He fed them generously who were his flocks,
Picked, shatterbrained, for food. Passed as a goat
Among his sheep, I cast off. Though hurled rocks
And prayers deranged by torment tossed our boat,
I could not silence, somehow, this defiant
Mind. From my fist into the frothed wake ran
The white eye's gluten of the living giant
I had escaped, by trickery, as no man.

Unseen where all seem stone blind, pure disguise
Has brought me home alone to No Man's land
To look at nothing I dare recognize.
My dead blind guide, you lead me here to claim,
Still waters that will never wash my hand,
To kneel by my old face and know my name.

[1] "Not any man . . . No Man"/In the *Odyssey*, Odysseus saves
himself from the Cyclops Polyphemus by telling him that his name
is No Man.

JAMES WRIGHT
(1927–1980)

Born in Martins Ferry, Ohio, Wright was encouraged to study literature by two of his teachers in vocational high school. He took his undergraduate degree at Kenyon College, studying with John Crowe Ransom, and an M.A. and Ph.D. at the University of Washington, where he was influenced by Theodore Roethke. He received the Pulitzer Prize for his *Collected Poems* in 1972. Other volumes included *Salt Mines and Such* (1971), *Two Citizens* (1973), and *The Blossoming Pear Tree* (1977). At the time of his death he was a professor or English at Hunter College.

To a Troubled Friend

Weep, and weep long, but do not weep for me,
Nor, long lamenting, raise, for any word
Of mine that beats above you like a bird,
Your voice, or hand. But shaken clear, and free,
Be the bare maple, bough where nests are made
Snug in the season's wrinkled cloth of frost;
Be leaf, by hardwood knots, by tendrils crossed
On tendrils, stripped, uncaring; give no shade.

Give winter nothing; hold; and let the flake
Poise or dissolve along your upheld arms.
All flawless hexagons may melt and break;
Why you must feel the summer's rage of fire,
Beyond this frigid season's empty storms,
Banished to bloom, and bear the birds' desire.

My Grandmother's Ghost

She skimmed the yellow water like a moth,
Trailing her feet across the shallow stream;
She saw the berries, paused and sampled them
Where a slight spider cleaned his narrow tooth.
Light in the air, she fluttered up the path,
So delicate to shun the leaves and damp,
Like some young wife, holding a slender lamp
To find her stray child, or the moon, or both.

Even before she reached the empty house,
She beat her wings ever so lightly, rose,
Followed a bee where apples blew like snow;
And then, forgetting what she wanted there,
Too full of blossom and green light to care,
She hurried to the ground, and slipped below.

RICHARD MOORE
(b.1927)

Richard Moore is a graduate of Yale, has been a pilot in the Air
Force, a Fulbright Scholar, a Fannie Hurst Professor at Brandeis
University, and presently teaches Liberal Arts at the New En-
gland Conservatory of Music. His poems and essays have ap-
peared in *The Atlantic Monthly*, *Harper's*, *The Hudson Review*,
The New Yorker, *Poetry*, *The Southern Review*, and many other
journals. Four collections of poetry have been published: *A
Question of Survival* (1971), the sonnet sequence *Word from the
Hills* (1972), *Empires* (1981), and *The Education of a Mouse*
(1983). Moore, who lives in Boston, has written in a great variety
of verse forms and feels that mastery of an external form can be a
liberation for the poet and a pleasure to the reader.

FROM WORD FROM THE HILLS

31: "Unable, father, still, to disavow"

Unable, father, still, to disavow
your stable world on two great girders trussed,
sexual continence and money lust,
I too have fingered the domestic plough
and sought with guile and fervor to endow
children with life and more than a bread crust;
and that is why, lazy and broke, I must
come pussyfooting to your sickroom now.

We're simple folk; beyond our gravel road
the populations of the world explode,

but we're contented with our modest portion.
Be happy—your ancestral line's been towed;
be glad—we've done our best to ease the load:
we've had one birth here, father, one abortion.

34: *"It took TV to civilize our village"*

It took TV to civilize our village
and bring our stubbled codgers up to date.
Up skyscrapers new notions percolate;
into our channeled valley drips the spillage,
where junkyards cover fields once used for tillage.
Our means are modest, but the needs are great
that softly sung commercials can create.
Some call it enterprise; I call it pillage.

When every crank and far-flung solipsist
knows about Prell and Dristan Nasal Mist,
who doubts the unity of Western Culture?
Tuned to elections, watching babies kissed,
viewing with awe the murdered anarchist,
what lone Promethean liver needs a vulture?

37: *"Though the new teacher is a trifle odd"*

Though the new teacher is a trifle odd,
the nuns are kind to me: never condemn
my heresies, nor know what bile and phlegm
stir up the student seedlings in my pod.
Through *Paradise Lost* yearly we still plod,
dwelling with love on each poetic gem.
I do my utmost to conceal from them
poetry's vilest monster, Milton's God.

It's risky, fathers, to send girls to school
these days, where they, neglecting things divine,
might listen to a poet, who will fool
away their hours, trying to define
innocence, gone when babes no longer drool,
and how it feels to club a porcupine.

DONALD HALL
(b.1928)

Born in New Haven, Connecticut, educated at Harvard and
Oxford, Donald Hall taught for twenty years at the University of
Michigan and currently lives in New Hampshire. He has written
critical studies on Marianne Moore and on the sculptor Henry
Moore and, in *Remembering the Poets* (1978), on Robert Frost,
Dylan Thomas, Eliot, and Pound. His editorial work includes
The Oxford Book of American Literary Anecdotes (1981). His
verse is collected in such volumes as *Exiles and Marriages*
(1955), *The Dark Houses* (1958), *The Alligator Bride* (1969), a
collection of new and revised poems; *A Blue Wing Tilts at the
Edge of the Sea* (1975), and *Kicking the Leaves* (1978).

The Funeral

It is the box from which no jack will spring.
Now close the box, but not until she kisses
The crossed, large hands which she already misses
For their caress, and on his hand the ring.
Now close the box, if we close anything.
She sees the wooden lid, and she dismisses
At least a hundred thoughtful artifices
That would enjoy the tears that they would bring.

The coffin does not matter. It was one
Like many in the row from which she chose it.
Now to be closed in it, he must become
Like all other dead men, deaf and dumb,
Blank to the small particulars that stun
Her mind all day. Black men, now come and close it.

ADRIENNE RICH
(b.1929)

Adrienne Rich was born in Baltimore and studied at Radcliffe. Her first volume of poetry, *A Change of World* (1951), a Yale Younger Poets selection, was published the year she graduated. *Diving into the Wreck* (1974) received the National Book Award for 1975. Her many volumes include *The Diamond Cutters* (1955), *Snapshots of a Daughter-in-Law* (1963), *Necessities of Life* (1966), *Leaflets* (1969), *The Will to Change* (1971), *The Dream of a Common Language* (1978), and *A Wild Patience Has Taken Me This Far* (1981). Her *The Fact of a Doorframe: Poems Selected and New, 1950–1984* appeared in 1984. Rich has also been active as a feminist. Her study *Of Woman Born: Motherhood as the Experience and Institution* appeared in 1976; her essays and speeches were collected in *On Lies, Secrets, and Silence: Selected Prose 1966–1978* (1979).

The Insusceptibles

Then the long sunlight lying on the sea
Fell, folded gold on gold; and slowly we
Took up our decks of cards, our parasols,
The picnic hamper and the sandblown shawls
And climbed the dunes in silence. There were two
Who lagged behind as lovers sometimes do,
And took a different road. For us the night
Was final, and by artificial light
We came indoors to sleep. No envy there
Of those who might be watching anywhere
The lustres of the summer dark, to trace
Some vagrant splinter blazing out of space.
No thought of them, save in a lower room
To leave a light for them when they should come.

THOM GUNN
(b.1929)

Thomson William Gunn was born and educated (Trinity College, Cambridge University) in England, where his first volume, *Fighting Terms*, appeared in 1954. He eventually settled in California, teaching at the University of California, Berkeley, for a number of years. His publications include *All My Sad Captains* (1961), *Moly* (1971), and *Jack Straw's Castle* (1976). His *Selected Poems: 1950–1975* appeared in 1976 and *The Passages of Joy* in 1982.

From the Highest Camp

Nothing in this bright region melts or shifts.
The local names are concepts: the Ravine,
Pemmican Ridge, North Col, Death Camp, they mean
The streetless rise, the dazzling abstract drifts,
To which particular names adhere by chance,
From custom lightly, not from character.
We stand on a white terrace and confer;
This is the last camp of experience.

What is that sudden yelp upon the air?
And whose are these cold droppings? whose malformed
Purposeless tracks about the slope? We know.
The abominable endures, existing where
Nothing else can: it is—unfed, unwarmed—
Born of rejection, of the boundless snow.

X. J. KENNEDY
(b.1929)

X. J. Kennedy was born in Dover, New Jersey, and for many years taught at Tufts University. His first book of poems was *Nude Descending a Staircase* (1961), for which he received the Lamont Award; his most recent, *Cross Ties: Selected Poems* (1985) received the Los Angeles Times Book Award. He and his wife Dorothy M. Kennedy live in Bedford, Massachusetts, where they write children's books and textbooks for college English.

Nothing in Heaven Functions As It Ought

Nothing in Heaven functions as it ought:
Peter's bifocals, blindly sat on, crack;
His gates lurch wide with the cackle of a cock,
Not turn with a hush of gold as Milton had thought;
Gangs of the slaughtered innocents keep huffing
The nimbus off the Venerable Bede
Like that of an old dandelion gone to seed;
And the beatific choir keep breaking up, coughing.

But Hell, sleek Hell hath no freewheeling part:
None takes his own sweet time, none quickens pace.
Ask anyone, *How come you here, poor heart?*—
And he will slot a quarter through his face,
You'll hear an instant click, a tear will start
Imprinted with an abstract of his case.

Robert Wallace
(b.1932)

Educated at Harvard, Robert Wallace is a Professor of English at Case Western Reserve University, where he edits Bits Press. His books include *Views from a Ferris Wheel* (1965), *Ungainly Things* (1968), *Critters* (1978), and *Girl Friends and Wives* (1984).

Under the September Peach

A hundred ruddy peach-moons ring the grass,
dark-jewelled with wasps, in whose oppressive hum
the dark machinery of ruin runs
in the sunny garden. Full half of summer's weight,

they gaze like desolate mirrors up into
the leafy heaven of the tree, where still
a hundred yellow-reddening planets swing
a zodiac, loose upon the string of space,

—and fall, by ones and twos, into this round
and glittering junkyard of the summer's air,
low circle of a spilled Hesperides:

whose tiny dragons gorge the rusting fruit
and peer, like eyes, from angry eaten caves
of sweetness, up, to see the still unfallen sky.

JOHN UPDIKE
(b.1932)

Born in Pennsylvania and educated at Harvard, Updike quickly established himself as a major novelist, short story writer, and man of letters. *Rabbit Is Rich* (1981), concluding the series of *Rabbit Run* (1960) and *Rabbit Redux* (1971), received a Pulitzer Prize. Other novels include *Couples* (1968), *Bech: A Book* (1970), *Marry Me* (1976), and *The Witches of Eastwick* (1984). Updike's numerous poems have appeared in such collections as *The Carpentered Hen* (1958), *Telephone Poles* (1963), *Midpoint* (1969), *Tossing and Turning* (1977), and *Facing Nature* (1985).

Love Sonnet

In Love's rubber armor I come to you;

$$
\begin{array}{l}
\quad\quad\quad b \\
\quad\quad oo \\
\quad\quad\quad\quad b. \\
\quad\quad c, \\
\quad\quad\quad d \\
\quad\quad\quad c \\
\quad\quad\quad\quad d: \\
\quad\quad\quad e \\
\quad f\!-\!- \\
\quad\quad\quad e \\
\quad\quad\quad\quad f. \\
\quad\quad\quad\quad\quad g \\
\quad\quad\quad\quad g.
\end{array}
$$

June Jordan
(b.1936)

Born in New York, June Jordan was educated at Barnard and the University of Chicago. She has taught at the City College of New York, Sarah Lawrence, Yale, and the State University of New York at Stony Brook. She was a Fellow at the American Academy in Rome in 1970–1971. Her novel, *His Own Where* (1971), was nominated for a National Book Award. Her books of poetry include *Things I Do in the Dark* (1977), *Passion* (1980), and *Civil Wars*. She has also edited a number of important anthologies.

Sunflower Sonnet Number One

But if I tell you how my heart swings wide
enough to motivate flirtations with the trees
or how the happiness of passion freaks inside
me, will you then believe the faithful, yearning freeze
on random, fast explosions that I place
upon my lust? Or must I say the streets are bare
unless it is your door I face
unless they are your eyes that, rare
as tulips on a cold night, trick my mind
to oranges and yellow flames around a seed
as deep as anyone may find
in magic? What do you need?

I'll give you that, I hope, and more
But don't you be the one to choose me: poor.

Sunflower Sonnet Number Two

Supposing we could just go on and on as two
voracious in the days apart as well as when
we side by side (the many ways we do
that) well! I would consider then
perfection possible, or else worthwhile
to think about. Which is to say
I guess the costs of long term tend to pile
up, block and complicate, erase away

the accidental, temporary, near
thing/pulsebeat promises one makes
because the chance, the easy new, is there
in front of you. But still, perfection takes
some sacrifice of falling stars for rare.
And there are stars, but none of you, to spare.

JUDITH MOFFETT
(b.1942)

Born in Louisville, Kentucky, Judith Moffett received her Ph.D.
from the University of Pennsylvania. The recipient of numerous
awards, she is a translator and a critic as well as a poet. Her
books of poetry include *Keeping Time* (1976) and *Whinny Moor
Crossing* (1984). "Now or Never," from her first book, is dis-
tinguished as a unified sequence of six sonnets.

Now or Never
I

They gave me in my kindergarten year
What seemed irrelevant, an Old Maid deck.
Gems, wrinkled skin, strange glasses on a stick,
Long gloves, pressed lips, and horrible orange hair,
No child, no husband ever to be hers,
That gaunt crone wasn't anything like me!
I got her meaning fast: *ignominy*
Is being single in a game of pairs.

How could I have imagined singleness,
Who called my mother's spinster aunt an old
"Witch-widder" heartlessly and was corrected
(A "maiden lady")? Nor had I suspected,
A child myself, that yearning for a child
Can raven even old maids like avarice.

II

Each morning of my tenth summer *swears Memory*
mythologizing as usual our washer disgorged a pulpy heap
of wet white strong cheap
fabric, ropy, smelling of soap, which it was my
job to untwist, shake out, nip
onto the lines high in windy sun
it never rained two corners to a clothespin,
then prop still higher. *Flap* Flap.

I plucked them down
stiffened, fragrant, mounding the basket knee-
high, to be cleverly doubled to eight
neat thicknesses by me each afternoon.
Diaper service was costly, convenient Pampers yet
to be invented. I was the diaper Service. *Me*

III

Those were the clean ones, but I don't think
I minded any of it;
a fragrance must exonerate,
somehow, a stink.

I've sloshed hundreds of filled diapers in
toilet bowls, not breathing;
what I remember is a sheathing
of powder on the changeling's clean skin.

And milkiness, patting his back
against my draped shoulder. For this, I see
the laundered airy diapers of Memory
peeling like lightning off the stack.

Not, not ever now, the crusty sour-
milk ones I very well know there were.

IV

There had to be. Doctors: "Your baby has
pyloric stenosis," a valve constriction which meant
he threw up a lot. Eventually he went
back to the hospital and was dosed with drops.

My mother broke to me the fabulous news
she was "expecting" (at last! after the years of hopes
and disappointing miscarriages!) in the Maternity
Shoppe of a big downtown department store:

"What's a 'maternity dress'?" "For ladies to wear
while they're pregnant." "Who're *you* buying one for?" "Me!"

I used to say, back in the irresponsible Fifties,
I wanted "a big family." Though I was one of the tree-
dwelling, androgynous little girls dolls bore,
I always liked even upchucky babies.

V

And all that windy, sunny diaper-summer—
His first, my tenth—I'd go out with our baby,
My little, little brother, walking. Maybe
His live weight on my heart induced the murmur
I always, lately, seem to hear. Returning
I'd feed him formula and sing, the rocker
Groaning a metronomic cadence, Shaker
Wisdom: *we come round right* I sang *by turning*.

Recalling what this battered snapshot shows,
The flannelette cocoon my sharp elbows
Bracket so bonily, a wash of joy
Transfigures all that gawkiness and spreads
Luminous circles right around both heads,
Mine, frowsy, and the fragile skull of the boy.

VI

so late as 65 a man has time   small
wonder age obsesses   my own
how inconceivably 31
pelvis stiffening ova going stale

Charlotte Brontë
died at 39 of TB
and the complications of a first pregnancy
having it would have killed her anyway

Eunice Kennedy Shriver
handily started her large family at 32
you don't know   can't know   you

fret   you're apprehensive   terrified
demons called mongolism and difficult birth invade
your peace   *now* you conclude *or never*

MARILYN HACKER
(b.1942)

Marilyn Hacker was born in New York City and has lived in a
great many places, including Mexico City, San Francisco, and
London. *Presentation Pieces,* her first book, published in 1974,
won the Lamont Prize and the National Book Award. Other
volumes include *Separations* (1976), *Taking Notice* (1980), and
Assumptions (1985). Hacker writes in a number of traditional
forms and is a major practitioner of the sonnet. "La Fontaine de
Vaucluse" is a sequence of seven sonnets.

FROM LA FONTAINE DE VAUCLUSE[1]

1. *"Azure striation swirls beyond the stones"*

Azure striation swirls beyond the stones
flung in by French papas and German boys.
The radio-guide emits trilingual noise.

"Always 'two ladies alone'; we were not alone."
Source, cunt, umbilicus, resilent blue
springs where the sheer gorge spreads wooded, mossed thighs:
unsounded female depth in a child-sized
pool boys throw rocks at. Hobbled in platform shoes,
girls stare from the edge. We came for the day
on a hot bus from Avignon. A Swed-
ish child hurls a chalk boulder; a tall girl,
his sister, twelve, tanned, crouches to finger shell-
whorls bedded in rock-moss. We find our way
here when we can; we take away what we need.

[1] Vaucluse is a department in the southeast of France; Avignon is
the capital.

7. *"We may be learning how to tell the truth"*

We may be learning how to tell the truth.
Distracted by a cinematic sky,
Paris below two dozen shades of grey,
in borrowed rooms we couldn't afford, we both
work over words till we can tell ourselves
what we saw. I get up at eight, go down
to buy fresh croissants, put a saucepan on
and brew first shared coffee. The water solves
itself, salves us. Sideways, hugging the bank,
two stocky women helped each other, drank
from leathery cupped palms. We make our own
descent downstream, getting our shoes wet, care-
fully hoist cold handsful from a crevice where
azure striation swirls beyond the stones.

Occasional Verses

"Your touch is abrasive. My blood seethes and smarts,"
said Sappho. Said Atthis, "Two pints and some darts."

"Stay," said Gaius, "it's keener than scandal when you—"
"I must go now," said Clodia. "The scandal was true."

"Your breasts are like melons, your mouth like dark plums,"
said Petrarch. Said Laura, "Why can't we be chums?"

"You move like a Phoenix on fire," said John.
"I'm off dancing," said Fanny. "You *do* carry on."

"Your glance is a torrent and I die of thirst,"
said William. Said Maud, "Revolution comes first."

"We're relations as well. . . ." Lytton coaxed Duncan Grant.
"We may *be* them," said Duncan, "but have them we can't."

I mull on poor poets who miffed their affairs
while you kip with the Muses discretely upstairs.

DAVID HUDDLE
(b.1942)

David Huddle's work has appeared in a number of magazines and journals, including *Esquire, Harper's,* and *The Hudson Review.* He is the author of two books, *Paper Boy* (poems) and *Only the Little Bone* (stories). He teaches at the University of Vermont. "Tour of Duty" is a sequence of sonnets dealing with Viet Nam.

FROM TOUR OF DUTY

Nerves

Training I received did not apply be-
cause Cu Chi District was not Fort Jackson.
Funniest thing, they had dogs like any-
where, used them for sandwich meat, I ate one
once, but I guess you want to know if I
ever shot somebody—didn't—would have
—curious about it, but my job gave
one duty, to ask questions. I'd lie

if I said some weren't women, children,
old men; I'd lie too if I claimed my mem-
ories weren't part of my life, but then

shame is natural, wear it, every day
think of bursting from sleep when mortars came:
crazy run to a dark hole, damp sandbags.

Words

What did those girls say when you walked the strip
of tin shack bars, gewgaw stores, barber shops,
laundries and restaurants, most all of which
had beds in back, those girls who had to get up
in Saigon before dawn to catch their rides to Cu Chi,
packed ten to a Lambretta, chattering, gay
in their own lovely tongue, on the dusty
circus road to work, but then what did they say?

Come here, talk to me, you handsome, GI
I miss you, I love you too much, you want
short time, go in back, I don't care, I want
your baby, sorry about that, GI,
you number ten. A history away
I translate dumbly what those girls would say.

LOUISE GLÜCK
(b.1943)

Educated at Sarah Lawrence and Columbia University, Louise
Glück was born in New York City. She has received a number of
fellowships, including a Guggenheim, one from the Rockefeller
Foundation, and another from the National Endowment for the
Arts. She has taught at Columbia, the University of Iowa, and
Williams College. Her books of poetry include *Firstborn* (1968),
The House on Marshland (1975), *The Garden* (1976), and *Descending Figure* (1980).

My Neighbor in the Mirror

M. le professeur in prominent senility
Across the hall tidies his collected prose
And poems. Returning from a shopping spree

Not long ago, I caught him pausing to pose
Before the landing mirror in grandiose semi-profile.
It being impossible to avoid encounter on the stairs
I thought it best to smile
Openly, as though we two held equal shares
In the indiscretion. But his performance of a nod
Was labored and the infinite *politesse* of rose palm
Unfurled for salutation fraud-
ulent. At any rate, lately there's been some
Change in his schedule. He receives without zeal
Now, and judging by his refuse, eats little but oatmeal.

BRUCE SMITH
(b.1946)

Bruce Smith was born in Pennsylvania and received his educa-
tion at Bucknell University. His books include *The Common
Wages* (1983) and *Silver and Information* (1985). He teaches at
Phillips Andover Academy. "In My Father's House" is a se-
quence of sonnets.

FROM IN MY FATHER'S HOUSE

Address

Street of Nectar, Street of Contingency,
Street of Fecundity like the moon's sea.
Street of First Kissing, Street of the Franchise,
Street of Some Money where his house is.
Boulevard of the Boy-in-Summer Rising
into the Sun. Street of Small Gashes
where his house is. Street of the Plangent,
Street of the Whips of Plantain, Place
of Illuminated Mother, Street of the Fallen
Motorcycle Cop, The Lane of One-Accounted-For,
Road of Want-More. Street of Rose Agony
where his house is. Concourse of the Party,
Street Impolitic, Street of Circumference, Wheel, Disc, Arc.

Street of Moonlighting, Street of His Tendons, Street of
    Duress,
Street of His Mansions, Street of His Sweetness, numberless.

O My Invisible Estate
—Vaughan

Where the afternoon sun blears the city.
Where the high-numbered streets zero
their dignity, we live without irony.
No house but a shadow
of a house, but when we need a shadow
this shadow is ours. The shadow
of a man and his two arms, tenderness
and some hunger that I was rocked in.
And whatever house has been in me since then,
a flesh made and unmade since then,
I find that every churchyard has a stone
that bears our name, Father. Imagine
the monuments to a name so common,
imagine that dark land is what we own.

Laundry

Not even the cops who can do anything could do this—
work on Sunday picking up dirty and delivering clean
laundry in Philadelphia. Rambling with my father, get this,
in a truck that wasn't even our own,
part ambulance, part bullet, there wasn't anything
we couldn't do. Sheets of stigmata, macula of love,
vomit and shit and the stains of pissing
another week's salary away, we picked up and drove
to the stick men in shirt sleeves, the thin
Bolshevik Jews who laughed out the sheets like the empty
speech in cartoons. They smelled better than sin,
better than decadent capitalism. And oh, we
could deliver, couldn't we, the lawless bags through the city
that said in his yawn, get money, get money, get money.

RICHARD KENNEY
(b.1948)

Richard Kenney was born in Glens Falls, New York, and was educated at Dartmouth. His poems have appeared in many magazines, including *The New Yorker, The Atlantic Monthly, Hudson Review, Poetry,* and *The Yale Review.* His first book, *The Evolution of the Flightless Bird* (1984), was published in the Yale Series of Younger Poets; his second book, *Orrery,* was published in 1985. "The Hours of the Day" is a sequence of twenty-four sonnets.

FROM THE HOURS OF THE DAY

In Retrospect

In fact, what change? The chimney of the spine
still burned its gray electric fire, where neural
fibers rose in braids above the heart's narrow
perch and frayed as if to part and yet held on,
held on; and cool morphology the life had followed
followed after all; and still the mortmain rule
of intellect unturned traced out its lines
across a window grid where green glass flowed
like rain, light left, and night flowed out to dawn—
the heal-all. Shamans' art. What change? One hero's awful
pitch and roll unsteadied by such ancient arcane
warps as compass points, or twice twelve hours—a fool's
abandoned pigeonholes, his handblown window panes . . .
Sand-painting here erased, in retrospect, by arc-

Light

crack—recall it vividly as first fabric
ripping in the distance, droplets that began
to spit my forehead and shoulders—I sat with a broken
neck and watched the first summer thunderheads
leap up the valley to the west like hydrophobic
spirits, erratic, rushing, a thick boiling brailing

up the sky's last light, and the world in a black hood.
A curtain of wind came several hundred yards ahead
of the rain, laid down the wild lilac trees. I heard
as a baby hears, the crack and fall; clapped eardrums felt
like new skin. Cumuli like radioactive stone crushed
in and shocked the earth a half hour after nightfall;
still the air smelled hot, a river; all through it I crouched,
a glistening bat under a black umbrella.

The Perfect Disc of the Moon

And clearly I recall the second day's end,
when just before its nightfall storm-light stabbed under
the towering recession of clouds that ringed across
the sky-sill, slaked an entire tall universe;
and in green light the ground itself fluoresced
like some intelligence unfixed, inhuman,
and dwindling—Crows went up like fists, a forest
flamed; in its adjacent field five heifers
stood against the fencewire, burst in a blind
and sudden gallop like misshapen horses,
ludicrous, senseless—*A long while later forced
eyes open in the flume of the queer stars . . .
like ancient long-throated birds, wild lilacs craned
across the perfect white disc of the moon.*

SHEROD SANTOS
(b.1949)

Born in Greenville, South Carolina, Sherod Santos attended the
University of California and the University of Utah, where he
received his Ph.D. He has received a number of awards for his
writing, including the Delmore Schwartz Memorial Award, the
Oscar Blumenthal Prize from *Poetry*, the Ingram Merril Award,
and the Discovery/*The Nation* Award. He was also the recipient
of a Guggenheim Foundation grant. *Accidental Weather* was
published by Doubleday in 1982 as part of the National Poetry
Series. "The Sheltering Ground," a sequence of six sonnets,
deals with the birth of a child.

FROM THE SHELTERING GROUND

1. *"First child, born out of breach in mid-May . . ."*

First child, born out of breech in mid-May, the hour
Of his arrival set that morning the water broke,
Sloughing off the body's dream-weight of a boy.
By late afternoon, you lay beneath a spiderless
Web of monitors and read the oscilloscopic
Etchings of the muscles contract, then the sensor's
Tone, the rapid *fa-lump, fa-lump, fa-lump*
Of his penumbral heart, then the image itself,
The sound patterns forming like a thumbprint
On the screen, and it was him, still transverse
And locked in his arterial room, the tiny negative
Imprint of rib-cage and lungs, the penis still secreted,
And the forehead drowsing where the sea-sounds
Of the blood sang all of the darkness together.

4. *"I bent to touch a damp cloth to your mouth . . ."*

I bent to touch a damp cloth to your mouth, you
Raised your head, and into mine another time
Weeks before when you'd startled from nightmare

And the image of him buried inside, the botched
Lungs wheezing that would not take air: your shallow
Breathing labored as if in thrall, you pitched over
In the dark, and in a moment you were back in the dream-
Field of the body to find him again, exposed as rock
And routed from his sheltering ground. And as you'd done
Those weeks before, you rolled your head a little in
My hand, and moaned, just once, and I could feel it then,
The shudder of the reach sink down inside and take
A handhold on the heel, and draw him out from that
Calyx of blood, into our burnished and immaterial air:

Married Love

As they sat and talked beneath the boundary trees
In the abandoned park, neither one mentioning
Her husband, or his wife, it seemed as though
Their summer shadows had detached themselves
In the confusion of those thousand leaves: but no more
Than they could call those shadows back from the air,
Could they ignore the lives they had undone,
And would undo once more, that afternoon,
Before giving in to what they knew, had always known.
And yet, in turning away, what they would say was not
That thing, but something else, that mild excuse
That lovers use of how things might have been
Had they met somewhere else, or in some better time,
Were they less like themselves than what they are.

Late November

All day pinecones drop like shot birds
off the tree limbs, the tea kettle sings
from the iron stove . . . from under the leaf-mold,
winter's stain spreads like kerosene.
The cattle stop to watch us on our sunset walks,
ice-glitter sputtering in the pine-tops
and gullies, the house windows flaming just once
and going out. Our eyes have begun
to deceive us now, as if the heart can't
stand the strain of the earth, as if the ice age
had begun its heave and the longnecks

arcing overhead each evening were calling
back some other season, calling back
to us, and that dying fire in the trees.

JULIA ALVAREZ
(b.1950)

Julia Alvarez was born in New York City but spent her childhood
in the Dominican Republic. She has won an American Academy
of Poetry Prize. In 1984–85 she held the Jenny McKean Moore
Visiting Lectureship in Creative Writing at George Washington
University. She now teaches at the University of Illinois at
Urbana Champaign. Her first book, *Homecoming* (1984), in-
cludes the sonnet sequence "33."

FROM 33

"Mother asks what I'm put to . . ."

Mother asks what I'm put to, that means men
in any declension except sex; it
means do I realize I am thirty-
three without a husband, house, or children
and going on thirty-four? Father extends
an invitation to come live with them,
there are two empty bedrooms I can write
in and handouts until I make it big
which means men at publication parties
asking me what mentors shaped my style
and has anyone told me how beautiful
I am having written something worthwhile?
Their drinks tinkle in their hands like keys
to doors closed at the closing of stories.

"HE: Age doesn't matter when you're both in love!"

HE: Age doesn't matter when you're both in love!
SHE: You say that now, wait till you've had enough.
HE: I love for keeps. I'll never let you down.
SHE: You lie, my dear, you'll lay me in the ground.
HE: Statistics say I'll probably die first.
SHE: Statistics say most couples get divorced.
HE: Better to love and lose than not at all.
SHE: Better to read the writing on the wall!
HE: You go by loss, you might as well not live.
SHE: Or live, single, and psychoanalyzed.
HE: It breaks my heart to hear you talk that way.
SHE: (Boy in her arms, wiping his tears away,
prescribes the cure for existential ache)
Come in, my sweet, and have some birthday cake.

"33 is the year that Jesus Christ"

33 is the year that Jesus Christ
took some big risks, the minister teases.
I've come to take the edge off loneliness
by being convinced that maybe god exists,
is with me in the empty bed, with
me when I can't do up my dress, with me
for bread and tunafish since recipes
depress me with leftovers, and just Is.
Wasn't he crucified at 33,
I ask, depressed, deserted by his friends,
divorced from God, subject to human laws?
Wasn't he the most single finally
at 33, meeting his lonely end?
Yes, the minister takes my hand, he was.

INDEX OF AUTHORS

INDEX OF TITLES

A

Index of First Lines

A

A book was writ of late called Tetrachordon, 121

A crown of ivy! I submit my head, 179

A hireling's wages to the priest are paid, 175

A hundred ruddy peach-moons ring the grass, 370

A leaf from Freedom's golden chaplet fair, 257

A lover is a slender, glowing urn, 202

A shilling life will give you all the facts, 320

A simple nosegay! was that much to ask?, 306

A sonnet is a moment's monument, 231

A sudden blow: the great wings beating still, 270

A while we wandered (thus it is I dream!), 261

A "woman with a past." What happier omen, 246

Across the brook of Time man leaping goes, 247

Ah, Christ, I love you rings to the wild sky, 311

Ah, Douglass, we have fall'n on evil days, 274

Alas, so all things now do hold their peace, 7

Alice is tall and upright as a pine, 131

All day I heard a humming in my ears, 227

All day pinecones drop like shot birds, 285

All Nature seems to work. Slugs leave their lair, 168

All were too little for the merchant's hand, 11

All you violated ones with gentle hearts, 346

Alone on Lykaion since man hath been, 262

Altarwise by owl-light in the half-way house, 340

Although we do not all the good we love, 109

Among the orchard weeds, from every search, 184

Amor, che nel penser mio vive e regna, xxiii

An old, mad, blind, despised, and dying king, 183

An old man in a lodge within a park, 207

And all that windy, sunny diaper-summer—, 375

And art thou he, now "fallen on evil days," 154

And clearly I recall the second day's end, 383

And every year a world my will did deem, 10

413

S